THE BAPTIST RIVER

Baptists
History, Literature, Theology, Hymns

General Editor: Walter B. Shurden, Mercer University

John Taylor, *Baptists on the American Frontier: A History of Ten Baptist Churches*
Edited by Chester Young
Thomas Helwys, *A Short Declaration of the Mystery of Iniquity*
Edited by Richard Groves
Roger Williams, *The Bloody Tenant of Persecution for Cause of Conscience*
Edited by Richard Groves; Edwin Gaustad, Historical Introduction
James A. Rogers†, *Richard Furman: Life and Legacy*
Lottie Moon, *Send the Light: Lottie Moon's Letters and Other Writings*
Edited by Keith Harper
James Byrd, *The Challenges of Roger Williams: Religious Liberty, Violent Persecution, and the Bible*
Anne Dutton, *The Influential Spiritual Writings of Anne Dutton: Volume 1: Letters*
Edited by JoAnn Ford Watson (Fall 2003)
David T. Morgan, *Southern Baptist Sisters: In Search of Status, 1845-2000*
(Fall 2003)
William E. Ellis, *"A Man of Books and a Man of the People": E. Y. Mullins and the Crisis of Moderate Southern Baptist Leadership*
(paperback Fall 2003; hardback 1985)
Jarrett Burch, *Adiel Sherwood: Baptist Antebellum Pioneer in Georgia* (Winter 2003)
Anthony Chute, *A Piety Above the Common Standard: Jesse Mercer and the Defense of Evangelistic Calvinism* (Spring 2004)
Annie Armstrong, *Rescue the Perishing: Selected Correspondence of Annie W. Armstrong*
Edited by Keith Harper (Spring 2004)
William H. Brackney, *A Genetic History of Baptist Thought* (Fall 2004)
Henlee Hulix Barnette, *A Pilgrimmage of Faith: My Story* (Fall 2004)
Anne Dutton, *The Influential Spiritual Writings of Anne Dutton: Volume 2: Discourses, Poetry, Hymns, Memoir*
Edited by JoAnn Ford Watson (Fall 2004)
Walter B. Shurden, *Not an Easy Journey: Some Transitions in Baptist Life* (Spring 2005)
Marc A. Jolley, editor, *Distinctively Baptist: Essays on Baptist History: Festschrift Walter B. Shurden* (Spring 2005)
Keith Harper and C. Martin Jacumin, *Esteemed Reproach: The Lives of Rev. James Ireland and Rev. Joseph Craig* (2005)
Charles Deweese, *Women Deacons and Deaconesses: 400 Years of Baptist Service* (BH&HS, 2005)
Pam Durso and Keith Durso, *Courage and Hope: The Stories of Ten Baptist Women Ministers* (BH&HS, 2005)
Anne Dutton, *The Influential Spiritual Writings of Anne Dutton: Volume 3: Autobiography*, Edited by JoAnn Ford Watson (Spring 2006)
Anne Dutton, *The Influential Spiritual Writings of Anne Dutton: Volume 4: Theological Works*, Edited by JoAnn Ford Watson (Winter 2006/2007)

THE BAPTIST RIVER

ESSAYS ON MANY TRIBUTARIES OF A DIVERSE TRADITION

Edited by W. Glenn Jonas Jr.

MERCER UNIVERSITY PRESS

MACON, GEORGIA

MUP/H353

1400 Coleman Avenue
Macon, Georgia 31207

Books published by Mercer University Press are printed on acid free paper that meets the requirements of American National Standard for Information Sciences—Permanence of Paper for Printed Library Materials.

Library of Congress Cataloging-in-Publication Data

The Baptist river : essays on many tributaries of a diverse tradition / edited by W. Glenn Jonas, Jr. -- 1st ed.
p. cm.
Includes bibliographical references and index.
ISBN-13: 978-0-88146-120-6 (paperback : alk. paper)
ISBN-10: 0-88146-120-2 (paperback : alk. paper)
1. Baptists--North America. I. Jonas, William Glenn, 1959-
BX6233.B37 2006
286--dc22
2006036380

Contents

Foreword vii
Preface xi
Acknowledgments xiv
1. Defining a Tradition: A River Runs Through It—*Glenn Jonas* 1
2. American Baptists—*Deborah Van Broekhoven* 20
3. Southern Baptists—*C. Douglas Weaver* 45
4. National Baptists—*Sandy D. Martin* 69
5. Independent Baptists—*Jerry L. Faught* 93
6. The National Association of Free Will Baptists—*William F. Davidson* 129
7. The Primitive or Old School Baptists—*John G. Crowley* 158
8. The North American Baptist Conference—*Philip E. Thompson* 182
9. Baptists in Canada—*William H. Brackney* 206
10. Seventh Day Baptists—*Don A. Sanford* 227
11. The Cooperative Baptist Fellowship—*Walter B. Shurden* 242
12. Baptist Americanus—*Lydia Huffman Hoyle* 269
Contributors 285

FOREWORD

Telling the Baptist story is usually connected to articulating the Baptist identity. Baptist historians and theologians, after discussing the diverse beginnings of the movement, especially the Calvinist-Arminian divide, seem to look for the common thread that weaves the movement together. For some, the thread is very small and consists of nothing other than adult believers' baptism by immersion. Many, such as H. Wheeler Robinson in *The Life and Faith of the Baptists* from 1927 or William Brackney in in *The Baptists* from 1994 identify four or five Baptist distinctives. By distinctives, these representative writers propose that Baptist identity is reflected in the movement's unique approach to believer's Baptist, local church autonomy, the final authority of the Bible, and a passion for religious liberty. To find a Baptist or a Baptist organization is to find a person or community that holds these values.

Other historians focus less on distinctives than on characteristics. Leon McBeth, for example, lists ten theological propositions that Baptists share with other Christians, ranging from the Trinity and Scripture to the doctrine of ministry and the idea of religious liberty. His story of Baptists, told in *The Baptist Heritage: Four Centuries of Baptist Witness*, then traces how Baptists have uniquely approached these ideas that they share with the wider Christian community.

Both the approach that focuses on Baptist distinctives and the approach that focus on Baptist commonalities with the wider Christian community look for the shared identity or common ground that all Baptists possess. In addition to Baptist distinctives, though, the Baptist movement is not uniform. Different Baptist communities take the shared principles of believer's baptism and local church autonomy and form very different congregations and denominational movements. These differences are centered around region. The creation of the Southern

Baptist Convention and what would become the American Baptist Church grew out of the national division over slavery, an ethical conflict that fell along a regional fault line. While both denominations expanded into the entire U. S. in the twentieth century, and while both had Baptist distinctives, Southern Baptists had their own unique identity, as did American Baptists.

Ethnicity also shaped and formed Baptist communities. The African-American community, while found in all Baptist denominations, formed the various National Baptist denominations in the late 1800s and again in the early 1960s. While it is easy to find the distinctives shared by National Baptists and Southern Baptists and Free Will Baptists, to understand Baptist identity fully, one needs to discover the uniqueness of the Nationals. In what ways is the National Baptist story unique and separate from the story of other Baptist families.

These differences of region and ethnicity are just two aspects that reflect Baptist diversity. A full understanding of Baptist identity mandates that we know more than Baptist distinctives and commonalities. The student of Baptist life needs to understand Baptist diversity. While the Baptist movement has much in common, it also has a breadth and diversity to it that cannot be discovered in a metanarrative of Baptist life.

Glenn Jonas' edited volume shifts from an interest in metanarrative to a telling of local stories. The local stories that the chapters in his book are the narratives of different Baptist denominations in America. Belief and distinctive provide only one window into Baptist identity. Baptists have lived out their story in different communities or denominations. Baptist identity has long needed a discussion of the different groups that are Baptist. This volume does that.

I get a series of questions in the Baptist history course that I teach that current volumes do not address or answer in sufficient detail (nor should they—such is not their focus). My students, in addition to asking about Baptist distinctives, wonder about the story of different Baptist subdenominations. With the emphasis on Baptist diversity, how is that diversity reflected in institutional life? What is a Free Will Baptist? A

Primitive Baptist? A North American Baptist? These are the kinds of questions that my students ask, in addition to others. This volume now provides them a place to begin to find that answer.

Mel Hawkins
Associate Professor of Religion
Carson-Newman College

PREFACE

There is an oft-quoted story attributed to Søren Kierkegaard about a fire that broke out in a theatre. The stage manager sent a clown out on the stage to warn the people. No one took the clown seriously, however, because they thought his warnings and gestures were merely his act. Referencing the story, John Claypool says "they heard the clown with their eyes."[1]

Baptists have been portrayed in a negative light recently because of incidents perpetrated by two pastors in North Carolina. The first involved Rev. Chan Chandler, pastor of East Waynesville Baptist Church, who led efforts to expel nine members of his congregation for refusing to support President Bush in the 2004 presidential election. The story gained national attention in May 2005, and the exposure coupled with the potential for legal action led to Chandler's resignation.[2]

The second incident involved Rev. Creighton Lovelace, pastor of Danieltown Baptist Church in Forest City, North Carolina, who posted a message that read "The Koran Needs To Be Flushed" on a sign in front of his church.[3] At first he refused to apologize even in the face of

---

[1] The story was originally told by Sören Kierkegaard in *Either/Or*, vol. 1, ed. and trans. Howard V. Hong and Edna H. Hong (Princeton: Princeton University Press, 1987) 30. For John Claypool's use of the story, see John R. Claypool, *The Preaching Event* (Waco: Word Books, 1980) 125. It is interesting to note how various preachers and theologians have embellished this story from its original form in Kierkegaard.

[2] See http://www.biblicalrecorder.org/content/news/2005/5_11_2005/ne110505 pastor.shtml (accessed 28 May 2005).

[3] See http://www.biblicalrecorder.org/content/news/2005/5_25_2005/ne250505 activist.shtml (accessed 29 May 2005). According to this article, Creighton graduated from high school in 2000 and claims to possess four educational degrees including a doctoral degree from "Slidell Baptist Seminary" in Slidell, Louisiana. According to Lovelace, he received all four degrees in just fifteen months. He is also a member of the Sons of Confederate Veterans and in 2001 circulated a petition proposing a constitutional amendment that would allow North Carolina to secede from the United States because of his concern that the nation might allow homosexual

massive criticism from community and Southern Baptist leaders. However, he quickly relented and changed the sign, saying, "Now I realize how offensive this is to them, and after praying about it, I have chosen to remove the sign. I apologize for posting that message and deeply regret that it has offended so many in the Muslim community."[4]

I worry sometimes that non-Baptists in the Christian world hear *Baptists* "with their eyes rather than their ears." By that, I mean it is easy to stereotype Baptists on the basis of the "clowns" who seem to receive much of the national media attention at times. Readers should be reminded, though, that although Baptists do have their share of "clowns," they still have a rich tradition of diversity. Not all Baptists are like the caricature.

The chapters that follow in this book are designed to demonstrate to the reader the remarkable diversity within the Baptist tradition by highlighting some of the major Baptist groups in North America. Deborah Van Broekhoven provides an essay on American Baptists that chronicles the development of the first national organization of Baptists in North America. Doug Weaver then writes about the Southern Baptist Convention, organized in 1845 due to Southern defense of slavery. Sandy Martin's essay on National Baptists describes the long, rich African American Baptist tradition in North America. Jerry Faught follows with an essay that highlights independent Baptists, a Baptist tradition often neglected in Baptist academia. William Davidson contributes an informative essay on the Free Will Baptist tradition in North America. John Crowley's article on Primitive Baptists brings to light a tradition that is often misunderstood. Philip Thompson chronicles the German Baptist tradition with his article on North American Baptists. Bill Brackney provides keen insights into the Baptist movement in Canada with his essay on Canadian Baptists. Don Sanford's essay brings to light the Seventh Day Baptist tradition and its distinctive

---

marriage and abolish churches. See http://speakout.com/petitions/1305.html (accessed 29 May 2005).

[4] See http://biblicalrecorder.org/content/news/2005/5_26_2005/ne260505apastor.shtml (accessed 29 May 2005).

contribution to the Baptist family. Walter Shurden chronicles one of the newest Baptist traditions, the Cooperative Baptist Fellowship, in his article. Finally, Lydia Hoyle provides a summation of other Baptist traditions in North America.

This book in no way attempts to be comprehensive. Rather, I have selected several of the more well-known Baptist traditions and have engaged, where possible, a representative historian from that tradition to explain its origin as well as any distinctive belief the tradition may have. My hope is that the reader will come to appreciate the broad diversity among Baptists and see this as the unique strength of the movement.

W. Glenn Jonas, Jr.
Buies Creek, North Carolina
May 2005

ACKNOWLEDGMENTS

Producing a book is never a solitary undertaking. I need to thank numerous individuals for their help in producing this book. First, I would like to thank all of the Baptist historians who contributed their valuable time to produce the articles that follow. Their expertise and professionalism is evident. Their attention to detail and accuracy made my job as editor much easier, and I am grateful to them.

A word of gratitude also needs to be said to Mr. Derek Hogan, Theological Reference Librarian and Instructor in New Testament at the Campbell University Divinity School. He provided valuable assistance in helping me to secure information as well as interlibrary loan materials that were necessary to complete this work.

My student worker for the past four years, Ms. Shelley Varner, was also extremely helpful in producing this book. She proved to be valuable as she read each chapter and happened to notice things here and there that I had missed. I owe her a debt of gratitude for her good work on this project over the last year.

Finally, a word of thanks goes to my family: my wife, Pam, and daughters, Hannah and Gracie. Thank you for your patience as I have talked about this project and as I have spent late nights trying to complete it.

Chapter 1

Defining a Tradition:

A River Runs Through It

W. Glenn Jonas, Jr.

What is the essence of *Baptistness*? In other words, what (if anything) is the essential characteristic shared by all Baptist groups? Baptist historians and theologians have attempted to identify distinctive Baptist principles for many years.[1] Since the takeover of the Southern Baptist Convention by fundamentalists in 1979, moderate Baptists in the South have been especially active in producing a plethora of books written for the laity attempting to describe Baptist principles on a more popular level.[2] Most of these efforts usually center on several classic principles

---

[1] An excellent discussion of some of these attempts by Baptist historians can be found in Bill J. Leonard, *Baptist Ways: A History* (Valley Forge: Judson Press, 2003) 2–10.

[2] Several good examples of this approach to defining Baptists on a more popular level are Alan Neely, *Being Baptist Means Freedom* (Charlotte: Southern Baptist Alliance, 1988); Gary E. Parker, *Principles Worth Protecting* (Macon GA: Smyth & Helwys Publishing, 1993); and William Powell Tuck, *Our Baptist Tradition* (Macon GA: Smyth & Helwys Publishing, 1993). The best discussion of Baptist principles for a lay audience, however, is Walter B. Shurden's *The Baptist Identity: Four Fragile Freedoms* (Macon GA: Smyth & Helwys Publishing, 1993). This book has been used widely in Baptist churches for a variety of study courses. Instead of listing a group of *principles* that define the Baptist tradition, Shurden synthesizes the entire Baptist tradition to the single concept of *freedom*. He then discusses how Baptists have lived out that freedom in four distinct ways: "Bible Freedom," "Soul

that are then touted as the definition of a *true* Baptist. These lists of Baptist principles usually include the following topics: baptism by immersion, regenerate church membership, local church autonomy, priesthood of the believer (sometimes referred to as liberty of conscience), religious freedom, separation of church and state, and biblical authority. Those groups that identify themselves as "Baptists" who may disagree with one or more of these principles are usually regarded in some way as counterfeit Baptists.

This approach seems to be lacking when one surveys the entirety of the Baptist tradition. For example, some Baptists in America believe in strict separation of the institutions of church and state. But there are other Baptists in America who refuse to use that terminology and argue that the founders of our country never intended such. Some Baptists insist on the priesthood of the believer, arguing that each person under the inspiration of the Holy Spirit can interpret Scripture for himself or herself. Other Baptists have such a strong belief in pastoral authority to the degree that the pastor is granted the responsibility of providing the congregation with the correct interpretation of Scripture. Or consider the practice of baptism by immersion. Other Christian groups that do not refer to themselves as "Baptist" share this practice. There are even some Baptist groups that do not insist on believer's baptism for church membership. Therefore, one is hard pressed to identify even believer's baptism by immersion as the distinctive characteristic of Baptists.[3]

More recently, Bill J. Leonard in his *Baptist Ways: A History* has suggested an entirely new approach for understanding Baptist identity. Acknowledging that "[n]umerous scholars have sought to delineate the

---

Freedom," "Church Freedom," and "Religious Freedom." Shurden also edited a multivolume series called *Proclaiming the Baptist Vision* (also published by Smyth & Helwys, 1993–1999) that includes volumes on the priesthood of all believers, the Bible, the church, religious liberty, and baptism and the Lord's Supper.

[3] Believer's baptism by immersion is the "functional essence of the Baptist identity," according to historian William Brackney. See his "Commonly (Though Falsely) Called': Reflections on the Search for Baptist Identity," in *Perspectives in Churchmanship: Essays in Honor of Robert Torbet*, ed. David Sholer (Macon GA: Mercer University Press, 1986) 71.

essence of the Baptists, with their conclusions often being as diverse as the distinctives they sought to define,"[4] he proceeds to suggest that "another way to describe the similarities and disparities in Baptist identity is to view classic distinctives as dynamics moving in tandem across a wide spectrum of belief and practice."[5] He suggests eight "dialectics" that serve to illustrate a tension among competing Baptist groups over each of the classic distinctives. These include authority of Scripture and liberty of conscience; local church autonomy and associational cooperation; congregational lay leadership and pastoral authority; instantaneous regeneration and gradual process; baptism and Communion as sacraments and symbols; statements of faith as confessional and creedal; religious liberty and Christian citizenship; theological and ecclesial diversity.[6]

Leonard's Baptist "ways" thesis allows for a greater sense of diversity within the Baptist family. He recognizes that even over the classic "distinctives," there is disagreement among Baptists. But the question still remains. Is there a common characteristic that runs through the Baptist tradition? I would contend that over four centuries of Baptist history, the essential quality that identifies Baptists is diversity through dissent. In other words, Baptist conflict spawns new Baptist traditions. This, in turn, creates Baptist diversity. Diversity-through-dissent therefore becomes the central identifying characteristic of the Baptist tradition.

From the beginning until the present, Baptist churches have divided and formed new Baptist churches, from which new Baptist movements often spring. Even the first Baptist congregation in Amsterdam, soon after it rejected infant baptism and accepted believer's baptism, divided over the pastor's desire to unite with the Mennonites. Since then, Baptists have always been a contentious, restless group of Christians.

The Baptist tendency toward controversy and division is so much a part of the tradition that Baptists ridicule themselves about it. There is a

---

[4] Leonard, *Baptist Ways*, 2.

[5] Ibid., 6.

[6] Ibid., 6–10.

humorous story about the Baptist who was stranded on a desert island. One day a ship came to the island and the shipwrecked Baptist ran out to greet it. "I'm so glad you're here," he said. "I've been alone on this island for five years." The captain replied, "If you're all alone, why do I see three huts?" The Baptist answered, "Well, I live in one and go to church in another." "What about the third hut?" asked the captain. "That's where I used to go to church." There is also an old saying: "Wherever there are two Baptists you'll find three opinions."

Historian Walter Shurden captures the essence of Baptistness by recognizing that "Baptists were the 'agitators' of the seventeenth century."[7] After the birth of the Baptist tradition, Baptists quickly began to challenge the *status quo*. They challenged the magistrates' authority over religious matters. They challenged the state church's insistence on religious uniformity. Shurden adds, "Baptists were born in the bosom of radicalism! They are born fighters because they were born fighting!"[8]

Historians Samuel Hill and Robert Torbet agree. In their book *Baptists North and South* they argue that the "total Baptist communion has no instrument of unity intrinsic to its structure." Consequently, Baptists are more likely to splinter than perhaps any other group simply because there is "neither bishop, nor general assembly, nor pope, nor creed to serve as a Baptist agent of cohesion or rallying center." Where Baptist unity has existed, it has been as the result of intentional efforts "motivated by a specific desire among some to practice the given spiritual unity of the Body of Christ," and not the result of any denominational "organizational structures."[9]

Four characteristics in the Baptist tradition make diversity-through-dissent inevitable. First, Baptists have a polygenetic origin. Second, Baptists are devoted to the concept of biblical authority and, on occasion, they tend to be Biblicists on some issues. Third, Baptist history

---

[7] Walter B. Shurden, *Not a Silent People: Controversies That Have Shaped Southern Baptists* (Macon GA: Mercer University Press, 1995) 2.

[8] Ibid., 1.

[9] Samuel S. Hill and Robert G. Torbet, *Baptists North and South*, (Valley Forge: The Judson Press, 1964): p. 64.

is replete with primitivism, the concept that the Baptist tradition is the restoration of true New Testament Christianity. Fourth, Baptists have always been advocates for freedom, both for the individual and the believing community. Taken together, these traits explain why Baptists have a penchant for controversy.

A Polygenetic Provenance

Unlike Lutherans who have Martin Luther and Methodists who have John Wesley, Baptists have difficulty discerning one founder to which the entire tradition can be traced. John Smyth was the founder of the earliest branch of English Baptists, the General Baptists. While they were the earliest form of the Baptist witness in the seventeenth century, about thirty years after their origin, another group called the Particular Baptists arose independently in England.

Arminian in their theology, General Baptists are so named because of their belief in *general* atonement, the concept that Jesus' death on the cross can be applicable for all humans. Furthermore, General Baptists arose from a radical expression of the separatist tradition. Educated at Cambridge (usually considered more radical than Oxford), John Smyth believed the Church of England to be the "Antichrist."[10] He was an agitator who became outspoken about the Church of England and Queen Elizabeth's *via media*, publicly denouncing all sorts of practices, but most frequently the clergy, whom he considered to be too similar to Catholic priests. He became so outspoken and bold that he was arrested and spent a short period of time in prison for refusing to conform to the practices of the Church of England.[11] One of Smyth's contemporaries

---

[10] W. T. Whitley, *The Works of John Smyth*, vol. 1 (Cambridge: Cambridge University Press, 1915) lxvi.

[11] H. Leon McBeth, *The Baptist Heritage: Four Centuries of Baptist* Witness (Nashville: Broadman Press, 1987) 32.

described him as "a learned man, and of good ability, but of an unsettled head."[12]

In 1606 Smyth made a formal break with the Church of England. He moved to Gainsborough and identified with a separatist congregation there, soon becoming its pastor. Encountering persecution, the congregation first divided into two different churches in order to be less conspicuous, but eventually both separatist groups decided to leave England and become expatriates in Amsterdam, Holland, where they could worship freely. Smyth's group, also led by a prominent layman named Thomas Helwys, arrived in 1607 and was befriended by a Mennonite named Jan Munter. Helwys and Smyth, along with the other English expatriates in their group, took jobs at Munter's place of business called the East India Bakehouse where they worked making a hardtack type of biscuit that was used on the numerous ships coming in and out of Amsterdam.[13]

The circumstances suggest that Smyth was influenced by the Mennonites and their distinctive practice of believer's baptism. Sometime in 1609 he baptized himself before the congregation, thereby publicly rejecting his infant baptism.[14] Then, he proceeded to baptize the other members of the group, giving birth to history's first Baptist church. Not long after this experience, however, Smyth began to regard this self-baptism as invalid because he believed it had no apostolic authority. He suggested that the group seek membership with the Mennonites and be baptized into their fellowship.

This unrest in Smyth's spirit eventually led to a significant amount of unrest in the congregation, so much so that they did what Baptists have been famous for ever since; they split! Smyth and some of the group remained in Amsterdam and sought membership with the

---

[12] Daniel Neal, *The History of the Puritans*, 4 vols. (London: Richard Hett: 1732–1738) 1:243, as cited in McBeth, *Baptist Heritage*, 33.

[13] McBeth, *Baptist Heritage*, 34.

[14] Smyth's *se-baptism* (self-baptism) was by the method of *affusion* or pouring. The practice of believer's baptism by immersion did not become standard until around 1641 when the Particular Baptists adopted immersion.

Mennonites. Smyth died of tuberculosis in 1612 unaffiliated with any church. Helwys, a much more stable leader, took the remnant of the group back to England and in 1612 and established the first Baptist church on English soil in the Spittalfields district outside of London.[15]

The Particular Baptists also arose in England and developed from a much more moderate expression of English Separatism. Calvinist in their theology, Particular Baptists got their name from their belief in *particular* atonement, the concept that Jesus' death is only for those whom God has elected.

The first Particular Baptists can be traced to a separatist congregation in London established in 1616. Historians usually refer to this church by using the initials of its first three pastors, Henry Jacob, John Lathrop, and Henry Jessey, or the "JLJ Church." Evidence suggests that this separatist church began having discussions about baptism as early as the 1630s and some of the members opted for believer's baptism about 1633. The church remained in harmony for the next five years until the group rejecting infant baptism separated in 1638, thereby creating the first Particular Baptist church. Records from this church, though sketchy, indicate that by 1641 their mode of baptism changed from affusion (pouring) to immersion.[16] Therefore, the Particular Baptists were the first Baptists to baptize by immersion. While General Baptists gave Baptists their understanding of the "meaning" of baptism (believer's baptism instead of infant baptism), the Particular Baptists provided the "mode" (immersion).

General and Particular Baptists continued in England separate from one another for the next two centuries. During the eighteenth century, Particular Baptists experienced numerical decline as a result of controversies over their Calvinist beliefs. An exaggerated form of Calvinism caused some Particular Baptists to reject efforts to evangelize. Andrew Fuller and William Carey in the late eighteenth and early nineteenth centuries, both proponents of a much more moderate form of

---

[15] McBeth, *Baptist Heritage*, 35–39.

[16] William H. Brackney, *Historical Dictionary of the Baptists* (Lanham MD: The Scarecrow Press, 1999) s.v. "Particular Baptists," 317–18.

Calvinism, are usually credited with bringing a renewal to the Particular Baptist tradition.

General Baptists, on the other hand, had problems from the theological left. Rationalism leading to universalism and anti-trinitarianism led to decline among General Baptists during much of the eighteenth century. Dan Taylor, greatly influenced by the Wesleyan revivals, began a movement called the New Connection among General Baptists that served to revive its numbers. In 1891, General and Particular Baptists formally united with each other in England.[17]

In addition to the influence of English Separatism on early Baptists, several Baptist scholars have maintained that the Anabaptist tradition also contributed to the birth of the Baptists.[18] The support for this argument is based more on circumstances than documentation, but the circumstantial evidence is strong. While in Amsterdam, the Smyth-Helwys group clearly developed a close association with Jan Munter and his fellow Mennonites. Although there is no specific document to indicate that Smyth developed his believer's baptism ideas from the Mennonites, it can be argued that he borrowed their mode of baptism (affusion); logically the close contact between the two groups led to influence. However, the dearth of documentation on the matter causes many historians to discount Anabaptist origin.[19]

While a variety of historians can be found who argue the presence of Anabaptist influence on the rise of the General Baptists, few have ventured to argue that Anabaptists influenced the rise of the later Particular Baptists. One Baptist scholar, Glen Stassen, argued convincingly that the theological foundation of the Particular Baptist tradition lay in the work of Menno Simons, a leading sixteenth-century Anabaptist leader. Elements of *The Foundation of Christian Doctrine*,

---

[17] See McBeth, *Baptist Heritage*, 153–99 for a discussion of the General and Particular Baptists in eighteenth-century England.

[18] McBeth, *Baptist Heritage*, 52–58.

[19] Excellent discussions of the historiography of this issue can be found in McBeth, *Baptist Heritage*, 49–63; Leonard, *Baptist Ways*, 10–15; and Robert G. Torbet, *A History of the Baptists*, 3rd ed. (Valley Forge: Judson Press, 1980) 18–21.

Simons's most widely distributed work, can be seen in the first confession of faith written by the Particular Baptists. Therefore, Stassen argues, the "Particular Baptists should not be ignored in our assessment of Anabaptist influence on Baptist origins."[20]

If Anabaptist influence was a part of the origin of the earliest two groups of Baptists, and enough evidence seems to suggest that it is a strong possibility, then the early Baptists came about as a synthesis of two divergent traditions: Dutch Anabaptism and English Separatism. This synthesis has created a tension in the Baptist tradition similar to the tension between General and Particular Baptists, which occasionally serves as root cause for disputes and diversity among different groups of Baptists.

A Bent Toward Biblicism

Growing out of English Separatism, Baptists shared a general disdain for non-congregational church governance. Baptist churches are free to govern themselves however they see fit. A local Baptist church may choose to cooperate with other Baptist churches to do missions, or that church may choose to carry out its mission commitments completely independent of other Baptist mission efforts. Furthermore, local Baptist churches choose their own congregational leaders and pastors.

For non-Baptists, especially those from a tradition with bishops governing the local churches, it may be unclear who or what holds authority for Baptists. In place of the authority of bishops, Baptists regard the Bible as central to their faith and practice. This concept has been evident from the beginning of the Baptist tradition. After a statement indicating that the local church has the sole responsibility of electing its leaders, John Smyth's *A Short Confession of Faith* (1610) states:

---

[20] Glen Stassen, "Opening Menno Simons's Foundation-Book and Finding the Father of Baptist Origins Alongside the Mother—Calvinist Congregationalism," *Baptist History and Heritage* 33 (Spring 1998): 34. Stassen published another version of this article in "Anabaptist Influence in the Origin of the Particular Baptists," *The Mennonite Quarterly Review* 36 (October 1962): 324–333.

> The doctrine which by the foresaid ministers must be proposed to the people, is the same which Christ brought out of heaven, which he, by word and work, that is, by doctrine and life, hath taught, which was preached by the apostles of Christ, by the commandment of Christ and the Spirit, which we find written...in the Scripture of the New Testament, whereto we apply whatsoever we find in the canonical book of the Old Testament, which hath affinity and verity, which by doctrine of Christ and his apostles, and consent and agreement, with the government of his Spiritual Kingdom.[21]

From this earliest confession of faith to the most recent Baptist confessions, the primacy of biblical authority has been evident in the Baptist tradition. In some cases, however, that attention to biblical authority has led to Biblicism. Biblicism can be defined as "the isolation of the authority of the Bible apart from and independent of engaging conversation with the insights and contributions of other areas of study."[22] Tending toward a literal interpretation of Scripture without the benefit of historical or literary contextual analysis, Biblicism understands the Bible as more than just a book of faith and theology. It also views the Bible as a book of scientific and historical truth, frequently in opposition to discoveries made by modern science and historians.[23]

The practice of "proof-texting" is one example in which Biblicism can be seen in the Baptist tradition. This practice, evident in Baptist confessions of faith, uses biblical passages to justify the various articles of faith described in the confession. While the intention for citing Scriptures within the confessions is to show that the doctrinal ideas are derived from biblical authority, unwittingly, a "move from biblical authority to Biblicism occurs in the essential identification of the

---

[21] William L. Lumpkin, *Baptist Confessions of Faith* (Valley Forge: Judson Press, 1969) 109.

[22] E. Frank Tupper, "Biblicism, Exclusivism, Triumphalism: The Travail of Baptist Identity," *Perspectives in Religious Studies* 29 (Winter 2002): 412.

[23] "Biblicism," *The Encyclopedia of Christianity*, 4 vols. (Grand Rapids: Eerdmans, 1999) 1: 255.

confessional statement and its biblical foundation together, the one equivalent to the other."[24]

Biblicism has led to conflict among Baptists. When the Bible is read literally without incorporating good principles of hermeneutics and then used to proof-text certain doctrinal ideas, a recipe for conflict is created. Frank Tupper observes that the "slippage between an appropriate referencing of the biblical traditions and an inappropriate proof-texting for doctrinaire compliance has often proven most notable in those articles asserting claims wherein different Baptists themselves cannot agree."[25]

The current debate among various Baptists about the role of women in ministry is illustrative of how Biblicism can lead to conflict and division. Many Baptists argue on the basis of Scripture references such as 1 Timothy 2:11–12 and 3:1–15 that God does not allow for women to occupy the role of pastor in a church. Other Baptists have the opposite opinion, arguing that God makes no gender distinction in calling people to pastoral ministry. They argue that the passages in 1 Timothy should be interpreted in their historical context rather than as a timeless principle for all ages. They cite biblical references such as Galatians 3:28 as providing the timeless principle. Both groups claim biblical authority but disagree vehemently on the outcome. Ultimately, this issue was one of several that led to a split in the Southern Baptist Convention in the late twentieth century.

Another issue that badly divided nineteenth-century Baptists in America was slavery. Baptists in the South, led by such prominent pastors as Richard Furman, argued that Scripture divinely ordained slavery. In a treatise written to South Carolina governor John Lyde Wilson, Furman argued,

> the right of holding slaves is clearly established by the Holy Scriptures, both by precept and example.... Had the holding of slaves been a moral evil, it cannot be supposed, that the inspired Apostles, who feared not the faces of men, and were ready to lay down their

---

[24] Tupper, "Biblicism, Exclusivism, Triumphalism," 412.

[25] Ibid.

> lives in the cause of their God, would have tolerated it, for a moment, in the Christian Church.... In proving this subject justifiable by Scriptural authority, its morality is also proved; for the Divine Law never sanctions immoral actions.[26]

On the other hand, Baptists in the North had a different view of the Bible's teaching on slavery. In 1845, the year that the Southern Baptist Convention was organized, two prominent Baptists, Richard Fuller from South Carolina and Francis Wayland from Rhode Island, debated this issue through written correspondence. Although much more irenic in their disagreements on this issue than many of their day, both men appealed to biblical authority. Wayland expressed hope that "[b]elieving as we both do that the Bible is a perfect rule of duty, if we can ascertain what it teaches, we may reasonably hope that our opinions may yet coincide."[27] Nevertheless, both men arrived at different conclusions about the Bible's teaching on slavery.

Fuller's approach was more Biblicist, arguing from a literal reading of both Old and New Testament texts. Wayland's approach was to see the texts in their original historical context and argue that ultimately the words of Jesus, "You shall love your neighbor as yourself" (Matthew 22:39) and "In everything do to others as you would have them do to you" (Matthew 7:12), comprise a "supreme law" of God that is the timeless truth contradicting the institution of slavery.[28]

A Propensity Toward Primitivism[29]

Early Baptists believed they had restored genuine New Testament Christianity. This primitivism was based on their rejection of infant

---

[26] Richard Furman, "Exposition of the Views of Baptists Relative to the Coloured Population in the United States in a Communication to the Governor of South Carolina," 2nd ed. (Charleston: A. E. Miller, 1838); online at http://alpha.furman.edu/~benson/docs/rcd-fmn1.htm (accessed 25 March 2005).

[27] Richard Fuller and Francis Wayland, *Domestic Slavery Considered as a Scriptural Institution* (New York: Lewis Colby, 1845) 49.

[28] Ibid., 29–30.

[29] The term "primitivism" is taken from Bill Leonard. See his *Baptist Ways*, 5.

baptism. Frank Tupper argues that because "all non-voluntary established churches practiced infant baptism, the decisive moment in the Baptist act of church restoration occurred in believer's baptism. Indeed, believer's baptism was the linchpin around which Baptist ecclesiology originated and revolved: 'The true church' practices 'true baptism.'"[30]

The importance of baptism in Baptist self-understanding can be seen in the earliest Baptist writings. John Smyth believed that he had discovered the true church when he rejected infant baptism. In 1609 he wrote a stinging criticism of the Church of England called *The Character of the Beast*, in which he argued that the Church of England, like the Roman Catholic Church, was a false church mainly because of its practice of infant baptism. Furthermore, he argued that the Separatists who withdrew from the Church of England could not consider their churches to be uncorrupted until they rejected the practice of infant baptism and established believer's baptism as their basis for constitution.[31] Smyth wrote,

> This therfor is the question: whither the baptisme of infants be lawful, yea or nay: & whither persons baptized being infants must not renounce that false baptisme, & assume the true baptisme of Chr: which is to be administred vppon persons confessing their faith & their sinnes: ...Let the indifferent reader judg of the whole & give sentence without partiality: & I doubt not but he shalbe constrained to give glory to God in acknowledging the error of baptizing infants, to have been a cheef point of Antichristianisme, & the very essence & constitution of the false Church.[32]

Smith's primitivism led him to believe that he was moving from a false church, constituted upon a false baptism, to the true New Testament Church based on believer's baptism.

---

[30] Tupper, "Biblicism, Exclusivism, Triumphalism," 415.

[31] H. Leon McBeth, *A Sourcebook for Baptist Heritage* (Nashville: Broadman Press, 1990) 18.

[32] John Smyth, *The Character of the Beast* (1609), as cited by McBeth, *A Sourcebook*, 19.

The most divisive Baptist movement resulting from primitivism is found in Landmarkism, which impacted the nascent Southern Baptist Convention in the middle of the nineteenth century. With its most prolific advocates, J. R. Graves, A. C. Dayton, and J. M. Pendleton, the Landmark Movement suggested that a local Baptist church is the only true expression of New Testament Christianity. Churches with other denominational stripes were not true churches at all, but were in fact pseudo-churches. Proponents of the movement advocated closed Communion (Communion could only be received by the members of the local Baptist church where it was administered), rejected "alien" baptism (baptism in churches other than Baptist), discouraged pulpit exchanges with non-Baptist ministers, and argued for an unbroken succession of Baptist churches back through church history to Jesus, John the Baptist, and the Jordan River. The Landmark controversy is arguably one of the most divisive movements ever to develop within the Baptist tradition.[33]

By attaching claims of primitivism to the Baptist tradition, some Baptist groups set themselves up for division. Discovering the essence of New Testament Christianity is elusive because of our limited knowledge of the church in the New Testament as well as cultural and historical differences between their time and ours. Bill Leonard has suggested that "Determining the marks of the true church, even in the New Testament, is no easy matter, and Baptists themselves divided over which distinguishing qualities were most biblical."[34]

---

[33] One of the classic treatments of Landmarkism is James E. Tull, "A Study of Southern Baptist Landmarkism in the Light of Historical Baptist Ecclesiology" (Ph.D. diss., Columbia University, New York, 1960). For a brief analysis and summary of the movement, see McBeth, *Baptist Heritage*, 447–61, and Shurden, *Not a Silent People*, 39–51.

[34] Leonard, *Baptist Ways*, 5.

A Fealty to Freedom

Born during the reign of King James I, who was bitterly opposed to religious dissent, Baptists developed a strong reverence for freedom of conscience. Soon after Thomas Helwys brought the first Baptists back to England from Amsterdam and established the first Baptist church on English soil, he wrote a treatise on religious freedom called *The Mistery of Iniquity*. Complaining about the king's antipathy toward Baptists and other dissenters, Helwys declared,

> wee do freely professe that our lord the King hath no...power over...consciences,...for our lord the King is but an earthly King, and if the Kings people be obedient & true subjects, obeying all humane lawes made by the King, our lord the King can require no more. For mens religion to God, is betwixt God and themselves; the King shall not answer for it, neither may the King be judg between God and man.... Let them be heretikes, Turks, Jews, or whatsoever, it apperteynes not to the earthly power to punish them in the least measure.[35]

In this paragraph, Helwys makes two important points that illustrate the early Baptist commitment to freedom of conscience. First, he indicates that a person's faith is exclusively between himself or herself and God. The individual's conscience is off-limits to any other earthly entity. Second, Helwys demonstrates that while the early Baptists desired freedom for themselves, they were also willing to fight for freedom for all, a novel idea in his day.

Walter Shurden argues that freedom is at the heart of the Baptist identity and has manifested itself in four different ways: Bible Freedom, Soul Freedom, Church Freedom, and Religious Freedom.[36] Shurden believes that the "Baptist passion for freedom is a major reason why

---

[35] McBeth, *A Sourcebook*, 72.

[36] Walter B. Shurden, *The Baptist Identity: Four Fragile Freedoms* (Macon GA: Smyth and Helwys, 1993).

there is so much diversity in Baptist life. Baptists differ, and their differences are often broad and deep."[37]

The freedom of the individual conscience before God is a celebrated concept in Baptist history. Charles Deweese indicates that it "fuels the Baptist engine of freedom."[38] Baptist confessions of faith throughout the four centuries of Baptist history have addressed the matter frequently. For example, the Standard Confession (1660), an English General Baptist confession, stated, "That it is the will, and mind of God...that all men should have the free liberty of their own consciences in matters of Religion, or Worship, without the least opposition, or persecution, as simply upon that account; and that for any in Authority otherwise to act, we confidently believe is expressly contrary to the mind of Christ."[39] E. Y. Mullins, in his classic *Axioms of Religion*, argued that commitment to the "competency of the soul in religion" represented the "historical significance" of the Baptist movement.[40] This should not be understood as advocating religious individualism, though. Mullins clarified, "individualism alone is inadequate because man is more than an individual. He is a social being. He has relations to his fellows in the Church, and in the industrial order, and in the State. We must comprehend these relations in our fundamental view."[41] Mullins believed, nevertheless, that soul competency was a bedrock feature for Baptists.

Another Baptist from Mullins's era was George W. Truett, who for forty-seven years served as the pastor of the First Baptist Church in Dallas, Texas. In a famous address he declared,

---

[37] Ibid., 2.

[38] Charles W. Deweese, "Doing Freedom Baptist Style: Liberty of Conscience" (Brentwood: Baptist History and Heritage Society, 2001) 1.

[39] Lumpkin, *Baptist Confessions of Faith*, 232–33, also cited by Deweese, "Doing Freedom Baptist Style," 5.

[40] E. Y. Mullins, *The Axioms of Religion* (Philadelphia: American Baptist Publication Society, 1908) 50–53.

[41] Ibid., 51.

> Out of these two fundamental principles, the supreme authority of the Scriptures and the right of private judgment, have come all the historic protests in Europe and America against unscriptural creeds, polity and rites, and against the unwarranted and impertinent assumption of religious authority over men's consciences, whether by church or by state. Baptists regard as an enormity any attempt to force the conscience, or to constrain men, by outward penalties, to this or that form of religious belief. Persecution may make men hypocrites, but it will not make them Christians.[42]

Echoing Truett, Bill Moyers, a modern observer of Baptists, declared, "Foremost among Baptist convictions—the reason for so much of the dissent that has marked Baptist history—is the right of the individual to follow the dictates of his or her conscience, free from the oppression of an overarching authority, secular or ecclesiastical."[43]

Baptists' support for freedom extends beyond the individual believer to the local church as well. Baptists believe that the local church is free to govern itself, call its ministers, contribute financially as it wills, discipline members, and set policies without any interference from a denominational hierarchy. This local church freedom is the natural progression from individual liberty of conscience. E. Y. Mullins indicates that "[a]ll souls are entitled to equal privileges in the church, just as all churches are entitled to equal privileges in the Kingdom of God. The individual precedes the group logically as well as in order of time, and the organization and government of the local church proceeds on the principle of the voluntary association of free individuals in obedience to Christ and for purposes set forth by him."[44]

Understanding this concept of church freedom in the Baptist tradition allows one to understand why Baptist churches so easily divide.

---

[42] George W. Truett, "Baptists and Religious Liberty," located on the Web site of the Baptist Joint Committee on Public Affairs, http://www.bjcpa.org/resources/publications/pub_truett_address.htm (accessed 23 May 2005).

[43] Bill Moyers, "Foreword," in W. R. Estep, *Revolution within the Revolution, The First Amendment in Historical Context, 1612–1789* (Grand Rapids: William B. Eerdmans, 1990) x, as cited by Deweese, "Doing Freedom Baptist Style," 4.

[44] E. Y. Mullins, *Baptist Beliefs* (Valley Forge: Judson Press, 1925) 65.

There is no governing authority over a local church except the membership of that church. Therefore, when disputes arise within the congregation, it becomes quite easy for the church to divide since no denominational authority exists to stop it.

A Tumultuous Tradition

Four key characteristics serve as the *fuel*, which, from time to time, has ignited controversy among Baptists. The polygenetic origin of Baptists has created a mixed theological tradition that sometimes tends to spotlight differences rather than unity. The attention that Baptists devote to biblical authority often leads to Biblicism in which various parties disagree with each other over ideas, all claiming support from the Bible. The primitivism held by many Baptists, that the Baptist tradition is the one most like the early church, often creates close-mindedness toward other Christian groups. Without balance from the broader Christian tradition, Baptists have often turned in on themselves. Finally, the devotion to freedom, specifically liberty of conscience, has created at times an environment in which conflicts can arise more freely than in other traditions.

The Baptist tradition is perhaps the most varied and diverse of all Protestant traditions. The title of this book, *The Baptist River: Essays on Many Tributaries of a Diverse Tradition*, uses the analogy of a river with tributaries as a way to describe the evolution of the Baptist tradition. In just three years, Baptists will celebrate their 400th anniversary. Throughout their history, Baptists have carved their way through the Protestant wilderness and have become a distinct *river* joining other rivers within the Christian religion. At times, some of the river's tributaries have flowed parallel to each other. Other tributaries have intersected each other, and still others have blended together. Yet, the Baptist river continues to flow. Those who travel this Baptist river often experience a lazy, peaceful journey. At other times, the journey is fraught with rapids and turbulence. Concerning the Baptist river, created by various tributaries, Bill Leonard writes, "Many Baptists seem surprised when disputes arise in their churches or denominational communities. While they well might be saddened by the divisions that have resulted from these confrontations, they should not be surprised. Dissent is one of the Baptist ways."[45]

[45] Leonard, *Baptist Ways*, 10.

Chapter 2

AMERICAN BAPTISTS

Deborah Van Broekhoven

Members of the Congregational and Anglican establishments in colonial America labeled Baptists as fanatics and disturbers of the public order.[1] One can find evidence in support of these accusations in the earliest history of American Baptists. Banished from Massachusetts to the more receptive climate of Rhode Island, the first generation had difficulty agreeing on theology or church order. Even under the pacific leadership of Obadiah Holmes and John Clarke, the Newport church (founded in 1644) suffered two different schisms, the second of which (in 1671) divided members over the question of whether Scripture dictated Sabbath rest and worship on Saturday or Sunday.[2] Arguably, it was this

---

[1] Lewis Peyton Little, *Imprisoned Preachers and Religious Liberty in Virginia* (Lynchburg VA: J. P. Bell Co., 1938), as referenced in Thomas E. Buckley, S.J., "Keeping the Faith: Virginia Baptists and Religious Liberty," *American Baptist Quarterly* 22 (December 2003): 425. On this point I owe a great debt to Dr. Edwin Gaustad and his many publications on early American Baptists. For comments on early drafts, I am grateful to Reid Trulson, Betty Layton, and Richard Pierard.

[2] Even in the denominational histories published for church membership classes or other promotional purposes, authors have had difficulty ignoring the struggle with which American Baptists organized, particularly at a national level. For a brief account of the Newport episode, see Don A. Sanford, *A Free People in Search of a Free Land* (Janesville WI: Seventh Day Baptist Historical Society, 1993) 3–6. For other sympathetic histories of the denomination, see Edward C. Starr, "American Baptist Convention," in *Baptist Advance: The Achievements of the Baptists in North America for a Century and a Half* (Nashville: Broadmans, 1964) 29–130, and Warren Mild, *The Story of American Baptists: The Role of a a Remnant* (Valley Forge: Judson

democratic insistence on the right of individual conscience and individual readings of biblical commandments that made it difficult for Baptists to organize as a denomination rather than a loosely organized movement.

Consequently, the numbers of Baptists rose dramatically in the late colonial and early national period, but the official birth of this Baptist movement was delayed until 1907. Only then did the national mission organizations, voluntary societies supported by a dues-paying membership, build on their custom of holding the anniversary meetings of their societies at the same time and place and agree to a more unified structure. Meeting at Calvary Baptist Church in Washington, D.C., those present agreed to a new umbrella structure, the Northern Baptist Convention.

As component parts of the new convention, the old societies retained their separate legal incorporations, mission programs, and names: the American Baptist Missionary Union (formed in 1814), the American Baptist Publication Society (formed in 1824), the American Baptist Home Mission Society (formed in 1832), the American Baptist Historical Society (formed in 1853), the Woman's American Baptist Home Mission Society (for Eastern women, formed in 1877), the Women's Baptist Home Mission Society (for Western women, formed in 1877), and two foreign mission societies for women, both founded in 1871. By 1913, there remained just two national mission societies for Baptist women, one for home and one for foreign mission work, and both focused on "woman's work for women."

In the new convention format, leaders and organizations in charge of various programs did not change, but the new method of cooperating and governing became more formal, working through two new features: a "General Board" and executive staff working for the convention. Both the board and the new staff were to coordinate and promote the mission

---

Press, 1976). For some comparative perspective, see Everett C. Goodwin, *Down by the Riverside: A Brief History of the Baptists* (Valley Forge: Judson Press, 2002), and Robert G. Torbet, *History of the Baptists* (Philadelphia: Judson Press, 1950; 2nd ed., 1963).

work of the former voluntary societies. Delegates or messengers from the states still attended an annual meeting, but they came as elected representatives of their state convention (or city "society") rather than as dues-paying members of the old societies. These delegates *de facto* added the new role of member of the over-arching societies. The president of the convention served as spokesperson and ceremonial head of the denomination, with Charles Evans Hughes, then governor of New York, elected as the first president. Of chief importance in the structure were the new executive staff positions of corresponding and recording secretaries, who promoted and coordinated mission education and giving, whether for home or foreign, men or women's work.

By 1911, the convention had also added a pension board—the Ministers and Missionaries Benefit Board, which remains the source of pensions for American Baptist (and other Baptist) ministers. At this same meeting, talks about consolidation and shared ministries ended with the convention voting to accept the merger of assets, ministers, and churches from the General Conference of Free [Will] Baptists—their one-time rival in New England and the Midwest. These changes reflect a transformation of fiercely independent and quarrelsome Baptists into a more unified, mainline denomination, albeit one with plenty of room for dissidents.

In fact, competition between the old societies continued, since the reorganization into a convention did not eliminate the old legal structure or the focus of each society on a particular type of mission work (overseas, home, or tract and Bible distribution). The new convention added another layer of national organization and redefined membership as that of congregations, not the dues-paying individuals who had previously made up the membership of the historical mission societies. In the new convention, the size of congregations or regional conventions determined representation on the General Board, not dollars contributed. The societies continued to serve their historic function of raising mission dollars and commissioning missionaries for service at home and abroad. But their board members gained a new role, as "general board" members with a voting interest in the business and policies of the other societies and their mission boards. Despite the new convention structure, member congregations continued to focus on the national programs run by the mission boards, their staff, and missionaries—a reality that led sociologist Paul Harrison to note that the denominational structure, particularly in contrast to other mainline denominations, remained weak.[3]

This new convention structure, however, had deeper roots, particularly in the eighteenth-century work of the Philadelphia Baptist Association (PBA) and its daughter churches and associations. Founded in 1707 after several years of informal meetings, PBA began when five congregations in New Jersey and eastern Pennsylvania pledged to meet annually for worship and consultation. The first such association of American Baptists, the PBA provided advice when congregations brought questions about church discipline, theology, and mission. Because the PBA was the oldest and most peaceful association of American Baptists, Baptists from Massachusetts and Virginia requested of PBA assistance in dealing with repeated jailings and fines and with the theological disagreements or conflicts in practices that congregations were unable to resolve on their own.

Religious persecution of Baptists eased after the American War for Independence, and in the generation following the war, PBA (along with the Massachusetts Baptist Missionary Society) sent missionaries into the Ohio Valley—a movement contested by virulently anti-mission Baptists (extreme Calvinist in their theology), who saw in the new missionaries outsiders from the Eastern establishment who, like corrupt priests in the time of Luther, were guilty of extracting money from simple frontier families. From the anti-mission perspective, these Baptist missionaries were disturbers of the peace, exploiters of the common folk, and guilty of promoting salvation through the good works of the new organizations, whether they promoted Bible-reading, Sunday schools, or temperance.

---

[3] Paul M. Harrison, *Authority and power in the free church tradition; a social case study of the American Baptist Convention* (Princeton: Princeton University Press, 1959).

The importance of PBA increased when in 1826 the new Baptist Tract Society moved from Washington, D.C., to Philadelphia. There the renamed American Baptist Publication Society (ABPS) enlarged its tract ministry and began publishing and distributing tracts and Bibles, along with newspapers. As early as the 1850s, the ABPS was publishing these materials in several languages for use both in the immigrant communities and in overseas missions.[4] Even as Massachusetts Baptists led in organizing support for Adoniram and Ann Judson and their work in Burma, the city of Philadelphia remained the solid center of publishing and home mission efforts through the nineteenth and twentieth centuries. When the denomination's Board of Educational Ministries closed in 2003, several of its ministries continued, including work with colleges and seminaries and the publication work of Judson Press (formerly the American Baptist Publication Society), a part of the operations of the American Baptist Home Mission Society since 2003.

PBA leadership was particularly important in creating spaces within this largely "white" denomination for African Americans and other minorities. In the difficult years after the Civil War and emancipation, "white" and "colored" Baptists struggled to accommodate both

[4] The history of these Baptist organizations is best traced in their annual reports, but there are several helpful summaries, including the special issue, "Chronology of the American Baptist Churches, USA," *American Baptist Quarterly* 14 (June 1995). Also helpful are Robert Torbet, *Venture of Faith: The Story of the American Baptist Foreign Mission Society and the Woman's American Baptist Foreign Mission Society, 1814–1954* (Philadelphia: Judson Press, 1955); Daniel Garden Stevens, *The First Hundred Years of the American Baptist Publication Society* (Philadelphia: The American Baptist Publication Society, 1925); Lempel C. Barnes, Mary C. Barnes, Edward M. Stephenson, *Pioneers of Light: The First Century of the American Baptist Publication Society* (Philadelphia: The American Baptist Publication Society, 1925); Charles L. White, *A Century of Faith* (Philadelphia: Judson Press and the American Baptist Home Mission Society, 1932); G. Pitt Beers, *Ministry to Turbulent America: A History of the American Baptist Home Mission Society Covering Its Fifth Quarter Century, 1932–1957* (Philadelphia: Judson Press, 1957); Bertha Grimmell Judd, *Fifty Golden Years: The First Half Century of the Woman's American Baptist Home Mission Society, 1877–1927* (New York: The Woman's American Baptist Home Mission Society, 1927).

integrated congregations and the increasing numbers of African American congregations.[5] In the District of Columbia, the legacy of slavery and master/servant relationships made integrated churches or associations particularly difficult. In that racial climate, both the American Baptist Home Mission Society (ABHMS) and the PBA worked closely with black churches, schools, and ministers. To some extent this mission in the South competed with pleas from Baptists in the Western U.S., where home missionaries traveled by foot, horseback, wagon, train, and (by the 1930s) automobile. This distribution of tracts, Bibles, and preachers did, however, include some Southern states. There, as well as in the West, these missionaries organized evangelistic services, Sunday schools, and churches.

While the work in the West remained important, after the Civil War, the ABHMS began shifting and adding funding to assist African Americans in the Southern states. Women's work among the freed people focused on ministries to women and children, as evidenced by the pioneer work of Joanna P. Moore, who, in the face of threatened violence from the white community, succeeded in recruiting and supporting hundreds of leaders for the low-profile home educational program she called "Fireside Schools." It is because of this history of concern about race relations that delegates to the 1911 Northern Baptist Convention heard an address by black churchwoman Nannie H. Burroughs on "Some Practical Ways of Solving the Race Problem." Interestingly, they also received lengthy recommendations from the Social Service Commission about how to encourage both rural and city churches to create ministries that targeted immigrants, the problem of child labor, and the saloon—the institution that "liberal" ministers

---

[5] Particularly good on this topic are James Melvin Washington, *Frustrated Fellowship: The Black Baptist Quest for Social Power* (Macon GA: Mercer University Press, 1986), and Evelyn Brooks Higginbotham, *Righteous Discontent: The Women's Movement in the Black Baptist Church, 1880–1920* (Cambridge: Harvard University Press, 1993). For the PBA perspective, see Robert C. Torbet, *A Social History of the Philadelphia Baptist Association: 1707–1940* (Philadelphia: Westbrook Publishing, 1944).

(including Walter Rauschenbusch and Shailer Mathews) saw as promoting excessive consumption of alcohol.[6]

In this same difficult period of race relations, Philadelphia Baptists did their part, not just by producing large numbers of home missionaries and mission dollars, but by welcoming into their association several black churches from as far south as Washington, D.C. As late as 1900, the count of church members for PBA included as many "colored" as "white" members. Still considered a "white" association by both black and white churches, PBA was positive in defending its integrated meetings and meals, and in 1894 had elected as its moderator the Rev. Theodore D. Miller, then pastor of the First African Baptist Church of Philadelphia.[7] It was this radical stand on race that led most Southern Baptists again to see Northern Baptists as "disturbers of the peace," with the consequence that talk of reconciliation and reunion between the Northern and Southern conventions went nowhere.

Strong support for a national denomination also came from Massachusetts and Virginia, with Baptists in both regions inspired by the

---

[6] Moore's autobiography, available on the "Religion of the South" Web pages of the University of North Carolina at Chapel Hill is *"In Christ's Stead;" on Life and Work Among the Negroes of the Southern States* (Chicago: The Woman's Baptist Home Mission Society, 1902). See also the *Annual of the Northern Baptist Convention, 1911, Containing the Proceedings of the Fourth Meeting* (Philadelphia: American Baptist Publication Society, 1911) especially 69 (for Burroughs) and 127–150 (for the Social Service Commission Report, along with reports on ministry to immigrant "foreigners.")

[7] Sorbet, *A Social History of the Philadelphia Baptist Association;* also Charles Brooks, *Official History of the First African Baptist Church* (Philadelphia, 1922)11. At various times in the nineteenth and early twentieth centuries, the terms "colored," "Negro," and "African" (not African American) were commonly used to denote Americans of African descent. The term "white" was less common, since it was assumed as the norm; i.e., only with the publication of John Boles, *Black Southerners, 1619–1869* (Lexington: University of Kentucky Press, 1983), did many (even among the scholarly community) understand that most readers, especially "white" readers, did not grasp the term "Southern" as applying to people of color, despite their life in "the South." More recently, historical studies have also analyzed the meaning of the term "white." See, for example, David Roediger, *Colored White: Transcending the Racial Past* (Berkeley: University of California Press, 2002).

vision of pioneer missionaries, notably William Carey, Luther Rice, Adoniram Judson, and Lott Cary. The earliest state "society" organization among American Baptists, the Massachusetts Baptist Missionary Society, formed in 1802 with the membership consisting of those willing to pay one dollar annually. The Boston Female Society for Missionary Purposes, organized in 1800 by Mary Webb (who from her youth was unable to walk or stand), provided a nearby model for the state mission society. The new state society commissioned and paid three men to undertake preaching tours in several states (and Canada) that brought gospel preaching to those without any regular minister. These early home missionaries also encouraged scattered Christians to organize new Baptist congregations or to affiliate with their brothers and sisters in more settled towns.

It was Congregationalists in Massachusetts, however, who with some financial support from Baptists, commissioned Adoniram Judson and Luther Rice to take the gospel to India. That these missionaries quickly became Baptists is due in part to the influence of British Baptists at the William Carey mission—an endeavor that both Congregational and Baptist readers had been following closely. Knowledge of Baptists in Massachusetts also influenced Judson and Rice. Judson himself credited a sermon printed in the *Massachusetts Baptist Missionary Magazine* (founded in 1803) as the source of his own vision for missionary service.[8] Renamed *American Baptist Magazine* in 1817, then renamed *Missions* in 1910, the publication continues today as *American Baptists in Mission*. The publication also included accounts of mission work in British India (of which Burma was then part). These Baptists had also contributed the better part of the $3,000 given by American Baptists in support of the

---

[8] Melissa Lewis and Mark Heim, "Editorial Introduction" to special issue, "Massachusetts: Mother of American Baptist Missions," *American Baptist Quarterly* 21 (March 2002): 4–9. I am grateful to Reid Trulson for pointing out that both Robert Torbet in *Venture of Faith* and Francis Wayland mention the role of this magazine in Judson's calling. See Francis Wayland, *Memoir of the Life and Labors of the Rev. Adoniram Judson, D.D., Vol. I* (Boston: Phillips, Sampson, & Company, 1853) 29.

Congregational mission to India. After discovering that key biblical texts supported believer's baptism, Judson's and Rice's knowledge of Baptist support for foreign missions made it easier to denounce pedobaptism, resign from the American Board of Commissioners for Foreign Missions, and press American Baptists to form a national organization able to support overseas mission work.

Missionary Luther Rice became the successful ambassador and fundraiser for that infant denomination. He returned home and in 1814 organized the first meeting of the General Missionary Convention of the Baptist Denomination in the United States of America for Foreign Missions, often dubbed the "Triennial Convention." The *Baptist Missionary Magazine* became the national organ for the new convention, as well as the new foreign mission society organized at that meeting. With the split of the denomination in 1845 over slavery, the remaining Northern Baptists renamed their mission society the American Baptist Missionary Union, a name that was changed in 1910 to the American Baptist Foreign Mission Society (the legal name for the current American Baptist Board of International Ministries).

Because Philadelphia had long been the printing and book distribution center in British America, Baptist leaders there easily stepped into a leadership role in creating, printing, and distributing other kinds of publications. Luther Rice worked with Noah Davis in Washington, D.C., to create in 1824 the Baptist General Tract Society. By 1826, Davis moved the operations to Philadelphia, the region from which Judson Press (the society's linear descendant) continues to operate. Philadelphia was the book and publishing center of the new nation, and there the printing operations of the tract society (soon renamed the American Baptist Publication Society, ABPS) grew to provide Bibles and tracts, Christian fiction, mission history, and Sunday school curriculum to millions.

By the 1850s, ABPS began printing materials in German and Swedish, languages of large immigrant communities. This commitment to publish in a variety of languages continued and expanded. By 1900 (and continuing well into the twentieth century), the enterprise produced dozens of "foreign" language publications for use in overseas work and with immigrant populations in the United States and Latin America. Stories published about overseas mission work often mentioned the ABPS papers and Bible picture cards, since these items were used as prizes and teaching tools by missionaries. One story, "What Miss Tingley Does with Papers," listed a dozen ways this missionary shared (and sometimes translated) these materials with pupils and teachers-in-training.[9]

The scope and quality of this publishing operation, combined with financial difficulties in the post-Civil War South, meant that decades after the Southern Baptist Convention formed, American Baptist Publication Society imprints continued to reach Baptists far south of the Mason-Dixon Line. Before the war this was possible because ABPS avoided titles that touched on the sensitive issue of slavery. After the war the practice continued, in part because Southern publishing houses were few and struggling and because ABPS agents, many of them Southerners themselves, provided colorful evangelistic and teaching aids in the form of tracts, Sunday school curriculum, and newspapers. Called colporteurs—a term adapted from the French term for carrying items over the neck—these agents were the backpackers and peddlers of their day. By 1900, most colporteurs used a horse or mule, wagon or cart—and in a few cases, a railroad "chapel" car—to carry their store of Christian literature.

Another reason the ABPS remained popular with some Southerners was their employment of "white" authors—a practice that drew criticism from African American leaders like William Simmons. Simmons himself was a home missionary for the Northern Baptists and a capable writer and educator. Initially the ABPS accepted this criticism and commissioned several pieces from African American authors. News of that change, however, resulted in a sharp reaction from Southern "whites." Bowing to the economic threat of a Southern boycott, the

---

[9] *Missions: A Baptist Monthly Magazine*, February 1920, 109. Rev. Claudius Buchanan's sermon, "The Star in the East," was republished for the Connecticut Bible Society in 1809.

publication society canceled the projects they had assigned to black authors.[10]

Despite this conservative policy by publication society executives, ABPS did publish quietly a few novels and many articles, sermons, and reports by black authors. White Southerners missed or overlooked the practice, but this reality certainly made it easier for the colporteurs who traveled the Southern states.[11] Regardless of the particular reason, many Baptists and Baptist churches (both black and white) continued to use American Baptist Publication Society materials. Only the rise of other Baptist publishing houses in the twentieth century seriously undercut the publication society's sales to Southern churches and ministers.

Both the American Baptist Missionary Union and the American Baptist Publication Society included some attention to their home readers and home missions, not just the more exotic overseas missions, but attracting funds for home mission work was more difficult. Commissioned in 1817 to evangelize the Missouri and Illinois frontier, John Mason Peck found his support dropped when he refused to focus on work among Native Americans. Peck secured some funding for his frontier ministry from the Massachusetts Baptists and worked with Jonathan Going to found the American Baptist Home Mission Society (1832). Peck is an excellent example of how individual leadership combined with help from the three societies stimulated church growth and more grassroots support for American Baptist mission work. His work with African American pioneer minister John Merry Meachum deserves more attention, as does his skill in building community through

---

[10]Washington, *Frustrated Fellowship*. My information on Simmons is drawn from his biographical file at the Valley Forge Archives Center, ABHS, and from *Pilgrimage of Faith: An American Baptist Timeline of People, Places, and Events* (Valley Forge: ABHS, 2001 ed.).

[11] Albert W. Wardin, Jr., *Tennessee Baptists: A Comprehensive History, 1779–1999* (Nashville: Executive Board of the Tennessee Baptist Convention, 1999) notes the importance of the American Baptist Publication Society publications and colporteur work.

the promotion, not just of Sunday schools and churches, but also of Bible societies, women's mite societies, and schools.[12]

The collapse of the Triennial Convention in 1845 over the issue of slavery remains the most longstanding and influential of the many schisms among Baptists in the United States. It was a schism that Adoniram Judson, Francis Wayland, and John Mason Peck all wished to avoid—along with public debate about slavery, which they saw as a controversial issue that, if discussed, would undermine support for Baptist mission work. At this time the anti-mission movement and other schisms had already undercut Baptist unity, particularly in western and southern regions of the U.S. By enacting a "gag rule" that limited discussion of slavery at Brown University (a rule common in other Northern Baptist institutions), Wayland hoped to seal off the aggravating and, to most Baptists, distracting issue of slavery—for which they saw no immediate solution. Their moderate approach was not successful, however, because many Baptists in the South supported slavery and pressed for the appointment of slaveholding missionaries—a red flag to even the most moderate of Northern Baptists. Some Northern Baptists—those radical enough to demand immediate abolition of slavery—were also dissatisfied and in 1843 formed the American Baptist Free Mission Society, an organization that reunited with the denomination after the Civil War. Northern leaders, however, failed to keep the controversy over slavery from disrupting mission work. When faced with a test case, the appointment of a slaveholding missionary, the Triennial Convention had enough Northern members to vote "no." Consequently, Southern Baptists left that 1844 meeting of the Triennial Convention and by 1845 had organized their own, the

---

[12] There is need for a new biography of Peck. The old standard is Rufus Babcock, ed., *Memoir of John Mason Peck* (Philadelphia: American Baptist Publication Society, 1864), which includes long excerpts from Peck's lost journals. For another view of Peck as community builder, see Deborah Van Broekhoven, "Illinois Baptists and the Agitation Over Slavery," *American Baptist Quarterly* 22 (March 2003): 18–32. This issue also reprints a copy of the ABHMS circular letter clarifying its position (alleged neutrality) on slavery and slaveholding (p. 32).

Southern Baptist Convention (SBC). That schism has proved to be irreparable, with the two regionally based conventions continuing to this day.[13]

After the Civil War, this ongoing concern among Northern Baptists to continue a close relationship with "white" Southern Baptists led, ironically, to tensions that resolved only with the establishment and strengthening of new Baptist publishers for Southern "whites" and for African American Baptists. These tensions developed because the American Baptist Publication Society wished to serve both newly literate African Americans and to recapture and enlarge its audience of Southern white readers. These two goals became incompatible when African Americans began pressing the publication society to employ some from their community as authors in its publications. While leaders in Philadelphia first agreed to this proposal and even solicited writings from leading educators and pastors, they quickly reversed themselves when Southern white customers threatened a boycott of ABPS materials. Backing down from their commitment to black authors, the publication society's move led to the organization of a publishing house for black Baptists—and arguably did little to slow the erosion of the market for ABPS materials among white Southerners, who increasing relied on publications from the SBC.

Despite these tensions, many black Baptists in the South continued to enjoy a close relationship with their white patrons in the societies that made up the Northern Baptist Convention. Early pioneers in interracial cooperation were Joanna P. Moore (1832–1916) and the Rev. Henry L. Morehouse (1834–1917). Moore was a young teacher in 1863 when she heard a visiting preacher describe the suffering of refugees from slavery. She quickly made plans, collected an offering from her Sunday school

---

[13] The definitive study is John R. McKivigan, *The War Against Proslavery Religion: Abolitionism and the Northern Churches* (Ithaca: Cornel University Press, 1984); see also Deborah Van Broekhoven, "Suffering with Slaveholders: The Limits of Francis Wayland's Antislavery Witness," *Religion and the Antebellum Debates Over Slavery*, ed. Mitchell Snay and John R. McKivigan (Athens: University of Georgia Press, 1998) 196–220.

and an unpaid commission from the Home Mission Society, and went south. Initially she served on Island #10 in the Mississippi River, where she found former slaves crowded into unsanitary and minimal shelters near Union military camps. Her work in literacy and domestic education, always along with Bible lessons, endeared her to thousands, particularly in the states of Louisiana, Tennessee, and Mississippi. She worked through threats (from precursors to the Ku Klux Klan) and established both a training school and retirement home for black women. Her vision for Fireside Schools, which were home-based, attracted strong support from women and less negative attention than her training school and Sunday school work had done. More at home in the black community than most white Northerners, Moore continued her work until her death in Nashville (TN), where her funeral attracted thousands, both black and white. According to her wishes, she was buried in a cemetery for African Americans.

Black churches and schools had no better friend among Northern Baptists than Henry L. Morehouse, corresponding secretary of the American Baptist Home Mission Society from 1879 until 1891. While primary schools that provided basic literacy did receive support, Morehouse was most concerned to assist in the creation of colleges and seminaries for African Americans. He insisted on the principle that W. E. B. Dubois later affirmed, that blacks were as capable as whites if provided the same level of higher education. Consequently, a great deal of home mission society funding went to support higher education—with twenty-seven colleges or seminaries established for the training of pastors and teachers.[14] After his term as corresponding secretary, Morehouse continued to serve in other capacities, for example, organizing in 1894 the Fortress Monroe Conference (VA) that dealt with rising tensions between Northern and Southern Baptists in their home mission efforts. Participants agreed to cooperate in support of black institutions in the South and to refrain from beginning new churches in

---

[14] Beverly Carlson, introduction to "Pursuit of the Promise: American Baptists and Black Higher Education, Part II," *American Baptist Quarterly* 12 (March 1993): 4–9.

areas where the other convention was already established. It is in this context, a laudable concern for peace and possibly sectional reconciliation, that the American Baptist Publication Society agreed to assign several of its agents to Southern states, accepting the condition that these missionaries be under the direction of the Southern Baptist Convention's appropriate state office. For example, the colporteurs commissioned and paid by the American Baptist Publication Society to work in Texas were supervised by staff of the Texas Baptist Convention.[15] This arrangement to work cooperatively with white leadership in some regions of the SBC helped heal wounds left by the Civil War and Baptist conflict over slavery, but it also undercut the practice of cooperative interracial work begun by Joanna P. Moore and her colleagues.

In 1950, when the Northern Baptist Convention was renamed the American Baptist Convention, the key leadership positions (corresponding secretary and recording secretary) were combined into one, general secretary, with Reuben Nelson serving in this key role. Both an elected office and full-time staff position, the general secretary served as the chief administrator and spokesman for the denomination, often fulfilling the added role of pastoral shepherd. Together the general secretary and the new "general" board sought to minimize competition and maximize cooperation between the various mission societies. With slight modifications, this convention structure remains in place, with the general secretary continuing to function both as a pastoral leader and chief executive for American Baptist Churches in the USA.

---

[15] Wilma Rugh Taylor, *Gospel Tracks Through Texas* (College Station: Texas A&M University Press, 2005); see also Wilma and Norman Taylor, *This Train Is Bound for Glory: The Story of America's Chapel Cars* (Valley Forge PA: Judson Press, 2000). Less known is the tension created when faculty or other missionaries working at black schools were charged both to provide an equal education for black students and be sensitive to the concerns of white citizens in the area. See, for example, the court records and related correspondence about the 1893 beatings of students and a faculty member, Rev. David Reddick, because of their connection to Bishop College, a school for "Negroes" in Bishop, Texas (American Baptist Home Mission Society record group, box 5, file 6, Valley Forge Archives Center, ABHS).

In 1955 the structure was streamlined even more, with the women's home and foreign societies merging their staff and programs into the older home and foreign mission societies. With this structure for woman's work gone, the newer National Council of American Baptist Women grew in importance. The NCABW and its immediate successor, American Baptist Women (more recently American Baptist Women's Ministries), created mission education materials, sponsored conferences, and coordinated the distribution of materials to local women's groups. Even within the integrated organizations for overseas and home missions, programs started by the separate women's societies continued, notably the support for urban "Christian Centers." Yet some women leaders who lived through the integration of women's and men's organizations by the 1960s were critiquing the change as one that had eliminated leadership positions for women. A series of study commissions on the role of women in the denomination, including in staff leadership positions, resulted in more women receiving appointment to leadership positions.[16]

By the 1950s, regional reconciliation had progressed enough for the leaders of major Baptist denominations to agree on a six-year campaign in celebration of the sesquicentennial of the Triennial Convention and its focus on creating a national structure in support of North American Baptist mission work. Representatives from the SBC, ABC, the two major conventions of National Baptists (African American), Seventh Day Baptists, North American Baptists (German), the Baptist Federation of Canada, and the Baptist World Alliance worked for more cooperation in their evangelism and education programs.[17] Ironically, this concern for cooperation with the SBC, in particular, helped undermine any unified approach to the campaign for civil rights for African Americans by the

---

[16] Elizabeth J. Miller, "AB Women's Gains and Losses Three Decades After the Integration of the Mission Societies," reprinted in the *American Baptist Quarterly* 20 (September 2001): 227–37. This is part of a special issue, "Leadership, Diversity, Global Concern: Celebrating Fifty Years of American Baptist Women's Ministries."

[17] The results included literature and evangelism campaigns, a joint convention in 1964, and a fine volume of historical essays, *Baptist Advance*.

American Baptist Convention. North Carolinian J. C. Herrin became the catalyst for change in the ABC when in 1959 he began working (despite earlier comity agreements to the contrary) in Southern states for the Northern-based publication society and home mission society. As "program associate," a title purposefully unclear, Herrin became a missionary for civil rights, working primarily in support of the student leaders, educators, and pastors in the movement, including Martin Luther King, Jr., Benjamin Mays, and dozens of others, black and white, Northern and Southern.[18]

Despite resistance from many of its member congregations, denominational leaders reached out to civil rights leaders in other ways. General Secretary Reuben Nelson issued an open letter inviting Baptists, regardless of race or region, to join in fellowship with members of the American Baptist Convention—a letter J. C. Herrin used to open dialogue with a number of progressive churches in the South, both "white" and "black." The Ministers and Missionaries Benefit Board was also proactive, providing moral and financial support to embattled pastors, including Martin Luther King, Jr.[19] In a notable example of support for improved race relations, Jitsuo Morikowa (Director of Evangelism), Elizabeth Miller (Director of Christian Social Concern), and Kenneth Cober (Director of Christian Education) journeyed south in 1964 to stand alongside the student and church leaders demonstrating for the integration of public facilities in St. Augustine, Florida.[20] Herrin's

---

[18] Initially, all of Herrin's funding came through a foundation grant (which he himself wrote) designed to improve race relations among college students in the South. As a white North Carolinian, Herrin's credibility with the black community was initially the result of the NC Baptist Convention firing Herrin from his post as chaplain at UNC-Chapel Hill—largely for his "liberal" stance on integration. There is only sketchy documentation of Herrin's work in denominational record, but the materials there complement the rich variety of student letters, project reports, and other letters in the personal papers of J. C. Herrin.

[19] John Saunders Bone, *"The Better Maintenance of the Ministry": The First Seventy-five Years, the Ministers and Missionaries Benefit Board* (New York: MMBB, 1987) 140–46.

[20] Ken Cober, "Personal Memories of the Civil Rights Movement [n.d.]," biographical file, Valley Forge Archives Center, ABHS. Other insights about this

closeness to the student demonstrators, particularly those from black colleges, led him to secure grants in support of scholarships for student leaders (including John Lewis and Stokely Carmichael), advanced training in finance for administrators of black colleges, and a voter registration program staffed by student leaders at Benedict College (South Carolina). J. C. Herrin resigned in 1971, his work having laid the foundation for the denomination adding a new, multiracial, black-led "Region of the South."

While work with the freed people of the South was a large part of home mission work between 1865 and World War II, an equal amount of funding and effort was directed at work with immigrants and Native Americans (a mission that prior to the Civil War had been conceived of and directed by the Foreign Mission Society). Assisted by the many "foreign" language missionaries and imprints of the American Baptist Publication Society, the home mission societies added to their earlier work with Chinese, German, and Swedish immigrants missionaries appointed to evangelize and organize churches among the Mexican, Portuguese, German, Italian, and Japanese immigrants. Other departments assisted evangelism programs and the construction of new church buildings.

By 1920 this work included ministry among the new wave of immigrants from Eastern Europe and required missionaries fluent in Russian, Czech, Romanian, and several other Slavic languages. An international seminary in New Jersey provided training for these home missionaries (most of them immigrants themselves), while the new American Baptist Seminary in Los Angeles provided similar training for Spanish-speaking missionaries. Founded earlier (in 1881, the same year as Spellman College), the Baptist Missionary Training School in Chicago continued to train women for home and overseas mission work. These capable and dedicated leaders began several Christian centers modeled after settlement houses like Chicago's Hull House, as well as

---

period I have gathered from conversations with J. C. Herrin. His comments, together with his papers, are a rich source of information about the behind-the-scenes infrastructure of the Civil Rights Movement.

centers for ministry in poor, rural areas of Appalachia. While trained primarily for work with women and children, BMTS graduates became leaders in all parts of the denomination—including the local church, overseas missions, and staffing of national and regional offices.

Along with this array of new programs, new congregations, and new missionaries, the denomination suffered setbacks in two areas. First, funding continued to rise and fall, as it had in the nineteenth century, reflecting the turns in the economic cycle. These financial problems were particularly difficult during the decades of the 1920s and 1930s, when missionaries were recalled and building projects often put on hold. Despite these cycles of expansion and retraction, financial support for mission work and missionaries continued strong through the 1920s, when the overseas missionary corps exceeded 800—the largest size ever in denominational history. These economic difficulties were compounded by a more intractable problem, theological controversy. This difficulty, which lasted for years, resulted in two major schisms and the withdrawal of several hundred congregations.

The first schism paralleled the conflict experienced in other denominations, each with "liberal" and "fundamentalist" wings struggling for control over the denomination's educational institutions, funding, and mission work. Stimulated by the publication of *The Fundamentals*, a series of books about "the fundamentals of the faith," what soon became known as the fundamentalists among Northern Baptists became concerned that their missionaries and denominational leaders might not subscribe to "fundamental" beliefs. After a decade of conflict over correct theology, the convention voted down the proposal to adopt the New Hampshire Confession of Faith (from 1833) as the denominational creed, instead emphasizing continued reliance on the Bible alone as a sufficient guide. This solution skirted the issue of biblical interpretation but did not resolve the issue for the fundamentalists. After repeated efforts to force a creedal statement, the fundamentalist faction in 1932 left the convention to form the General Association of Regular Baptist Churches. During this period, leaders like Helen Barrett Montgomery and especially Harry Emerson Fosdick epitomized the mainline, "liberal" stand of many in the convention, arguing that Christians could use new methods of biblical interpretation without endangering their evangelical faith.

Chosen to lead the denomination during this period of conflict, laywoman Helen B. Montgomery epitomized the "liberal" but still evangelical center of the denomination. Elected in 1920 as the first woman president of the Northern Baptist Convention (or any major Protestant body), Montgomery valued both the personal study of the Bible and the social gospel. Well known for her ecumenical history of women's mission efforts, *Western Women in Eastern Lands* (1910), Montgomery had led in the merger of the denomination's regional mission societies (in 1909 and 1913), resulting in just two women's national societies, one each for home and foreign missions. She also worked with Lucy Peabody and Martha McLeish (mother of the poet, Andrew) to improve leadership training for the many young women who joined the multiplying chapters of the World Wide Guild. They all were part of the ecumenical Federation of Women's Boards of Foreign Missions (now Church Women United), with Montgomery preparing mission education materials for use in associated mainline denominations.

A graduate of Wellesley College, Montgomery used her skill in ancient languages to translate the New Testament into the everyday language of her generation—an accomplishment she completed in 1924 as a centennial present for its publisher, the American Baptist Publication Society. Montgomery's pacific spirit, along with her love of Scripture, mission work, and mission education, spread enthusiasm for Bible study and missions, dampening the fundamentalist criticism and delaying the coming schism almost one generation.[21] A better-known

---

[21] For an outline of Montgomery's achievements, see Conda Delite Hitch Abbott, *Envoy of Grace: The Life of Helen Barrett Montgomery* (Valley Forge PA: ABHS, 1997), and Winthrop Hudson's biographical sketch in *Notable American Women, 1607–1950* (Cambridge MA: Belknap Press of Harvard University Press, 1971) 566–68. As the leading mission educator of her day, much of her work is published in the various periodicals of American Baptists and ecumenical

social gospel advocate, Walter Rauschenbusch, evinced a similar pacific and pious spirit and willingness, which in the company of returning missionaries (including his own sister, Emma, an appointee to India) retained the loyalty of most congregations in the historical denomination.[22]

The second schism destructive of public peace and ministry in the denomination occurred in 1947, the product of a competitive "conservative" missionary society forming within the convention. This was a greater blow to the denomination, since this time conflict was over the quality of the corps of overseas missionary appointees, some of whom, critics argued, were theologically liberal and unsuited to the task of evangelism. A similar argument had rocked the foreign mission society almost 100 years earlier, when in the 1850s the society was torn (but not split) over disagreements about whether missionaries could engage in indirect evangelism (i.e., educational work) or just direct, personal evangelism. In the 1930s and 1940s, however, the conflict was not over evangelism methods but over biblical interpretation. Discussing the Bible in the context of sociological and historical analysis, for example, was acceptable to "liberals," but less so to "conservatives," regardless of the concern conservatives shared with liberals for providing solutions to social ills like child labor and the abuse of alcohol.[23] In an attempt to provide a place for spiritual refreshment (and retreat from

---

organizations, but much more is also documented in the records of the Rochester public schools and those of her home congregation, Lake Avenue Baptist Church, Rochester, NY.

[22] Christopher H. Evans, *The Kingdom Is Always But Coming: A Life of Walter Rauschenbusch* (Grand Rapids MI: Eerdman's, 2004).

[23] A helpful introduction to these schisms are the various entries on "liberalism," "Conservative Baptist Association," and other Baptist leaders as found in Bill J. Leonard, *Dictionary of Baptists in America* (Downer's Grove IL: InterVarsity Press, 1994), and William H. Brackney, *Historical Dictionary of the Baptists* (Lanham MD: Scarecrow Press, 1999). For earlier Baptists, see William Cathcart, ed., *The Baptist Encyclopaedia*, 2 vols. (Philadelphia: Louis H. Everts, 1881). I am using these terms because they were employed in the debate, but with great reservations, since the meaning of these terms, both then and now, was elastic and inconsistent—often with contemporary understandings of these value-laden but slippery terms.

denominational quarrels), Luther Wesley Smith spearheaded the drive to create a summer conference center at Green Lake, Wisconsin—a ministry that continues to this day.[24]

Since the 1970s, broad shifts, cultural fragmentation, and the growth of para-church organizations has undercut denominational loyalties and funding, even while a growing number of ethnic congregations (especially Hispanic and African American) have continued to affiliate with American Baptist Churches (ABC). The denomination responded to these changes with a series of reorganizations, resulting in the current name, American Baptist Churches in the USA, and a shift from annual to biennial conventions. More importantly, the general board of the denomination (rather than the biennial convention) began setting ABC policy at its semi-annual meetings. These changes have been complicated by the multiplication of special-interest groups and ethnic caucuses, each aware that their growing numbers (both in total and as a percentage of denominational membership) entitled them to greater representation on boards and executive staff positions. The leaders and board members of most member bodies now include individuals from a colorful range of backgrounds. In the twenty-first century, the denomination's demographic reality is such that there is no majority group; i.e., the increasing numbers of African American, Hispanic, and other ethnic Baptist congregations now outnumber the traditional "white" congregations, and some congregations are beginning to work self-consciously toward a worship and leadership style that welcomes a range of ethnic members.

In 2003 the denomination suffered a major blow when its Board of Educational Ministries closed. Only a limited amount of its programs merged into the operations of the home mission society. These two remaining "foreign" and "home" mission boards continue to pursue

[24] John A. Barbour and Lawrence H. Janssen, *40 Years of a Closer Walk: The American Baptist Assembly* (Chicago: Commercial Production Corp., 1983); see also the more recent history by Wilma R. Taylor, *Walking on Water: Celebrating Sixty Years of Ministry* (Ripon: Green Lake Conference Center, 2004).

their original objectives, fostering a national consciousness about mission through hundreds of mission projects, publications, and missionaries. A second blow fell in 2004, when a slow decline in mission funding for national programs dropped sharply, the result of a new agreement allowing states and regions to retain a greater percentage of dollars raised through the four major offerings, each promoted by national and regional organizations within ABC, but collected annually by member congregations. These financial blows were not the only threat to the denomination. A kind of anti-federalism in state and regional conventions threatens to undermine any shared sense of mission, with churches in the far West leading in the creation of a new, less denominational kind of home mission organization, the Great Commission Network. Disagreements about whether the adoption of a creedal statement and a uniform code of conduct (particularly in regard to homosexual practices) have also undermined American Baptist unity.

With the multiplication of voices, sharp cuts to the overarching office of general secretary, and autonomous organizations the organizers of support for "home" and "foreign" missions, confusion is common, even among the most loyal grassroots members. Displaying the chief weakness of Baptist polity throughout history, the denominational staff and clergy are often unclear about how to define who is in charge of a given program or policy. Truly this remains a thoroughly Baptist organization, weak in its national structure, but still strongly committed to pursuing its evangelistic mission through varying types of partnerships. With each congregation (and each Baptist organization, region, and individual) free to pursue its own pragmatic path of mission and discipleship, including through organizations outside the denominational structure, the future of projects coordinated by national staff remains uncertain. At any given meeting, there continue to be issues that "disturb the peace" among those gathered.

These periodic disturbances, sometimes resulting in schism, seem in part a result of the Baptist emphasis on separation of powers at the national level, along with an emphasis on the power of individuals and congregations to choose their own leaders and programs. A given congregation may not understand the historical role of the program boards (as societies) in their founding or in the creation of their understanding of Christian mission in the world, and so be inclined to rely on local leaders or more specialized, nondenominational organizations to shape their mission. Yet that sense of mission as the core of Baptist beliefs and work remains central to the national consciousness among American Baptists, with the American Baptist Foreign Mission Society, the oldest and best known of the "societies" and the organization recognized for promoting mission support among congregations. This reality holds true for most congregations, not withstanding the longtime presence of a department for mission support and education housed in the office of general secretary. These "Ministers of World Mission Support," however, have always been deployed throughout the regions, where they also receive financial support and supervision. The difficulty of this method for mission education and promotion, coordinated through the weak central offices in Valley Forge, has been acknowledged and the old system largely dismantled, but the shape of a new system is not yet clear.

Despite this organizational upheaval, churches from most regions responded generously once their members learned that missionaries might be called home because of insufficient funds. Giving for international mission work increased by $1.4 million, a 34 percent increase over the previous year. This upsurge enabled the Board of International Ministries (formerly the American Baptist Foreign Mission Society) to keep its 126 full-time missionaries in place and to continue working with more than 170 partner organizations and churches spread over 71 countries. At the same time, predictions that absorbing some staff and programs from the defunct Board of Educational Ministries would undermine the effectiveness of home mission work have so far proved unfounded. The Board of National Ministries continues to support the work of Christian centers, refugee resettlement, seminarian education, church renewal, and new church planting. In 2004, Judson Press (formerly the American Baptist Publication Society) produced a small profit for the first time in memory. This resilience, together with the outpouring of support for tsunami relief ($1.8 million was collected in only two months) is an expression of vitality. Indeed, the predictions of imminent death for this venerable denomination may be premature.

Chapter 3

SOUTHERN BAPTISTS

C. Douglas Weaver

The Southern Baptist Convention was formed on 8 May 1845 in Augusta, Georgia. Baptists in the South split from their Northern counterparts primarily over the issue of slavery. Storm clouds had been brewing for several years.

Baptist voices against slavery could be heard in the late nineteenth century in the South. As cotton became king, however, the South became profoundly committed to slavery and developed a biblical defense for it. At the same time, abolitionist voices increasingly made noise in the North. Ultimately the two visions for society could not coexist.

In 1814, Baptists North and South had created the Triennial Convention for the purpose of supporting foreign missions. As tensions exacerbated over the issue of slavery in American society, Baptists attempted to maintain cooperation in mission endeavors. To do so, the Triennial Convention proclaimed an official stance of neutrality on slavery, i.e., slaveholding was not a test of fellowship. After the American Baptist Anti-Slavery Convention was formed in 1840 and declared that Southern churches should confess the sinfulness of holding slaves, the Triennial Convention still asserted its neutrality on the issue the following year.

Nevertheless, Baptists in the South were suspicious. Georgia Baptists offered the name of a slaveholder for a mission appointment as a "test case," but the Triennial Convention simply refused to consider the application because the nature of the test violated its stated neutrality. The tension burst in 1844, however, when Baptists from Alabama demanded an explicit avowal that a slaveholder could be appointed as a missionary. In turn, the board of managers of the Triennial Convention replied that they would never appoint a slaveholder. Neutrality had failed on both sides, and the result was the decision of Baptists in the South to form a new organization.[1]

Upon the creation of the Southern Baptist Convention (hereafter SBC), William B. Johnson, the newly elected president, said the separation from Baptists in the North was not over doctrine but over missions. Slavery, he said, was a civil issue.[2] Consequently, some Baptists have suggested that missions was the key to the formation of the SBC. The issue was clearly, however, the right for slaveholders to do missions. The majority of messengers to the first convention in Augusta were from Georgia. The fact that they held slaves at a rate six times higher than the average Southerner revealed a definite economic interest in the maintenance of a biblically based slavery.[3] The defense of slavery—what has been called the "original sin" of Southern Baptists—necessitated a new religious organization.[4]

---

[1] General surveys of the history of the Southern Baptist Convention include W. W. Barnes, *The Southern Baptist Convention, 1845–1953* (Nashville: Broadman Press, 1954); Robert A. Baker, *The Southern Baptist Convention and Its People, 1607–1972* (Nashville: Broadman Press, 1974); and Jesse Fletcher, *The Southern Baptist Convention: A Sesquicentennial History* (Nashville: Broadman and Holman Publishers, 1994). Histories of the broader Baptist tradition that have information about Southern Baptists include Leon McBeth, *The Baptist Heritage: Four Centuries of Baptist Witness* (Nashville: Broadman Press, 1987), and Bill J. Leonard, *Baptist Ways: A History* (Valley Forge: Judson Press, 2003).

[2] William B. Johnson, "Appeal to the Public," in Robert A Baker, ed., *A Baptist Source Book* (Nashville: Broadman Press, 1966) 118–22.

[3] Robert Gardner, *A Decade of Debate and Division: Georgia Baptists and the Formation of the Southern Baptist Convention* (Macon GA: Mercer University Press, 1995) 30.

[4] See E. Luther Copeland, *The Southern Baptist Convention and the Judgement of History: The Taint of Original Sin* (Lanham MD: University Press of America, 1995).

Schism over slavery was not unique to Baptists. Both Methodists and Presbyterians split over the issue. Historian C. C. Goen noted that the creation of separate Southern denominations, while not causing the split of the United States, helped pave the way for it. "Broken churches" were precursors of a "broken nation."[5]

The SBC was organized on a convention model rather than the societal mode (an organization with one purpose such as foreign missions) used by the Triennial Convention and other Baptist agencies located in the North. As a centralized convention, Southern Baptists desired to support both foreign and home mission boards. For several decades, however, many Southern Baptist churches continued to use some Northern agencies like the American Baptist Publication Society, and the nascent Southern mission boards essentially functioned as societies vying and struggling for funds. As the post-bellum decades progressed, a general consensus developed that gave structure to the Southern Baptist identity. Historian Bill Leonard has demonstrated that a sense of Southern Baptist distinctiveness was cultivated and maintained by denominational loyalty, a commitment to Southern culture, and a universal sense of mission rooted in individual religious experience.[6]

Southern Baptists found commonality in a universal sense of mission. Baptists were diverse in some theological concerns (some were strict Calvinists; others affirmed a general atonement in their evangelistic practices) and worship styles, but the focus upon individual religious experience was universal among them. They were mission-minded, evangelistic, and generally focused on personal morality rather than the sins of society. Church discipline was most often enforced against personal sins such as drinking, dancing, and card playing. Consequently, Southern Baptists normally avoided the "social gospel"

---

[5] See C. C. Goen, *Broken Churches, Broken Nation: Denominational Schisms and the Coming of the American Civil War* (Macon GA: Mercer University Press, 1985). See also Mitchell Snay, *The Gospel of Disunion: Religion and Separatism in the Antebellum South* (Chapel Hill: University of North Carolina Press, 1997).

[6] Bill J. Leonard, *God's Last and Only Hope: The Fragmentation of the Southern Baptist Convention* (Grand Rapids: Eerdmans, 1990) 11–17, 43–44.

concerns that characterized Baptists in the industrial North in the latter half of the nineteenth and early twentieth centuries. Holiness was usually a function of individual beliefs, not social activism. A "social Christianity" was practiced, e.g., mountain schools and orphanages were established, but Southern Baptists were at best "passive reformers" who focused on converting individuals rather than transforming businesses and other social structures.[7] As historian Martin Marty has said, Southern Baptists became the "Catholic Church in the South."[8] As the "established church," their focus on revivalistic conversion and their acceptance (and promotion) of a segregated Jim Crow society defined Southern evangelicalism.

From the outset, Southern Baptists found unity in a commitment to a cultural identity. To be Baptist was to be Southern. To be Southern was to defend and contend for a racial orthodoxy of white supremacy that prevailed in the antebellum period and continued in the segregated world of the Jim Crow South. Segregation was built upon the same "biblical" rationale as slavery. God designed the races to be separate; moreover, African Americans were considered innately inferior. H. H. Tucker, influential editor of the Georgia Baptist paper *The Christian Index*, expressed the typical sentiment of white Southern Baptists: "We do not believe that all men are created equal as the Declaration of Independence declares them to be; nor that they will ever become equal in this world."[9]

Before the Civil War, numerous Southern Baptist churches were biracial (with balconies or separate seating for slaves), but in the post-bellum period the freed African Americans quickly sought their own churches and were supported in this effort by whites. Southern

---

[7] Keith Harper, *The Quality of Mercy: Southern Baptists and Social Christianity, 1890–1920* (Tuscaloosa: University of Alabama Press, 1996) 53, 73, 116.

[8] Martin Marty, quoted in Leonard, *God's Last and Only Hope*, 3.

[9] Paul Harvey, *Redeeming the South: Religious Cultures and Racial Identities Among Southern Baptists, 1865–1925* (Chapel Hill: University of North Carolina Press, 1997) 31.

Baptists—usually out of paternalistic concern—did provide some support for evangelization and education of African Americans.[10]

The belief in white superiority was seen, however, even in ministry efforts. The promotion of mountain schools was encouraged because the children in the Appalachian region were of pure Anglo stock. On the foreign mission field, mission policy gave priority to converting European whites who could then help American whites convert the world. According to J. F. Love, appointed executive secretary of the Foreign Mission Board in 1915, only whites had the capability of converting all the races.[11]

Southern Baptists supported the "Myth of the Lost Cause," the Southern response to the Civil War.[12] While the North had won the war, the South had not been defeated; it had just received a divine chastening for future use. Characterized by white superiority, chivalry, and personal moral virtue, the Southern way of life was the key to withstanding the assault of a Yankee America that was becoming ever more secular and liberal. Yankee religion that promoted racial/social equality was especially feared because it would result in the "mongrelization of our noble Anglo-Saxon race."[13]

Modern historians have said that the social attitudes of Southern Baptists (and other Southerners) were "culturally captive," especially in the area of race relations. Or, borrowing a phrase from the biblical prophet Amos, Southern Baptists were "at ease in Zion."[14] Southern

---

[10] Donald Mathews, *Religion in the Old South* (Chicago: University of Chicago Press, 2000) 193.

[11] Copeland, *The Southern Baptist Convention and the Judgement of History*, 37. Harper, *Quality of Mercy*, 82–88.

[12] See Charles R. Wilson, *Baptized in Blood: The Religion of the Lost Cause, 1865–1920* (Athens: University of Georgia Press, 1980).

[13] Harvey, *Redeeming the South*, 17, 22–23, 31.

[14] See John L. Eighmy, *Churches in Cultural Captivity: A History of the Social Attitudes of Southern Baptists* (Knoxville: University of Tennessee Press, 1972). See Rufus Spain, *At Ease in Zion: Social Attitudes of Southern Baptists, 1865–1900* (Nashville: Vanderbilt University Press, 1961). Paul Harvey prefers a more reciprocal process between church and culture in the South. Churches were not only

Baptists not only defended the status quo of a Jim Crow South; they also promoted it. To be Baptist was to be Southern.

By the end of the nineteenth century, Southern Baptists were developing a strong sense of denominational loyalty around a common programmatic identity/piety (a Foreign Mission Board, a Home Mission Board, a Sunday School Board, and a theological school named The Southern Baptist Theological Seminary). More elaborate programs and agencies were created along the way to provide a "one-stop shop" for Baptists to live the Christian life.

The work of I. T. Tichenor at the Home Mission Board was pivotal. The agency struggled for survival but moved to Atlanta in 1882 from Marion, Alabama, and gained solid footing under Tichenor's leadership (1882–1889). Tichenor, the former president of what is now Auburn University, convinced his fellow Southerners to support a Southern mission board rather than dividing their loyalties with the older American Baptist Home Mission Society. Some analysts credit Tichenor with saving a struggling convention and securing the identity of Southern Baptists.[15]

In similar fashion, James M. Frost garnered support for a Sunday School Board that developed from the work of the HMB in 1891. Previous attempts at producing a Southern literature were ineffective, but Frost, leader of the Sunday School Board for two decades (1896–1916), succeeded in promoting the use of literature written by Southern Baptists for Southern Baptists. Once the American Baptist Publication Society broached the idea of black authors, Frost's goal of a doctrinally correct Southern literature found more ready acceptance. By 1910, the ABPS had ceased its work in the South.[16]

The cultivation of a denominational consciousness was also seen in the missionary work of Southern Baptist women. Ladies Aid Societies,

---

captive to Southern culture but were key formers of that culture. See Harvery, *Redeeming the South*, 4.

[15] Kimball Johnson, "Isaac Taylor Tichenor," *Encyclopedia of Southern Baptists*, 1416. Fletcher, *Southern Baptist Convention*, 94.

[16] Harvey, *Redeeming the South*, 30.

trailblazers in women's work, raised money (often as sewing circles) to rebuild churches devastated during the Civil War. Their fundraising efforts also supported missions, cared for the poor, and helped pay ministers whose salaries were often in arrears.[17]

The development of an organized woman's missionary union among Southern Baptists began in earnest in the 1870s. A "Woman's Mission to Woman" movement began in 1868 in Baltimore and was enthusiastically received by Baptist women throughout the South. In 1872, Henry A. Tupper, the new corresponding secretary of the Foreign Mission Board, ushered in a new day when he began the approval of female missionaries, and he strongly encouraged the organization of women's missionary groups in local churches. Two years later, with Tupper's encouragement, "central committees" were created to coordinate mission efforts in states.

Some pastors had fears that women's suffrage was on the horizon and invoked the biblical proof text "let the women keep silent in the church" toward expanded involvement of women in Southern Baptist life. In 1885, women messengers from Arkansas were disqualified as messengers to the SBC's annual meeting, and their participation was excluded through a constitutional amendment until 1918.

Consequently, a national missions organization, the Woman's Missionary Union, was officially organized as an auxiliary to the Southern Baptist Convention in 1888. While the women wanted to participate in Baptist missions life at the national level, Annie Armstrong, the first corresponding secretary of the infant organization, attempted to calm the waters when she declared that the women did not desire an independent women's organization with no ties to Southern Baptists. As an "auxiliary" group, the "WMU" immediately became the financial backbone of Southern Baptist mission efforts. When the Gospel Mission movement—a missions ideology that promoted missions solely by local churches rather than national mission boards—threatened

---

[17] Catherine Allen, *A Century to Celebrate: History of Woman's Missionary Union* (Birmingham: WMU of the SBC, 1987) 17–18.

the work of the Foreign Mission Board in the 1890s, Armstrong insisted upon allegiance to the Southern Baptist way of cooperation.[18]

If Southern Baptists have saints, Annie Armstrong, and even more so Lottie Moon, have been bestowed with the honor. Moon, an almost legendary figure in Baptist missiology, was a missionary to China, serving from 1873 until 1912. Her correspondence with local women's groups did much to create a passion for Southern Baptist missions. She so identified with the Chinese that she adopted their dress and essentially starved herself to alleviate the poverty of the girls she taught. Moon's suggestion to have a special offering for missions was heeded by Annie Armstrong, and the annual Lottie Moon Christmas offering became (and still is) the most influential financial support for foreign missions in Southern Baptist life. Subsequently, a home missions Easter offering was named after Annie Armstrong.[19]

The most significant threat to the development of a denominational loyalty based on a common programmatic identity was an extreme local church ecclesiology called Landmarkism. The movement, led by J. R. Graves, editor of the *Tennessee Baptist* from 1843 until 1893, was initiated in the 1850s and attacked the young Convention's centralized method of doing missions. Graves argued that only local churches, not mission boards, should do missions because there were only local churches, no universal church, in the New Testament. Graves also rejected alien immersion, baptism administered by non-Baptists, and advocated closed Communion, the restriction of the Lord's Supper to other Baptists. According to Graves, the local Baptist church was the true New Testament church since only Baptists could trace a direct succession of

---

[18] See C. Douglas Weaver, "From Saint to Sinner: Missionary Pioneer to Gospel Mission Convert: The Legacy of Martha Loftin Wilson," *Viewpoints: Georgia Baptist History* (2002): 71–85. Martha Wilson, leader of women's missions in Georgia, upset Armstrong when she failed to give exclusive loyalty to missions coordinated by the Foreign Mission Board of the SBC.

[19] For information about Lottie Moon, see Catherine Allen, *The New Lottie Moon Story* (Nashville: Broadman Press, 1980). For information about Annie Armstrong, see Bobbie Sorrill, *Annie Armstrong: Dreamer in Action* (Nashville: Broadman Press, 1984).

churches back to Jesus and John the Baptist. Because Baptists churches were the only genuine Christian churches, other churches were considered religious societies and their ministers did not have a valid gospel ministry. Landmarkism spread throughout Southern Baptist ranks through the work of Graves as well as through the fictional novel *Theodosia Ernest* by A. C. Dayton and the *Church Manual* (still available in Baptist bookstores in the late twentieth century) by J. M. Pendleton.

The Landmark legacy upon Southern Baptist life has been significant. Graves's goal to abandon mission boards in favor of exclusive local church missions was defeated at the 1859 meeting of the SBC, and Landmarkers ultimately formed their own group in 1902. Still, Southern Baptists' suspicion of other denominations is a legacy of the Landmark extreme focus on the local Baptist church. The practice of closed Communion and the rejection of alien immersion also reigned for decades and are still practiced by some Southern Baptists.[20]

The late nineteenth century was an era of intense denominational competition and biblical restorationism (gospel primitivism). Whereas some churches like the Disciples of Christ claimed to restore the New Testament Church, Baptists agreed with Graves that they were *the* New Testament Church. The Whitsitt Controversy—the resignation of William H. Whitsitt as president of Southern Baptist Theological Seminary in 1898—revealed the strength of the Landmark account of history. Whitsitt's position, that Baptists could not trace their origins back to the New Testament but were birthed in the 1600s in England as part of English Protestantism, was so fiercely criticized that his resignation was necessary for the survival of the seminary.[21]

As Southern Baptists progressed into the twentieth century, loyalty to a centralized denomination that unified around common programs,

---

[20] For a good summary of Landmark beliefs, see Leon McBeth, *Baptist Heritage*, 446–61. Landmarkism is cited as an example of gospel primitivism in Richard Hughes, *The American Quest for the Primitive Church* (Champaign: University of Illinois Press, 1988).

[21] See Rosalie Beck, *The Whitsitt Controversy: A Denomination in Crisis* (Ann Arbor: University Microfilms, 1985).

especially missions, triumphed in Southern Baptist life. At the same time, Landmark perspectives helped keep Southern Baptists isolated from the "taint" of ecumenical cooperation with other denominations. Denominational statesman J. B. Grambell of Texas typified the Southern Baptist attitude: "Southern Baptists do not ride a horse unless they hold the bridle reins."[22]

Organizational efficiency was a goal of most denominations in the first half of the twentieth century. Southern Baptists have been dubbed "Business Baptists" for their adoption of the "corporate" model during this era of significant numerical growth and an increasingly centralized organization.[23] Numerous agencies developed and executive officers were added; the influential executive committee (the Convention's operating center when it was not in annual session) was established in 1917 with its first full-time executive secretary-treasurer Austen Crouch ten years later. The Sunday School Board also named its first executive secretary in 1917. Several new agencies that were established included the Annuity Board (1918), the Baptist Brotherhood (1926), the Baptist Student Union (1928), and the Education Commission (1928).

The expansive organizational growth of the SBC was also seen in the development of new theological schools. The growth in the southwest region of Southern Baptists was manifested in the creation of a new seminary in Texas in 1908, Southwestern Baptist Theological Seminary, under the leadership of B. H. Carroll. Additional seminaries were established in New Orleans (1917); San Francisco (Golden Gate,

---

[22] Timothy George, "Southern Baptist Relationships with Other Protestants," *Baptist History and Heritage* (July 1990): 31.

[23] The phrase "business Baptists" was used by E. Glenn Hinson in his church history lectures at Southern Baptist Theological Seminary in the 1980s. Hinson also used the phrase in the article "The Baptist Experience in the United States," *Review and Expositor* 78 (Fall 1981): 190–204. See also Samuel Hill in Nancy Ammerman, ed., *Southern Baptists Observed: Multiple Perspectives on a Changing Denomination* (Knoxville: University of Tennessee Press, 1993) 31–32, for additional information about the "corporate" model of organization.

1944); Wake Forest, North Carolina (Southeastern, 1951); and Kansas City (Midwestern, 1957).[24]

Denominational efficiency and evangelistic fervor produced rapid growth of the Southern Baptist Convention. By the end of the nineteenth century, Southern Baptists surpassed the Methodists and became the largest religious group in the South. Membership in churches grew from one million in the 1870s to 2 million in 1906 and 3 million after World War I. At the end of World War II, Southern Baptists counted 5,865,554 members. Benefiting from the baby boom and the post-war religious revival in America, as well as creative organized evangelistic endeavors like "A Million More in '54," membership totals climbed to 8,169,491 in 1954 and then 9,731,591 in 1960. New state conventions in western "pioneer" areas like Arizona (1928), California (1940), Hawaii (1943), and Alaska (1946) revealed that Southern Baptists were south, north, east, and west. State conventions began to dot the North—the historic center of American Baptist life—in 1979 (New York).[25]

Southern Baptists also developed an efficient fiscal operation to manage their burgeoning corporate structure. The $75 Million Campaign, a Convention-wide fundraising effort to celebrate the SBC's seventy-fifth anniversary, raised $58 million (1919–1924). While SBC finances experienced difficulties because of spending based on total pledges ($92 million), the fundraising campaign was still the largest by far in Southern Baptist history and pointed to the economic potential of the SBC. The most significant move toward denominational efficiency was the creation of the Cooperative Program (1925), a unified budget administered by the executive committee that supported all of the Convention's agencies (1925). Previously, the various SBC agencies had separate budgets and often competed for funds. With a unified plan, Southern Baptists developed an even stronger loyalty to Convention programs since each church—no matter the size—could rightly say it was helping to fund each and every agency. Giving to state Baptist

---

[24] Hill, in Ammerman, ed., *Southern Baptists Observed*, 31–32.

[25] Fletcher, *Southern Baptist Convention*, 318–19, 403–404.

conventions developed along the same unified plan. Most Southern Baptists do not consider it an exaggeration to call the Cooperative Program the most effective stewardship method in Christian history and consequently often judge loyalty to the Convention by the percentage of a church's budget that is allocated to Southern Baptist ministries.

Organizationally efficient and numerically strong, Southern Baptists cultivated a sense of "chosenness" throughout the twentieth century. Americans had long claimed an identity of "manifest destiny" as God's "city on a hill." In the exuberant aftermath of World War I and the nation's "calling" to spread democracy, Southern Baptists spoke confidently of the unique role of the South and their own missionary mandate. Noted Louisiana Baptist minister M. E. Dodd told the 1919 meeting of the SBC that "the Baptist hour of all the centuries has sounded." The following year, influential Kentucky Baptist Victor Masters spared no hyperbole in his assessment: "As goes America, so goes the world. Largely as goes the South, so goes America. And in the South is the Baptist center of gravity of the world."[26]

Conflict has characterized Baptist life. With a focus on the independence of the local church, a strong bent toward individualism, and a heritage of anti-creedalism and dissent, Southern Baptists have engaged in numerous contentious debates. Walter Shurden, in a book describing Baptist controversies, said Baptists are "not a silent people."[27]

Whenever Southern Baptists have argued, theological conflict has not been far behind. At the time of the formation of the SBC, Baptists in the South claimed that the split with Northern Baptists was not over doctrinal concerns. As the post-bellum period transpired, however, Southern Baptists frequently pointed to the growing liberalism of "Yankee" faith. Southern Baptists embodied Southern conversionist evangelicalism and denounced the new developments in the historical-critical study of the Bible that became popular with biblical scholars.

---

[26] James J. Thompson, Jr., *Tried as by Fire: Southern Baptists and the Religious Controversies of the 1920s* (Macon GA: Mercer University Press, 1982) 11.

[27] Walter B. Shurden, *Not A Silent People: Controversies that Have Shaped Southern Baptists* (Macon GA: Smyth and Helwys, 1995).

Crawford Toy, who began espousing the new methodology in his Old Testament classes, was forced to leave Southern Baptist Theological Seminary in 1879.

Throughout Baptist history, Baptists have summarized their beliefs in confessions of faith. In the nineteenth century, local Southern Baptist churches and Baptist associations adopted confessional statements. At the same time, Southern Baptists declared that these confessions were not creeds because the Bible was the sole Baptist creed. S. G. Hillyer, a professor at Mercer University in the late nineteenth century, described the relationship of confessions to the Bible in the life of local churches.

> The Baptists of Georgia, from the very beginning of their development in this State, acknowledged no authority in matters of "faith and of practice," except the Scriptures. It is true, each church had what was called its abstract of principles or its confession of faith. But this abstract, or confession, was adopted by each church, as an independent body, for itself, and it was held to be valid only so far as its subscribers believed it to be in harmony with the Bible. In controversies with their opponents, Baptists never appeal to the confessions found in their church records, but directly and exclusively to the inspired Word.[28]

In the 1920s, theological conflict erupted in Northern churches in what is called the fundamentalist-modernist conflict. Since Southern Baptists had few theological modernists, they only experienced a "lighter" version of the Northern conflict. The dominant issue was evolution, and teachers at denominational schools were the targets. Much of the discord came from the sensationalistic antics of fundamentalist J. Frank Norris, pastor of First Baptist Church, Fort Worth, Texas. Norris called respected Baptist leaders like G. W. Truett the "Sanhedrin," and Norris's church was excluded from the Baptist General Convention of Texas in 1922, primarily for his censoriousness.

---

[28] S. G. Hillyer, *Reminiscences of Georgia Baptists* (Atlanta: Fotte and Davies Co., 1902) 219–20.

"Norrisism" became synonymous with a lack of charity and unwillingness to cooperate.[29]

E. Y. Mullins, president of Southern Baptist Theological Seminary in Louisville and the leading theologian in Southern Baptist life, told the 1922 annual meeting of the SBC that denominational schools should teach the historic beliefs of the Christian faith. Evolution should not be taught as fact; at the same time, he argued for "firm faith and free research." In order to maintain unity (and efficiency) in the SBC, denominational loyalists led in the adoption of a new confession of faith, the *Baptist Faith and Message* (1925). The confession, largely written by Mullins, affirmed the sole authority of the Bible for "all religious opinions" but did not mention evolution specifically because the "confession committee," none of whom affirmed evolution, did not believe a theological confession needed a statement on science. Detractors continued to press for an explicit anti-evolution statement, however, and the Convention passed the "McDaniel Statement" the following year. The confession had little impact in Southern Baptist life for several decades.[30]

Southern Baptist voices for freedom of conscience and religious liberty were not rare in the Convention's first 100 years. They continued to warn against establishment religion, a concern articulated by the earliest Baptists of the seventeenth century. One frequent manifestation of the call for religious freedom—and one reason for it—was the persistent Protestant aversion to Catholicism. In 1871, for example, when prominent pastor Richard Fuller resigned from Seventh Baptist Church, Baltimore, the church selected William Brantley of Second

---

[29] Shurden, *Not a Silent People*, 58–60. L. R. Scarborough, one of Norris's primary opponents, penned a tract titled "Fruits of Norrisism" and charged Norris with intolerance and a lack of charity. See Baker, *A Baptist Source Book*, 196–97.

[30] E. Y. Mullins, quoted in Baker, *A Baptist Source Book*, "The Memphis Articles of 1925," 204–205. See also Phyliss Rodgerson Pleasants, "Myth: Baptists Are Scientific Creationists," *Baptist Myth Series*, ed. Doug Weaver, Walter Shurden, and Charles Deweese (Nashville: Baptist History and Heritage, 2003). George McDaniel, president of the SBC in 1926, was pastor of First Baptist Church, Richmond, Virginia.

Baptist Church, Atlanta. When the Georgia church complained that their strategic ministry in the growing Southern city was being damaged, Seventh Baptist Church retorted that surely someone could be found to pastor in Atlanta. Ministry in Baltimore was especially strategic since the city was the center of American Catholicism and its "gross error."[31]

Anti-Catholicism persisted during the first half of the twentieth century. Despite the gradual centralizing of the Southern Baptist Convention, most Southern Baptist congregations were largely rural and were resistant to the increasing urbanization that Catholic immigration portended. Catholics were considered to be a threat to individualism, democracy (will the Pope try to rule America?), and morality (the sin of alcohol consumption). Consequently, Baptists joined other Southerners in harshly denouncing the candidacy of Al Smith for the presidency of the United States in the election of 1928 and then the election of John F. Kennedy in 1960. With the establishment of better relations between Protestants and Catholics as a result of the changes implemented through the Catholic council, Vatican II (1958–1963), some Southern Baptists began dialoguing with Catholics. At the close of the twentieth century, Catholicism was still called a "false gospel," but cooperation occurred on conservative pro-life social issues.[32]

Southern Baptists' call for religious liberty and the separation of church and state especially found expression in the ministry of pulpit stalwarts like George W. Truett of First Baptist Church, Dallas. Truett became one of the most legendary Baptist ministers in the Convention's history. Like E. Y. Mullins, he served as president of both the SBC and the Baptist World Alliance. One of the legacies of his career was the speech "Baptists and Religious Liberty," given on the steps of the capitol in Washington, D.C., at the seventy-fifth anniversary convention in 1920. Truett declared that Baptists "have never been a party to oppression of conscience.... Christ's religion needs no prop of any kind

---

[31] C. Douglas Weaver, *Second to None: A History of Second-Ponce de Leon Baptist Church, 1854–2004* (Nashville: Baptist History and Heritage, 2003) 23.

[32] Thompson, *Tried as by Fire*, 167–68.

from any worldly source, and to the degree that it is thus supported is a millstone hanged about its neck."[33]

Support among Southern Baptists for religious liberty resulted in the formation of a Public Affairs Committee in 1936. The PAC later developed into the Baptist Joint Committee on Public Affairs (mostly funded by Southern Baptists but an agency that included other Baptist groups in America). The BJCPA became a strong voice for the separation of church and state, including support for the 1963 Supreme Court decision declaring the unconstitutionality of state-sponsored prayer in public schools. The SBC discontinued membership in the BJCPA in 1991.

Southern Baptists, as well as other Christian groups in the South, believed in white superiority and considered segregation to be the accepted, i.e., biblical, way of life throughout the first half of the twentieth century. A minority of progressive Southern Baptists, however, pushed for racial equality. Clarence Jordan, one of the founders of the interracial commune Koinonia Farm (1942), and Walter Johnson represented the more radical dissenters who tired of denominational bureaucracy and institutionalism.[34] When the Supreme Court ruled in the groundbreaking 1954 case, *Brown v. Board of Education*, that "separate but equal" facilities were unconstitutional, denominational leaders supported the decision. A denominational call to integrate local churches was not trumpeted until 1968, however.

As the Civil Rights Movement continued into the sixties, progressive voices within the Southern Baptist Convention were found at the Christian Life Commission, under the leadership of Foy Valentine. Baptist youth learned about "race relations" in the work of Baptist Student Unions at the college level; at the seminaries, young Southern Baptist ministers were influenced by the progressive prophetic stands of seminary professors Henlee Barnette and T. B. Maston. At the

---

[33] George W. Truett, "Baptists and Religious Liberty," in H. Leon McBeth, ed., *A Sourcebook for Baptist Heritage* (Nashville: Broadman Press, 1990) 469, 472.

[34] David Stricklin, *A Genealogy of Dissenters: Southern Baptist Protest in the Twentieth Century* (Lexington: University Press of Kentucky, 2000) 35–40.

local level, most churches were resistant to integrated worship or integrated church memberships. A few churches slowly integrated; others refused to seat African Americans and fired pastors who pushed the issue. If any group within the local church pioneered better race relations, it was the Woman's Missionary Union. Already in the 1940s, some women's groups were doing study courses that talked about racial justice.[35]

During the last four decades of the twentieth century, Southern Baptists continued to inculcate a strong commitment to the denomination in the midst of an increasingly pluralistic environment. The seventies were marked by the height of denominationalism. Baptist young people continued to attend Baptist camps and continued to learn missions in Baptist versions of the Boy Scouts (Royal Ambassadors) and Girl Scouts (Girl's Auxiliary). The year 1976, proclaimed the "year of the evangelical" by secular journalists, witnessed a devout Southern Baptist from Plains, Georgia, Jimmy Carter, elected as president of the United States. As the challenges of postmodernism and its de-emphasis on traditional denominations surged to the forefront of "doing church" in America, some Baptists responded by moving away from explicit usage of denominational labels. At the end of the twentieth century, Baptist youth often said they were Christian first, evangelical second, and Baptist third. The megachurch/community church phenomenon, which became persuasive in evangelical America, also impacted Southern Baptist life. The Southern Baptist congregation at Saddleback Church (Lake Forest, California) with pastor Rick Warren is one of the largest churches in America.[36] Throughout the twentieth century, Southern Baptists continued their evangelistic efforts and missionary passion. Support for the Cooperative Program, especially the work of the Home

---

[35] Leon McBeth, "Southern Baptists and Race Since 1947," *Baptist History and Heritage* (July 1972): 159, 165. For the work of local WMUs, see C. Douglas Weaver, *Every Town Needs a Downtown Church: A History of First Baptist Church, Gainesville, Florida* (Nashville: Baptist History and Heritage, 2000) 69–70.

[36] See www.saddleback.com (accessed 23 May 2005). The church's Web site does not make mention of anything Baptist.

and Foreign Mission Boards, was the pride and joy of most Southern Baptists. Bold Mission Thrust, an initiative to share the gospel with every person on earth by the year 2000, began in 1977. By 2004, Southern Baptists sponsored more than 5,000 home missionaries and more than 5,000 foreign missionaries serving in 153 countries. Numerical advance continued to characterize Southern Baptists. Membership grew from 13,196,979 in 1980 to 15,044,413 ten years later. The number of Southern Baptist churches increased from 35,404 to 37,974 during the same period. The latest statistics (2004) report more than sixteen million Southern Baptists in more than 42,000 local churches. At the dawn of a new century, Southern Baptists claim the title of the largest Protestant body in the United States.[37]

A significant element of the recent growth of Southern Baptists is among ethnic minorities. While almost a completely white denomination in 1970, by 2000 ethnic minorities totaled 20 percent of Southern Baptists. African American growth has been significant. The Convention added 1,600 African American congregations in the 1990s to have more than 2,700 in 2002. In 1995, Southern Baptists offered their first official apology to African Americans for "historic acts of evil such as slavery." Superceding the observance of Race Relations Sunday (1965), an annual Racial Reconciliation Sunday dots the denominational calendar at the beginning of the twenty-first century.[38] It should be added, though, that while the SBC has grown in the number of African American congregations that affiliate with it, there remain relatively few Southern Baptist "white" churches that are integrated.

The central story of Southern Baptists during the last decades of the twentieth century, however, does not focus upon missions, evangelism, or ethnic diversity. The fundamentalist-moderate conflict, or the "Conservative Resurgence" as it is called by the victors, quickly

---

[37] Fletcher, *Southern Baptist Convention*, 318–19. See www.sbc.net (accessed 23 May 2005).

[38] Amy Green, "Southern Baptist Surprise! Why Are So Many African Americans Attracted to a Church That Was Once Identified with White Racism?" *Christianity Today*, 48/9 (September 2004): 54.

overshadows any analysis of ministries. The "official" beginning of the "Controversy" was the election of Adrian Rogers, pastor of Bellevue Baptist Church, Memphis, Tennessee, as SBC president in 1979. Tremors of the religious earthquake, however, dated back to the early sixties and the "Elliott Controversy." Ralph Elliott, a professor of Old Testament at Midwestern Baptist Theological Seminary, suggested in his book, *The Message of Genesis*, that Genesis 1–11 was "theological history." The importance of the stories—such as that of Adam and Eve—was the theological message they told, not whether they were literal history. Published by Broadman Press, the official press of the Sunday School Board of the SBC, the book caused a backlash of protest among some Baptists. Elliott was branded a liberal who did not believe the Bible. Although the Sunday School Board never reissued the book, they initially defended it. They argued that they published a variety of works that reflected the diversity of theological views held by Southern Baptists. Midwestern Seminary eventually fired Elliott, not over his use of modern historical critical methods of biblical study, but for insubordination. He refused to revise the book, and he refused to promise that he would not republish with another press.[39] The Convention's response to the Elliott affair was the adoption of the 1963 *Baptist Faith and Message* confessional statement. In this revision of the 1925 statement, the Bible was described as "truth without any mixture of error," a phrase whose meaning later became a point of contention in SBC affairs. As with the 1925 confession, denominational loyalists

[39] Numerous books on "the Controversy" have been written. For a moderate perspective, consult Bill J. Leonard, *God's Last and Only Hope: The Fragmentation of the Southern Baptist Convention* (Grand Rapids: Eerdmans, 1990); Walter B. Shurden, *Not a Silent People: Controversies that Have Shaped Southern Baptists* (Macon GA: Smyth and Helwys, 1995); and Bruce Gourley, *The Godmakers: A Legacy of the Southern Baptist Convention?* (Lebanon TN: Providence House, 1996). For the conservative viewpoint, see James Hefley, *The Conservative Resurgence of the Southern Baptist Convention* (Hannibal MO: Hannibal Books, 1991); James Hefley, *Truth in Crisis*, vols. 1–5 (Hannibal MO: Hannibal Books, 1986–1989); and Jerry Sutton, *The Baptist Reformation: The Conservative Resurgence in the Southern Baptist Convention* (Nashville: Broadman and Holman, 2000).

sought to unify the Convention with this voluntary confession. Herschel Hobbs, an influential denominationalist from Oklahoma, emphasized the voluntary and non-creedal nature of the confession in a preamble. Most local churches ignored the confession, however, as they addressed ministry needs in the rapidly changing 1960s. A second flare-up occurred with the publication of the *Broadman Bible Commentary* series at the end of the decade. In 1970, the SBC criticized the volume on Genesis, primarily because the author, British Baptist G. Henton Davies, said that God's command to Abraham to sacrifice his son, Isaac, could not be taken literally. Charges of liberalism rose again, and the commentary was rewritten by popular Bible teacher Clyde Francisco of Southern Seminary.

With the election of Adrian Rogers as SBC president in 1979, the transformation of the Southern Baptist Convention began in earnest. A political strategy to elect a series of SBC presidents who affirmed biblical inerrancy—called the *sine qua non* of orthodox evangelical theology—was devised by architects Paige Patterson of the Criswell Biblical Institute and layman Judge Paul Pressler. According to the plan, the Convention presidents used their appointive powers to select committees that remade trustee boards of SBC institutions into havens of conservative theology. While many of the elections were close, the plan was remarkably successful. By 1990, the "inerrancy movement" controlled the SBC. Leaders felt that a new reformation had occurred; they believed they had successfully purified denominational agencies (defunding one, the Baptist Joint Committee) and theological seminaries of liberalism and, by doing so, restored Southern Baptists' historic conservatism. While the Convention still contained "dissenters," these Baptists would no longer have leadership opportunities unless they affirmed the "conservative resurgence" and its theological parameters.

Conservative versus liberal was not how the dissenters/losers viewed the conflict, however. Fundamentalist versus moderate was more accurate. While theological differences existed, moderates thought the conflict was more of a political power struggle. The real issue was "control versus freedom."[40] Conservatives were actually intolerant fundamentalists because they demanded doctrinal conformity—as they defined it. W. A. Criswell, revered pastor of First Baptist Church, Dallas, and "grandfather" of the modern SBC fundamentalist movement, referred to moderates as "skunks" for their liberal odor.[41] Moderates unsuccessfully warned of a "galloping creedalism" pervading the non-creedal legacy of Southern Baptists. Moderates affirmed that they believed in the Bible as much as fundamentalists. They affirmed the trustworthiness of the Scriptures for faith and practice and objected to the insistence upon inerrancy since the word referred to the original manuscripts of the Bible, which no longer exist. They also opposed the increasingly political connotation of the word "inerrancy"; its use was becoming a creedal litmus test. Moderates unsuccessfully pressed their case to maintain "unity amidst diversity" for the sake of cooperative missions and evangelism, in their view the heart of Southern Baptist life. Fundamentalist Southern Baptists, however, opted for doctrinal agreement and accountability as the defining characteristic of Baptist cooperation.

While the "Controversy" was over at the national level by 1990, skirmishes continued during the next decade at the state and local levels. A few dissenting churches (or individuals in SBC churches) formed the Cooperative Baptist Fellowship (CBF), which eventually distanced itself completely from the SBC. Southern Baptist leaders viewed the CBF with disdain. The crowning achievement of the victory against moderates came with the adoption of a revision of the 1963 confession, called the 2000 *Baptist Faith and Message*. New items included a statement that excluded women from the pastorate, a practice moderates increasingly supported, and a statement on the submission of the wife to the husband in family life. Denominational employees and seminary faculty were required to subscribe to the confession.

---

[40] Shurden, *Not a Silent People*, 83, 86.

[41] Walter B. Shurden and Randy Shepley, eds., *Going for the Jugular: A Documentary History of the SBC Holy War* (Macon GA: Mercer University Press, 1996) 235.

The "Controversy" produced some additional consequences. Some independent fundamentalist Baptists joined forces with Southern Baptists after the defeat of the moderate group, the most notable addition being the founder of the Moral Majority, Jerry Falwell. Citing theological liberalism as the primary reason, Southern Baptists distanced themselves from mainline Protestant churches and other Baptists (withdrawing from the Baptist World Alliance in 2004). At the same time, Southern Baptists cooperated more extensively with other conservative evangelical groups in missions and in the public arena (pro-life concerns, "family values," and Republican politics).

Southern Baptist Distinctives

Southern Baptists do not claim a separate list of Baptist distinctives. They affirm the "classic" list of defining traits that includes believer's baptism by immersion, personal religious experience, salvation through Christ alone, missions and evangelism, priesthood of believers, religious liberty, congregational church government, the importance/autonomy of the local church, confessionalism, the sole authority of the Bible for faith and practice, and the Lordship of Christ. What is distinctive is the way some of the distinctives function as Southern Baptists enter the twenty-first century.

- Priesthood of believers still means all Christians have direct access to God, but its corollary, "soul competency" (*the* distinctive for E. Y. Mullins), is criticized for allowing private interpretation of the Bible, a gateway to heresy. The priesthood of the laity is also paired with and subordinated to the authority of the pastor—the "ruler" of the local congregation.
- Biblical authority means an affirmation of biblical inerrancy—the Bible is "without error" in all areas of reality (e.g., including historical and scientific detail). Consequently, inerrancy necessitates the exclusion of women from the pastorate (and often from the deaconate).

• Confessions have more creedal force, especially in the employment of denominational employees.

• Religious liberty no longer translates into a strict separation of church and state. Support for the placing of religious symbols such as the Ten Commandments on public property is commonplace.

• Cooperation in missions and evangelism is to be with other conservative evangelical or "doctrinally orthodox" Christians.

• Local churches are autonomous, but associations, and the state and national conventions, demand doctrinal accountability for participation.

As they have throughout their history, Southern Baptists are known for their passion and commitment to missions and evangelism. They seek to be biblical in faith and practice and desire to embody the "New Testament Church." The essential defining characteristic of twenty-first-century Southern Baptists is a doctrinal consensus of conservative evangelical inerrantist theology. Unified in doctrinal orthodoxy, Southern Baptists are committed to evangelizing the world for Jesus Christ. The sense of chosenness, a trait found throughout their history, still inspires the Southern Baptist vision. In hyperbolic terms, Adrian Rogers expressed this optimism regarding the significant role of Southern Baptists in God's future providence:

> This is going to sound like megalomania, but I believe that the hope of the world lies in the West. I believe that the hope of the West lies in America. I believe that the hope of America is in Judeo-Christian ethics. I believe that the backbone of that Judeo-Christian ethic is evangelical Christianity. I believe that the bellwether of evangelical Christianity is the Southern Baptist Convention. So I believe, in a sense, that as the Southern Baptist Convention goes, so goes the world.[42]

---

[42] Fletcher, *Southern Baptist Convention*, 333–34.

Chapter 4

NATIONAL BAPTISTS

Sandy D. Martin

The National Baptist family includes the National Baptist Convention, USA, Inc. (founded in 1895), the National Baptist Convention of America (1916), the Progressive National Baptist Convention (1961), and the National Missionary Baptist Convention (1988). Telling the National Baptist story is significant for a number of reasons. First, the National Baptists, constituting the largest segment of African American Baptist and black Christian traditions in the U.S. and one of the largest in American religion overall, deserve presence on the pages of history.[1] Second, examining black Baptist history, particularly the National Baptists, provides great information and understanding of black religion, history, and culture. As is true of practically all human societies, people are understood most profoundly when we comprehend the interaction and, in some cases, the inseparable nature of the relationship between religion and other aspects of culture. Third, while black Baptists are indeed black, they are also assuredly Baptists who have struggled with many of the same issues as have non-black Baptists, such as foot-washing, Calvinism, issues of religious freedom and tolerance, and struggles for and over extra-congregational governance and association. Therefore, a full appreciation of Baptist history, in the U.S. and the world, is certainly difficult to achieve without acknowledging the

[1] For a description of the major black religious bodies and issues confronting them, see C. Eric Lincoln and Lawrence H. Mamiya, *The Black Church in the African American Experience* (Durham NC: Duke University Press, 1990).

contributions and activities of this large family of National Baptists.[2] The Baptist movement is not a white phenomenon with blacks attached to the margins, but it is now and has always been a multiracial reality, even when in the hearts and minds of many the idol of race has triumphed over the God of Jesus Christ; even when politically, socially, economically, and ecclesiastically the particularity of human preference has dwarfed the universality of God's creation. Finally, the story of the National Baptists lends increased understanding to the study of American religion and world Christianity. The African American Baptist tradition has been not only a racial but also a national and international phenomenon.

In this chapter we shall explore the history of African American Baptists under the following headings: (a) conversions and the earliest congregations, 1619–1830; (b) the origins of associations and conventions, 1830–1865; and (c) achieving national unity, 1865–present. As some readers may already know, the first continuous, successful national organization of African American Baptists began in 1895 with the formation of the National Baptist Convention. Neither the Southern Baptist Convention, which emerged in 1845, nor the American Baptist Churches, which trace their united, collected origins back to the early 1900s, can most fully explain their denominational existence without going back to colonial America and even England and continental Europe. Likewise, the National Baptist Convention and churches emanating from it must include the earliest conversions and organizations of independent black churches, associations, and conventions in recounting their histories because the formation and endurance of these conventions are culminations and organizational expressions of the independent religious efforts of Baptists who preceded them.

---

[2] A wonderful example of the holistic telling of the Baptist tradition is Bill Leonard's *Baptist Ways: A History* (Valley Forge PA: Judson Press, 2003).

Christian Conversions and the Earliest Congregations, 1619–1830

While the first Baptist church on the African continent was founded by black Baptists from North America, most specifically from Canada, we have no record that Baptist fellowships existed on the continent prior to the late 1700s. Unlike their white counterparts, American blacks first encountered that denomination in the United States. In examining the records of seventeenth-century white Baptists and predominantly white associations, we find the occasional mention of Africans in America who embraced the Baptist tradition, sometimes as enslaved and other times as freed people. But black Baptists—as most American Christians black, white, or red—did not enter the church in great numbers until the First and Second Great Awakenings. The awakenings were series of revivals that swept the colonies (and later the States). The First Great Awakening may be traced back to colonial New Jersey in the late 1720s with the preaching of Theodore Frelinghuysen. Spreading beyond the middle colonies into New England, the revivals reached the Southern colonies with great strength in the 1740s. Blacks were present, as enslaved and freed people, throughout the colonies, though more greatly represented in some areas than others. It is not surprising, therefore, that in the earliest days of the Great Awakening blacks in the colonies also came to Christianity through this evangelical movement.[3]

As we shall see, some of these conversions to Baptist Christianity eventuated in the formation of independent black groups in the middle states and New England. But because the race was largely enslaved in North America, the great majority of blacks resided in the South into the early twentieth century. It is in this region that the greatest number of blacks embraced Christianity, the Baptist tradition in particular, and

---

[3] As examples of colonial and early national period references to African American presence among Baptists and the concern over slavery on the part of white Baptists, see Terry Wolever, ed., *The Life and Ministry of John Gano*, vol. 1 (Springfield MO: Particular Baptist Press, 1998) 61; and A. D. Gillette, ed., *Minutes of the Philadelphia Baptist Association*, Baptist History Series 22 (Paris AR: The Baptist Standard Bearer, n.d.) 247 (in the 1789 minutes) and 307 (1795 minutes).

became members of Baptist fellowships. Some scholars question the traditional claim that the awakenings effected huge increases in church memberships. This writer, however, still subscribes to the conventional view. While some might challenge the growth in white church membership statistics as a result of the revivals, it is practically universally understood that these awakenings greatly augmented the growth of black church membership.

The same factors that attracted whites to evangelical Christianity also drew blacks and Native Americans. First, the catechetical method, involving instruction and learning of prayers and creeds, proved fruitful in some circumstances but a hindrance in others. The relative scarcity of ordained clergy, the low level of literacy among all races, and other factors rendered the catechetical approach less attractive for the mass of plain, struggling people, enslaved or free. Evangelicals preached and witnessed to a God with whom even the illiterate and the enslaved could have direct, personal experience, including being called to ministry. More specifically, regarding African Americans, it helped the evangelical cause that some of the most outspoken opponents of slavery during the eighteenth century were evangelicals, some of whom, like David Barrow of Virginia, literally freed their slaves of physical bondage and themselves of what they regarded as a spiritual bondage of slaveholding. This antislavery strand in evangelicalism strengthened the inherent revivalistic emphasis on the universal accessibility of God's grace for everyone regardless of background or condition. In addition, elements of evangelicals, such as the emphasis on the immediate presence and power of God, were greatly reminiscent of traditional african religion(s) and, thus, evangelicalism proved a successful vehicle in transitioning Africans to Christianity.[4]

As African Americans embraced Christianity, three principal forms of ecclesial fellowships developed among them. First, most black

---

[4] For a description of the impact and appeal of revivals on colonial and early national period African Americans, see Albert J. Raboteau, *Slave Religion: The "Invisible Institution" in the Antebellum South* (New York: Oxford University Press, 1978) especially 128–50.

Baptists, prior to the Civil War, fellowshipped in biracial or multiracial churches. In some instances blacks represented a minority, and in others they constituted a majority of the total memberships in churches that sometimes had nearly four or five times as many blacks as whites. The First Baptist Church of Richmond, Virginia, is a prime example of a multiracial church composed of an overwhelming majority black membership prior to the Civil War. No wonder that after the Civil War the white members in such churches often withdrew, leaving the buildings to the black memberships. There were varying degrees of treatment of blacks by their white counterparts in these multiracial churches. Concisely, we may characterize the relationships between blacks and whites as thus: (a) Black Baptists in such churches came closer to racial equity, including the opportunities to practice some forms pulpit ministry, than they did in most non-evangelical fellowships or in general society. (b) Individual black ministers here and there enjoyed unparalleled opportunities for leadership, having their freedom bought so that they might more freely preach the gospel. (c) Black members generally faced restraints on their freedom in the churches—such as segregated seating, common refusal to ordain black ministers, and discrimination in the administration of church ordinances—which intensified as the nation moved further from the pre-Revolutionary and Revolutionary eras (ca. 1750–ca. 1780).[5]

In addition to the mixed race fellowships, black Baptists also worshipped in the context of the invisible institution. The invisible institution refers to all religious practices of African Americans, especially the enslaved, that occurred beyond the observation of whites. Often blacks, unsatisfied with the worship style or lack of freedom in mixed race churches, met in secret in slave cabins, the woods, creeks, or any secluded place where they could more freely serve God and relate to each other with greater honesty and meaning. Albert Raboteau does an excellent job focusing on the invisible institution during the antebellum

[5] Carter G. Woodson, *The History of the Negro Church* (Washington, D.C.: Associated Publishers, 1972) 34–60.

period, and one can see evidence of this phenomenon as early as the eighteenth century.[6]

The third form of black Baptist fellowship occurred in independent black congregations, organizations operated by and largely for African Americans. To be sure, the mixed race congregations and the invisible institution contributed significantly to the eventual formation of the National Baptist organizations. But the most immediate context for the rise of independent black Baptist denominationalism was the independent or separate black congregations. The same factors that encouraged the rise of the invisible institution and led ultimately to the formation of black Baptist associations and conventions animated the rise of the independent congregations. African American Baptists sought contexts in which they could worship God and fellowship with each other devoid of the racially discriminatory and, in some instances, spiritually confining atmosphere of the mixed race but white-controlled churches. Like their white counterparts, black Baptists saw missions, especially overseas missions in lands predominated by African peoples, as vitally integral to their understanding of Christianity. And, like some of their white siblings, African American Baptists sought to aid the antislavery cause or at least offer a testimony against the system.[7]

One great controversy in black Baptist history has been identifying the earliest organized separate black congregation. Rather than focus on the origins of particular churches, let us instead point to three main areas of eighteenth-century black independency. Some scholars have noted the existence of the Bluefield Baptist Church, later taking the name First African Baptist Church, in Virginia. This church may have been organized as early as 1758. Others have discounted the historical priority of this congregation on two grounds. First, they claim, it was organized by white ministers and, thus, was not in the truest sense an independent black congregation. Second, they point out that the congregation itself was disrupted with the membership moving to different locales. The

---

[6] Raboteau, *Slave Religion*, esp. 211–18.

[7] James M. Washington, *Frustrated Fellowship: The Black Baptist Quest for Social Power* (Macon GA: Mercer University Press, 1986) 23–45.

First African Baptist Church in Savannah, Georgia, founded in 1788, is most generally accorded the title of the oldest black church, Baptist or non-Baptist, in the U.S. and the world, given the fact that the earliest black churches were Baptist. The claim to historical priority is strong for this congregation because of clear documentation and continuous, uninterrupted history.[8]

But the historical priority of First African is challenged by the First Bryan Baptist Church also located in Savannah, which sees itself as the legitimate heir of the original group founded by Andrew Bryan. It seems that following a dispute, the pastor and most of the congregation moved to the present location of the First African Baptist Church, leaving the majority of the deacons and the remaining membership at the original site. Weakening First Bryan's claims is the fact that the other group and the pastor had the majority of the membership and retained the original name while the First Bryan group originally surrendered the name of First African and instead accepted the title Third African from the white-controlled Sunbury Association in the 1830s, changing it only subsequently to First Bryan. But First Bryan has received official recognition from the National Baptist Convention, USA, Incorporated that it stands on the site of the original church, though the NBCI has not attempted to solve the dispute between these two churches. Furthermore, one could legitimately raise the question of whether the pastor, Andrew Marshall, and the majority membership effectively departed from the identity of the First African Church as founded by Andrew Bryan because (a) they left the original church site; (b) both the majority of the deacon board and the Sunbury Baptist Association defined Marshall as doctrinally heretical for his apparent support of Alexander Campbell's teaching; (c) the association, demonstrating the

[8] For discussions of the origins of black Baptist churches, see Woodson, *Negro Church*, 34–38; Washington, *Frustrated Fellowship*, 7–11; Raboteau, *Slave Religion*, 139–42; Andrew Billingsley, *Mighty Like a River: The Black Church and Social Reform* (New York: Oxford University Press, 1999) 13–21; and Mechal Sobel, *Trabelin' On: The Slave Journey to an Afro-Baptist Faith* (Westport CT: Greenwood Press, 1979) 99–108, 250–51.

extraordinary power whites had over blacks during the era of slavery, declared the Marshall group excommunicated and dissolved as a valid Baptist church; and (d) people representing the First African church in the association continued to do so, albeit under the newly mandated name of Third African.[9] It is probably best to take the position that they both are equally the heirs of the original fellowship and should share whatever distinction is accorded to the original First African church.

Another area contending for the birth site of the oldest black congregation is upcountry from the coastal area of Savannah, the eastern Georgia/western South Carolina area of Augusta-Silver Bluff. In the past, scholars recognized the Silver Bluff Baptist Church in South Carolina across the river from Augusta as being the first organized black church. But contrast was drawn between the first organized church (Silver Bluff) and the congregation that had an unbroken history (the Savannah churches). Founded between 1773 and 1775, according to traditional accounts, the Silver Bluff church underwent disruption during the American Revolution. Some members journeyed down to the Savannah coastal area, others migrated across the river to Augusta, and some remained in the Silver Bluff area and later reconstituted a church—according to usual historical accounts. Church traditions in that Augusta-Silver Bluff area, however, have dissented from this depiction. An Augusta group, the present-day Springfield Baptist Church, maintains that it is the reconstitution of the original Silver Bluff group. Likewise, church members in the Silver Bluff area across the years have insisted that the organized church group there either did not totally disappear or that it was reconstituted earlier than the 1790s, the usual date given.

---

[9] In addition to discussions by Washington, Raboteau, Billingsley, and Sobel referenced in a previous footnote, see James M. Simms, *The First Colored Baptist Church in North America Constituted at Savannah, Georgia, January 20, A.D. 1788* (originally published by Philadelphia: J. B. Lippincott Company, 1888) and found on "Documents of the South" Web site of the University of North Carolina at Chapel Hill, copyrighted 2000. See 13–126 of the text as originally paginated.

The question of historical priority is indeed an important one but accompanied with dangers. Focusing solely on the priority question as it relates to the visible, institutional formation of communities runs the risk of omitting equally compelling and significant stories of other African Americans who even earlier affirmed and maintained the Christian faith, including its Baptist version, but did not during these earliest times develop separate organizational structures. Second, focusing on historical priority of visible, institutional structures overlooks the dynamic role played by the "invisible institution," those religious activities practiced by African Americans that largely went unobserved by whites. Actually, directing our attention to the invisible institution raises the whole question of how we define a church. Would it not be in keeping with the earliest history of the Christian faith itself if we recognized any community of people who reverence Christ as Savior and maintain fellowship as constituting churches? Third, too much attention to the question of historical priority of institutions risks separating African American Christians from the larger world of Baptists and Christianity. The black church, Baptist and otherwise, did not develop in a solely black environment but also in interaction with white and red (Native American) Christians and in an international context, as we shall see later in this chapter. Fourth, seeking to pinpoint one congregation as the oldest might be subsequently compromised or dislodged if evidence emerges demonstrating the priority and continuity of a tradition hitherto overlooked. Finally, an exclusive or near-so concentration on the question of institutional priority runs the peril of promoting competition among and between specific fellowships of believers at the expense of recognizing a far greater movement taking place—that is, the emergence of independent black Christianity, including black Baptists, and its impact on other churches, the nation, and the world.

Because of different approaches to defining the church, interpretation of historical data, and what constitutes evidence, it is virtually impossible to prove to any of the respective advocates of historical priority of the individual churches that their position is incorrect. For these and other reasons, this chapter proposes a new model for addressing the question of historical priority of African American Baptist congregations, one that perhaps will not satisfy the contending parties but will hopefully broaden the question and point to important ecclesial interconnections. I contend that the Silver Bluff Baptist family of churches constitutes one of the earliest, uninterrupted, continuous, verifiably existing black Baptist (and Christian) communities and that out of this Silver Bluff fellowship emerged specific organizational groupings of churches: the Silver Bluff Baptist Church, presently in Beech Island, South Carolina; the First African and the First Bryan Baptist churches in Savannah; and the Springfield Baptist Church in Augusta.

While the earliest origins of black Baptist churches lie in the states of Georgia, South Carolina, and Virginia, the black congregational movement soon spread to other colonies (subsequently states). By the end of the first decade of the nineteenth century, black Baptist congregations were located in practically every state of the union. The Second Colored or African Baptist Church amicably emerged from the First African in Savannah in 1802. During these early years we find First African Baptist Churches in various places, including Philadelphia; the Gillfield or Second African Baptist Church in Petersburg, Virginia; African or Joy Street Baptist Church in Boston, Massachusetts; Stone Street Baptist Church in Mobile, Alabama; Abysinnian Baptist Church in New York City; African Baptist Church in Claiborne County, Mississippi; and the Calvary Baptist Church in Bayou Chicot, Louisiana. During the 1810–1840 period (and thereafter), black Baptist churches continued to appear throughout the nation and territories, including First Colored Baptist Church in Trenton, New Jersey; Wood River Baptist Church in Wood River, Illinois; White Bluff Colored Baptist Church in Chatham County, Georgia; First African Baptist Church in South Richmond, Virginia; First African Baptist Church in St. Louis, Missouri; First African Baptist Church, Lexington, Kentucky; Mount Zion Baptist Church in Ridge Prairie, Illinois; First African Baptist Church in New Orleans; Union Colored Baptist Church in Cincinnati, Ohio; St. Anne's Primitive Baptist Church in Deland, Florida; First

Baptist Church (Colored) in Hartford, Connecticut; First Colored Baptist Church in Washington, D.C.; and Meeting Street Baptist Church in Providence, Rhode Island.[10]

This is a limited listing of African American independent Baptist congregations until 1840 but remains helpful in conveying a number of important points about the forerunners of the National Baptist conventions. First, black Baptist congregations flourished with African American Christians wherever they could, establishing separate communities of worship. This independent movement was more easily done by free or freed blacks, of course, but the Savannah churches and a number of others indicate that even in the South amid slavery it was possible to maintain some degree of black Baptist congregational autonomy. Second, the above listing of black churches shows amazing geographical spread. Black people, mainly because of enslavement, were located in major colonial and national areas, from New England to the deepest South and into the Midwest and expanding Western settlements. This geographical distribution also shows the results of African American migration, refugees from slavery as well as people, families, and groups involved in the general movement from more settled areas to the ever-expanding frontier. Third, bringing this listing of black groups down to the 1840s buttresses the observation that during the 1830s and 1840s African American Baptists had sufficiently institutionalized locally that they were now prepared to move to the next level of organization, the regional associations.

Before advancing to a discussion of black regional associations, let us note that these African American Baptists were in fact Baptist. Sometimes in our zeal to respect the uniqueness of the forces and trials they faced, we run the danger of classifying them as *tertium quid*, somewhere between being true Baptists and non-Baptists. Though their African background and social location as a largely enslaved and universally oppressed race rendered their Baptist identity a great measure of distinctiveness, the fact of distinction does not disqualify

---

[10] Sobel, *Trabelin'*, 250–53.

them as authentically Baptist any more than the peculiarities of German, Welsh, or Irish backgrounds would so categorize those Baptists. We see the validity of their Baptistness amply demonstrated by their historical contemporaries, for example, in Savannah. When Andrew Marshall permitted Alexander Campbell access to the pulpit at First African and proceeded to express opinions that at the least gave the appearance of approbation, the diaconate of the church took strong exception. The Sunbury Association, ruling that Marshall and the group that exited the church properties were not true Baptists, continued communion with and accepted representation from the non-Marshall minority remaining at the original site, Third African Baptist Church and eventually First Bryan Baptist Church, as well as the Greater Ogeechee and Second African Baptist Churches.[11]

Furthermore, in buttressing the point of their genuine Baptistness, most African American Baptists lived in the enslaved South and continued in worship, at least at regularly prescribed times, with white-controlled, though certainly not always predominantly white, congregations. In some instances, especially in the South, African Americans vastly outnumbered whites with ratios of two, three, or even excess of four to one. A number of interesting statistics from South Carolina prior to 1850 demonstrate this phenomenon. In the First Baptist Church of Charleston, only 261 of the 1,643 members were white; the Second Baptist Church in Charleston had a closer ratio, 312 blacks to 200 whites, but still a black majority. The Georgetown Baptist Church had 298 African American and only 33 white members. In addition, these churches were members of associations where white memberships were only half the size of black memberships. Of course, some areas with predominantly white memberships had large black minorities. For example, the Bethel Baptist Association in 1838 had a total membership of 1,502 whites compared with 637 African Americans, and by 1843 there were 1,804 whites and 1,000 blacks, actually a small numerical gain by African Americans. Nor was this fellowshipping of

---

[11] Simms, *First Colored Baptist Church*, UNC-Chapel Hill, esp. 97–126 of original text.

black Baptists with white-controlled associations unique to the South. After a number of African American congregations were founded in Washington, D.C., in the 1830s and 1840s, a prominent congregation originally founded by Sampson White in 1839 found reception by the Philadelphia Baptist Association, preferring this group to Southern associations that supported enslavement.[12]

The recognition of the "regularity" of African American Baptists by their white counterparts also finds expression in the purchase of enslaved black preachers' freedom and in their calling to pastor biracial or white churches. Admittedly, these occurrences were rare especially prior to the 1840s, but they transpired with sufficient frequency to advance the point under discussion. The Gloucester Baptist Church in Virginia, a white congregation, invited the black William Lemon to serve as pastor in the early 1800s. Blacks and whites in a Portsmouth, Virginia, congregation in the late 1700s worshipped together with a surprising degree of racial equality and at one point called Thomas Armistead, an African American, to serve as pastor. The same church, after a period of dissension and disarray over the issue of free will, found unity with the ministry of Josiah Bishop. Both whites and blacks were deeply impressed with his preaching, and the church supplied the funds so that Bishop bought his liberty and later that of some other family members.[13] Another enslaved preacher, Uncle Jack, found favor with whites—who arranged his licensing and bought his freedom and some farmland—and successfully converted many of them.[14] Joseph Willis, born free in South Carolina, established a biracial church in the Mound Bayou, Mississippi, area in 1805. A man with moderate education, Willis relocated to Louisiana where he was ordained in 1812 and became the founder and the first moderator of the Louisiana Baptist Association in 1837.[15]

Black Baptist activities in the area of missions also underscore this group's commitment to Baptist polity and doctrine and cooperation with

---

[12] Woodson, *Negro Church*, 94–98.

[13] Ibid., 45–46.

[14] Ibid., 47.

[15] Ibid., 74.

their white counterparts. Thomas Paul, a Baptist minister and church organizer in the Northeast, formally requested in 1823 that the Baptist Missionary Society of Massachusetts appoint him as a missionary to Haiti. The predominantly white body heartily approved of his mission plans, and he served for half a year in Haiti. While the Haitian president and other officials warmly received him and though he did succeed in reviving some church people, Paul's lack of fluency in French greatly hampered his work and forced a disappointed missionary to return to the States.[16] One year after the Baptist Triennial Convention formed, a white deacon, William Crane, and two black ministers, Lott Carey and Colin Teague, organized the Richmond African Baptist Missionary Society in 1815 to promote missions work in West Africa. Working with the Triennial Convention and later the Southern Baptist Convention, this society, through its advocacy and fundraising for the cause, drew attention to a continent largely ignored by American white Baptists. Actually, the society worked with the Baptist Convention and the American Colonization Society in helping to place Carey and Teague in Liberia in 1822.[17] This combination of black emigration and mission interests is also reflected in the fact that the Providence Baptist Church in Richmond relocated to Monrovia in 1822.[18] Though subsequent years would reveal that the African American colonists largely lived separate lives from the indigenous Africans, there were significant efforts by some to spread the Christian faith among traditional African peoples.

The presence of strong missionary interest, foreign and domestic, points to another indicator of the Baptistness of these early African American Christians. The formation of the black Baptist movement took place in an international context, as a part of a global movement on the part of Baptists of all races. From the Silver Bluff/Savannah nexus of black Baptists, we see the spread of Baptist Christianity into other parts of the world. Both George Liele and David George, as we have noted,

---

[16] Ibid., 76–79.

[17] Sandy D. Martin, *Black Baptists and African Missions: The Origins of a Movement, 1880–1915* (Macon GA: Mercer University Press, 1989) 18–19.

[18] Sobel, *Trabelin'*, 251.

relocated to the Savannah coastal area after the disruption of the Silver Bluff community during the middle 1770s. Sometime after Andrew Bryan's baptism, Liele journeyed to Jamaica, where he established the first Baptist church, white or black, on the British island. Through the impact of Liele's work, missionaries were sent to West Africa during the 1840s, and evangelistic outreach to Central America, Haiti, and Cuba began in the 1870s. Liele was not the only black British loyalist who migrated to the Caribbean area during the Revolutionary era; Frank Spence left Florida in 1780 with another loyalist contingent and began work in Nassau, Bahamas. Ten years later a refugee from slavery in Charleston, South Carolina, having made it to Augustine, Florida, likewise sailed to Nassau. Both men helped to establish Baptist churches, presumably the first ones, in the Bahamas. In addition, William Hamilton began a Baptist church in Trinidad and Tobago in 1816; he, too, had emigrated from the States, in his case via Bermuda.[19]

Another British loyalist and Baptist church founder who came from the United States was David George. A friend and ministerial colleague to Liele, George left the Savannah area in 1782 for Nova Scotia, Canada, where he established a Baptist church. The challenges of environmental conditions and racial proscriptions, combined with an intense desire to spread the gospel to Africa, encouraged him to journey with a community of black Nova Scotians to the British colony of Sierra Leone, which, like Liberia, was a haven for Africans escaping or rescued from the oceanic slave trade. George helped establish in Sierra Leone the first Baptist church on the continent.[20] It should be emphasized that their correspondence with non-black Baptist officials and leaders in the United States and England demonstrates their sense of fidelity to global

[19] Clement Gayle, *George Liele: Pioneer Missionary to Jamaica* (Nashville: Bethlehem Book Publishers, Inc., 2002) especially 70–85.

[20] For an informative biography of George along with original letters from him, see Grant Gordon, *From Slavery to Freedom: The Life of David George, Pioneer Black Baptist Minister* (Hantsport NS: Lancelot Press, 1992).

Baptist principles, polity, identity, and fellowship.[21] Thus, from the southern area of what would become the United States, particularly around Savannah, would emanate Baptists who carried the faith to the Caribbean, Central America, Nova Scotia, and the African colonies of Liberia and Sierra Leone between 1780 and 1880.

The Rise of Associations and Conventions, 1830–1865

Exactly why did African Americans separate from white Baptists and form independent black congregations and later associations and conventions? First, African American Baptists, as other black Christians, sought fellowships where they could worship, witness, and perform their ministries without the encumbrances of racial discrimination. While the early white evangelicals showed a great degree of openness to African Americans, their openness overall was not progressively enlarged but in some instances actually diminished during the 1780s–early 1800 era, the time of the rise of many black congregations in various denominations. These racial proscriptions include establishing and/or continuing segregated seating, segregation at the Communion table, a sense on the part of African American church people that their spiritual needs were going unmet by white clergy and the larger white-controlled churches, and a refusal of white authorities to ordain black clergy. Second, many African American Christians believed that white churches paid insufficient attention to evangelizing African Americans and dealing with the temporal conditions they faced. Third, African Americans often desired greater freedom to worship as they pleased without restrictions placed on them by their white counterparts. This freedom of worship included styles that might have reflected the pattern of traditional

[21] For correspondence by black Baptists to white Baptist officials, see Milton C. Sernett, *African American Religious History: A Documentary History*, 2nd ed. (Durham NC: Duke University Press, 1999) 44–51; George Liele and Andrew Bryan's letters; and Gordon, *From Slavery to Freedom*, 198–215, for letters by and/or about David George addressed to John Rippon.

African religion and the liberty to pray, speak, and preach more boldly against slavery.

A fourth reason for the rise of independent black congregations and later associations and conventions was the dedication on the part of African Americans to continue more sustained overt or subtle attacks on the system of slavery. Many of the earliest white Baptists who evangelized in the Southern colonies/states, such as David Barrows, were antislavery in sentiment; some literally freed their slaves. Some white preachers faced great hostility and bodily harm because of their preaching against slavery. This antislavery stance certainly factored in the attractiveness of evangelicalism, including the Baptist variety. A number of churches and associations during the 1780s took strong positions against slavery, defining it as an evil that must be extirpated. But during the 1790s and early 1800s, many white church people, especially in the Southern states where slavery was most profitable, had defied or renounced that position. Black and white antislavery Baptists had principally two choices other than remaining in contexts where their lives would be continually threatened or taken from them. They could support colonization of blacks in the hope that slaveholders would be more amenable to emancipating the enslaved with the assurance that the enslaved would be colonized in Africa or some foreign land. This colonization strategy often went hand in hand with foreign or overseas missions. The other choice for these antislavery proponents was that they themselves immigrate from the South to places where the populace was more hospitable, or at least not as vehemently opposed, to their activities.

Along with other factors, the quest to free African Americans from slavery contributed immensely to the establishment of the first associations and conventions.[22] Southern free blacks, those emancipated or freed, and refugees from slavery migrated to the Northern and

---

[22] Washington, *Frustrated Fellowship*, 3–45, for a discussion of the attractiveness of evangelicalism and the antislavery and abolitionist stances of both blacks and whites, including the role of abolitionism in the founding of black Baptist associations and conventions.

Midwestern states and territories. Combining their dedication to humanitarian concerns, missions (foreign and domestic), and antislavery positions, they proceeded to establish the earliest black associations in the Midwest during the 1830s. The earliest black Baptist association of record was the Providence Baptist Association, formed in 1834, in Berlin Cross Roads, Ohio. Robert Townsend, James B. Steward, Jacob Ward, and Kendall Carter were among those who sought greater Baptist unity among six churches in the state to achieve the goals of fostering education, missions, and antislavery. The association's antislavery stand evidences itself more prominently in the title of the group in 1859 when it was known as the Providence Antislavery (Colored) Baptist Association and by that time had grown to fifteen churches. Two years following the founding of the Providence Association, another black Ohio group of churches formed the Union Association or the Association of the Regular Baptist Churches of Color in Ohio with Reuben Malvin as moderator and Charles B. Satchel as clerk. In the southwestern portion of the neighboring state, Illinois, John Livingstone and others established the third black Baptist association, the Wood River Baptist Association, in 1839. Originally named the Colored Baptist Association and Friends of Humanity, this group demonstrates its commitment to antislavery because both black and white antislavery Christians often described themselves as "Friends of Humanity," perhaps an influence of the Society of Friends or Quakers who themselves were the earliest denominational opponents of slavery.

While Ohio and Illinois were free states, they were not always inviting places for African Americans. It is clear that some antislavery sentiment on the part of many whites was intimately linked with anti-black feelings. Indeed, refugees from slavery and other free blacks often found that Northern communities had laws restricting their movements or even denying them the right of domicile. Hence, blacks migrated farther north, even across the U.S.-Canadian border. Among these settlers and descendants of settlers were Baptists in Michigan and west Canada who formed the Baptist Association for Colored People, more popularly known as the Amhertsburg Baptist Association, in 1841. The

Amhertsburg Association was home to some of the greatest lights in the black Canadian abolitionist movement, including Anthony Binga, Sr., and William Troy. One of their number, Samuel Davis, delivered an attack on slavery at the National Colored Convention meeting in Buffalo, New York, in 1843 that was equal in intensity to that delivered by the famed Henry Highland Garnett.

There were other movements toward black Baptist denominational unity during the years preceding the Civil War. On the East Coast, the American Baptist Missionary Convention was founded in 1840. Founded in New York City at the Abyssinian Baptist Church, convention members elected Sampson White, pastor of the New York congregation, as their first president. Black Baptists had grown discouraged with the manner in which they were insufficiently included in the affairs of the American Baptist Antislavery Convention, an interracial group. This new group sought to take a stronger stand against slavery and promote African missions, though during its early years most work was done on the home front. In 1858 William John Barnett journeyed to Sierra Leone as a missionary of this convention. In the Midwest, another convention formed out of the Wood River Association. The Western Colored Baptist Convention was formed in 1853 in St. Louis, Missouri. For six years it did not convene (1859–1864). In 1864 the Wood River Association rejuvenated the convention, and it took the name Northwestern and Southern Baptist Convention. This new name indicates the concern of black Baptists for denominational work both in the West and among their racial siblings becoming free in the South due to the successes of Union forces there. With both the American Baptist Missionary Convention and the Western Colored/Northwestern and Southern Baptist Convention, we see a move of African American Baptists to effect union beyond the local association to the broader regional or even national level.[23]

---

[23] See Washington, *Frustrated Fellowship*, 3–45, for the discussion on the founding of independent black churches and associations. Also see Leroy Fitts, *A History of Black Baptists* (Nashville: Broadman Press, 1985) 60–65.

The Achievement of National Unity, 1865–Present

By any calculation, the Civil War and Reconstruction periods made a great impact on all of the U.S., including the churches. For white churches, the slavery debate, Civil War, and Reconstruction were events that created and/or maintained barriers between Christians of the North and South. For black Christians, the slavery debate was an opportunity to express solidarity with their oppressed racial kin across geographical and political lines; the Civil War was the occasion of reunion between Southern and Northern Christians; and Reconstruction was the promise of a new day for blacks throughout the nation and its territories. For African American Christians, including Baptists, the Civil War was the exodus, God's acting in history to free the oppressed. Historians point out a number of things that highlight this black belief in the Civil War period as an exodus event, including many enslaved black Christians' fervent conviction that God would one day bring an end to chattel bondage, the identification of the Union forces with the army of God, and the profound, religiously liberating experiences of freedom with the victory of Union armies and the issuing of the Emancipation Proclamation.

While some might point to other events, such as the independent church movement in the late eighteenth and early nineteenth centuries, as being the exodus event for African American Christians, most African Americans of the time memorialized the Civil War-Emancipation occurrence as the Jubilee. Even today, many black churches assemble on 31 December of each year for "watch night" services, welcoming in the New Year. Unfortunately, the current practice has been divorced from its original meaning, i.e., the enslaved awaiting the arrival of 1 January 1863, when according to Lincoln's Emancipation Proclamation the enslaved in the Confederacy would become free. Some have claimed that such a proclamation actually freed no slave because it was not possible for Union forces to enforce a law in areas they had not conquered. But this contention misses three crucial points: (a) those enslaved blacks who had already escaped to Union lines were no longer "contrabands," who might be returned according to the discretion of the military commander, but free people; (b) as the Union military captured an area, there was no longer any question that the formerly enslaved were now at least physically free of chattel slavery; and (c) the very announcement that the U.S. government had recognized their right to be free brought to the enslaved a psychological victory, hope for the future, and validation that God was acting to liberate them.

Despite the circumscriptions the newly freed still faced and the setbacks that would come in the decades ahead, emancipation brought an end to chattel slavery; and freedom, thought limited in many ways, delivered opportunities to the enslaved and those who labored on their behalf, black and white, that were hitherto not known. Religious freedom took on a whole new and more complete meaning as the African Americans chose their own denominational affiliations, gathered themselves into churches, and constructed places of worship. As a result of this newly found freedom, black Baptist organizing continued and even advanced to new levels.[24] The military conflict had barely ceased when Baptists began organizing state conventions, with Virginia, South Carolina, and North Carolina being among the first. Fidelity to regional Baptist associations continued and even expanded. In the West, the Baptist General Association of Western States and Territories emerged in 1873 and was successful in placing missionaries in central Africa in the 1880s. The New England Baptist Convention, formed one year later, represented Northeastern black Baptists' commitment to the spread of the gospel and the uplift of the black race. And, importantly, new stronger efforts were made to effect national conventions of Baptist forces.

One can see the thrusts toward national union with the formation of the Consolidated American Baptist Missionary Convention in 1866, a glorious but ultimately unsuccessful attempt to unite the Northwestern and Southern Baptist Convention with the American Baptist Missionary

---

[24] In support of the following discussion on the formation of post-Civil War state, regional, and national conventions, see Martin, *Black Baptists*, 107–29; Fitts, *History of Black Baptists*, 69–79; and Washington, *Frustrated Fellowship*, 83–157.

Convention. William W. Colley's unpleasant experiences with Southern white Baptists on the mission fields in West Africa in the 1870s constituted one factor that led him and his fellow Virginians to pioneer the formation of the Baptist Foreign Mission Convention (BFMC) in Montgomery, Alabama, in 1880. Both the National Baptist Convention, USA, Incorporated, and the National Baptist Convention of America have traditionally identified their birthdates with the formation of the BFMC. For a ten-year period, the BFMC sponsored missionaries in West Africa, but economic difficulties ended the enterprise in 1893. African American Baptists organized the American National Baptist Convention (ANBC) in 1886 to conduct domestic missions and the Baptist National Educational Convention (BNEC) in 1893 to promote education. By 1894, black Baptists had come to realize the need for one national convention, modeled after the Southern Baptist Convention, that would incorporate all black American Baptists into one organization that would meet their myriad obligations—education, home missions, overseas missions, publications, etc. That year the BFMC adopted a proposal, which proved successful, to unite the ANBC, the BFMC, and the BNEC as one convention with a number of boards carrying out the respective duties of the merging organizations.

The first National Baptist Convention came into existence in Atlanta, Georgia, in 1895. This national convention of African American Baptists, unlike previous ones, would survive. Given that the first black Baptist congregations emerged possibly as early as the 1750s and certainly by 1788, and the earliest associations appeared in the 1830s and 1840s, why did it take so long for African American Baptists to achieve national unity? There are at least three reasons. First, black Baptists, like many of their white counterparts, greatly valued the tradition of local polity or church governance to the point of fearing and resisting organizations above the congregational level and certainly beyond regional groupings. The first white-controlled group, the Triennial Convention, did not emerge until 1814, and even this organization was devoted almost mainly to foreign missions. The Southern Baptist Convention (SBC) achieved total unification of its work only in 1845, and at that point the SBC was virtually a regional body—more a large association than a national convention. The Northern Baptist Convention (forerunner of the American Baptist Churches) consolidated its work in the first decade of the twentieth century. It, too, was virtually a large regional association. Thus, the 1895 appearance of the NBC did not chronologically place it too far afield (but perhaps ahead) of its white counterparts. This commitment to local congregational autonomy and distrust of larger, overarching bodies obviously characterized white as well as black Baptists.

Second, sectional tensions contributed to the delay in the formation of a truly national convention of African American Baptists. Certainly the conflicts did not reach the level of white Southerners' and Northerners' antebellum conflicts over slavery. But historical data abundantly testify that Baptists in particular and blacks in general experienced sectional conflict in the aftermath of the Civil War.[25] Often Northern black Baptists felt convinced that they knew what was best for their Southern siblings, that Northerners were the best caretakers of purest Christianity.

Third, evidence suggests that African Americans were torn between the universalist ideals of the Christian faith and their particularistic needs as a race of people in a racially conscious society. That is, many blacks held out hope that some merger or cooperation with whites was possible, that true Christians should transcend the race line. It is not that they expected social intermingling of the race to occur in the near future, but some did seem to evince a belief, or at least a hope, in some type of unity between the races at the association or convention level. But perhaps more important than a belief that such an institutional merger with whites was possible were the divisions that occurred among blacks themselves over the extent to which they should cooperate with, or even depend on, the support of whites. Combined with one or both of the previous reasons, this issue of black-white cooperation apparently contributed to a delay in the formation of a national black convention

[25] Washington's *Frustrated Fellowship* and Fitts's *History of Black Baptists* amply demonstrate the presence of sectional tension in African American Baptist history.

and factored in secessions from the NBC after it was organized, represented by the formation of the Lott Carey Baptist Convention from the NBC in 1897.

Perhaps more important than the reasons for the delay in the formation of a truly viable national convention of African American Baptists were the reasons for the successful organization of the National Baptist Convention in 1895. First, African American Baptists in the post-Civil War period believed that a union of forces would better equip them to carry out the work of missions, education, and other denominational work. In unity there was strength. Second, African Americans continued to live in a race-conscious society that often limited their full and free participation, even in religious affairs. In particular, during the post-Reconstruction period with the rapid rise of Jim Crow legislation, segregation, disfranchisement, economic privations, and the spread of racial terrorism, blacks felt the need to unite for defense and mutual support. And, finally, African Americans of various denominations, including black Baptists, in the late 1800s and early 1900s were motivated by the sense of racial divine calling. As far back as the late eighteenth century, African American Christians had been guided by the conviction that God had especially prepared them to be the means by which Christianity and "civilization" would be spread to all peoples of African descent, at home and abroad—that they would be instruments by which black peoples would be both spiritually and temporally uplifted or liberated. This view was expressed clearly in the interpretation of Psalm 68:31 as a prophecy that African peoples would rise religiously and politically.

This accomplishment of national unity of African Americans in the National Baptist Convention in 1895 was not to continue, however, without divisions and conflicts.[26] In 1897, the Lott Carey Baptist Convention, especially represented in the states of Virginia, North

---

[26] For historical outlines of the continuing conflicts and development of new denominational bodies from the National Baptist Convention during the 1897–1988 period, see Fitts, *History of Black Baptists*, 79–106; and Lincoln and Mamiya, *Black Church*, 20–39.

Carolina, and the middle Atlantic seaboard, organized with the conviction that the foreign mission program could operate more efficiently, a sense that stalwart supporters of African missions had been marginalized, and the belief that greater efforts should be made to cooperate with white Baptists in the pursuit of missions. In 1915–1916, a dispute over the control of the publishing house associated with the NBC eventuated in the separation of the forces into the National Baptist Convention, USA, Incorporated (NBCI) and the National Baptist Convention of America (NBCA). During the 1950s and early 1960s, the NBCI struggled with two issues that produced another split: the question of "tenure" for the convention president (specifically Joseph H. Jackson), that is, term limits; and the role of the convention in the Civil Rights Movement. Despite indications on his part that he favored a two-term limit as president, Jackson, beginning in the mid 1950s, continued to seek and win reelection, sometimes employing parliamentary tactics that some critics found unjust. Connected with the tenure question was the debate over to what extent the NBCI should become actively involved in the Civil Rights Movement as represented by Martin Luther King, Jr., stressing civil disobedience, mass protests, government support, and extensive integration of institutions in society. Jackson, while embracing an integrated society for both religious and political reasons, favored less emphasis on mass protest and civil disobedience and greater attention to the use of the courts, self-help, economic empowerment, and the maintenance of black institutions. After unsuccessful attempts to dislodge Jackson as convention president, a group convened in 1961 to form the Progressive National Baptist Convention with the intent of combining traditional denominational work with a more activist civil rights agenda. In 1988, the NBCA faced a serious division in its ranks when once again the management of the publishing house came under dispute. In that year a new organization emerged: the National Baptist Missionary Convention.

Chapter 5

INDEPENDENT BAPTISTS

Jerry L. Faught

In the early twentieth century, as Baptists in America formed extensive denominational machinery and created a religious establishment of their own, a splinter group arose from within Baptist ranks whose leaders did not seek to reform Baptist conventionism. Rather, they aspired to refound the Baptist tradition—to restore what had become corrupted. Although an acceptance of some degree of diversity had been normative for Baptists throughout their history, the so-called independent or separatist Baptists aimed to redefine the Baptist tradition on the basis of doctrinal, moral, and ecclesiastical uniformity. In their pursuit to establish pure Baptist churches, independent Baptists opposed Baptist denominationalism because they believed it influenced churches to compromise essential and clearly defined New Testament doctrines, destroyed local church autonomy, and had no biblical basis. Convention machinery, the concept of a universal church, and theological liberalism were all modern innovations that must be repudiated if the Christian faith were to continue unadulterated.

These ideas have persisted as the movement has matured. Current leaders often describe their churches as "Independent, Fundamental, Premillennial and Baptistic."[1] In 1987, Bill Leonard described the movement as a coalition of "fiercely autonomous local congregations whose constituents are theological fundamentalists, Baptist in practice,

[1] Nancy T. Ammerman, *Bible Believers: Fundamentalists in the Modern World* (New Brunswick NJ: Rutgers University Press, 1987) 21.

and who follow a separatist approach to other denominational bodies."[2] Despite their aversion to conventionism, independent Baptist leaders have formed their own organizations, frequently referred to as fellowships.[3] For the most part, Independents cooperate through the participation of their pastors in these state or national fellowships, although some churches refuse to affiliate with any of the organized fellowships.

Despite their separatist outlook, a segment, beginning in the 1950s, started to associate with other evangelicals such as Billy Graham to advance the modern revival movement. In the 1970s, others became influential on the American political and social scene as some Independents softened their separatist stance and formed associations with like-minded outsiders in order to influence the moral culture of America. While these ecumenical activities have brought tension from within the ranks, at the same time, the movement, which lacked powerful influence and prominence in its early years, has recently become one of the most dynamic and controversial forces in Baptist life in America. Although their main strength is in the South, independent Baptists have around 4,700 churches with a membership of about 2 million.[4] Although most congregations are small (between 100 and 500 members), "non-convention" Baptists claim some of the largest Sunday schools and churches in the United States.

---

[2] Bill J. Leonard, "Independent Baptists: From Sectarian Minority to 'Moral Majority,'" *Church History* (December 1987): 505.

[3] For Independents, the word "convention" or "denomination" indicates control over local churches that maintain membership in the organization. The word "fellowship" signifies that each church is autonomous and can determine what programs it will support.

[4] Albert W. Wardin, ed., *Baptists around the World* (Nashville: Broadman & Holman, 1995) 371, 394, 403. Southern groups have about 4,500 churches with a membership of about 1,935,000, while northern groups have more than 2,000 churches and a membership of about 200,000. As Wardin notes, it is difficult to gain exact figures on membership for separatist fundamental fellowships. Fellowship directories list cooperating churches and pastors but do not give membership statistics. Also, many churches are related to more than one fellowship.

The independent Baptist movement emerged in the early twentieth century during the fundamentalist-modernist controversy. Fundamentalism surfaced in America in the nineteenth century and emerged as a clear movement by the first two decades of the twentieth century.[5] During the second decade of the twentieth century, wealthy Presbyterian laymen financed, published, and distributed a series of twelve small paperback volumes titled *The Fundamentals: A Testimony to the Truth*.[6] This series, which stressed common beliefs of fundamentalists that were based on the concepts of biblical literalism and biblical inerrancy, marked the beginning of the movement and helped to popularize it.[7] Although a number of fundamentals of the Christian faith were articulated in the booklets, fundamentalists have often been identified by five nonnegotiable doctrines of Christian orthodoxy. These five points of doctrine, which do not sufficiently represent the whole range of fundamentalist theology, are the inerrancy of Scripture, the divinity of Jesus, the Virgin Birth, Jesus' death on the cross as a substitute for our sins, and Jesus' bodily resurrection and literal, imminent Second Coming.[8]

---

[5] C. Allyn Russell, *Voices of American Fundamentalism: Seven Biographical Studies* (Philadelphia: The Westminster Press, 1976) 15.

[6] *The Fundamentals*, 12 vols. (Chicago: Testimony Publishing Company, 1910–1912). Curtis Lee Laws, editor of the *Watchman-Examiner*, an unofficial, conservative, Baptist publication, coined the term "fundamentalist" in 1920. See the *Watchman-Examiner*, editorial, 1 July 1920.

[7] Stewart G. Cole, *The History of Fundamentalism* (Westport CT: Greenwood Press, 1931) 52–62. Nearly three million copies of the volumes were distributed to thousands of Christians who welcomed them gladly. Cole credits the volumes, frequent Bible and prophecy conferences of the day, and World War I as important factors contributing to the emergence of Fundamentalism.

[8] Justo Gonzalez, *The Story of Christianity*, 2 vols. (San Francisco: Harper, 1985) 2:257. Gonzalez states that these five fundamentals were first articulated at the Niagara Conference of 1895. According to E. R. Sandeen, however, Stewart Cole (1931) carelessly made the assertion that the Niagara Conference adopted the five fundamentals, but the only statement produced by the Niagara group was issued in 1878 and contained fourteen points. The Niagara Conference adopted no five-point statement. See Ernest R. Sandeen, "Toward a Historical Interpretation of the Origins of Fundamentalism," *Church History* (March 1967): 79. Fundamentalist historian George W. Dollar noted that serious

Fundamentalism did not arise in a historical vacuum. Although several factors may have contributed to the rise of Fundamentalism, the greatest reason the movement came into being was the challenge of Protestant liberalism.[9] In general, liberals, not a monolithic group, denied biblical literalism and inerrancy and sought to reformulate traditional theological concepts to make them more amenable to the modern scientific mind. According to many liberals who considered themselves to be committed Christians, this could be done without sacrificing the religious truth of the Christian faith. A small number of liberals, sometimes called modernists, saw Christianity merely as one religion among many and the Bible as one of many great books.[10]

Fundamentalism saw liberalism or modernism as a threat to the essence of Christianity. Therefore, fundamentalists instituted a militant program to rid the SBC (Southern Baptist Convention) and the Northern Baptist Convention (NBC)[11] of what they perceived as liberal tendencies in the two major national denominations. The independent Baptist movement came into existence when a well-organized company of fundamentalists, failing to take over either of the two major national bodies of Baptists, retreated from denominational life and either established their own separate organizations or refused to associate with any entity beyond the local church level. The independent Baptist movement, then, arose as a principal sub-group within Fundamentalism during the fundamentalist-modernist controversy. Because liberalism made more inroads among Baptists in the North than in the South, the battles were more tumultuous among Northerners.

---

injustice has been done to Fundamentalism by associating the movement only with the "Famous Five" and ignoring other important articles of faith. See Dollar's *A History of Fundamentalism in America* (Greenville SC: Bob Jones University Press, 1973) 72–73.

[9] George M. Marsden, "Defining Fundamentalism," *Christian Scholar's Review* (Winter 1971): 141–51.

[10] Gonzalez, *Story of Christianity*, vol. 2, 256.

[11] The NBC became the American Baptist Convention in 1950 and American Baptist Churches, USA, in 1972.

Northern Independent Baptists

Fundamentalists in the North initially followed the strategy of identifying liberals in the NBC and attempting to expurgate them from the convention. To accomplish this goal so that they could readily reshape the denomination into a fundamentalist entity, they formed two significant organizations. The Fundamentalist Fellowship, organized in 1920, consisted of mostly moderate fundamentalists, while the militant faction created the Baptist Bible Union of North America (BBU) in 1923. From these two organizations a number of other significant independent organizations have arisen.

Founded in 1920 by Northern fundamentalists in Buffalo, New York, during a pre-convention rally, the Fundamentalist Fellowship, as it first came to be known, held its meetings immediately before annual sessions of the NBC to rally messengers for the fundamentalist agenda.[12] Hoping for an opportune moment to impose their views on the NBC, they prepared a conservative confession of faith known as the Goodchild Confession, which was based on the Philadelphia and New Hampshire confessions. For some reason, the group never asked the NBC to adopt the creed.[13] Yet, clearly the Fundamentalist Fellowship existed to purge liberals from the denomination. J. C. Massee, prominent pastor and moderate fundamentalist leader in the group, remarked, "we must therefore eliminate those men who have put in jeopardy the spiritual life and purpose of the denomination."[14] The inability of the Fundamentalist Fellowship to achieve its aims led the body eventually to separate from the NBC.

In 1946, the Fundamentalist Fellowship changed its name to the Conservative Baptist Fellowship, but since 1965 it has been called the Fundamental Baptist Fellowship of America. Since the 1950s, the FBF has been critical of and has refused to cooperate with other conservative

---

[12] H. Leon McBeth, *The Baptist Heritage* (Nashville: Broadman Press, 1987) 756.

[13] Stewart G. Cole, *History of Fundamentalism*, 68.

[14] Joseph M. Stowell, *Background and History of the General Association of Regular Baptists* (Hayward CA: Gospel Tracts Unlimited, 1949) 12.

evangelicals who have actively supported Billy Graham crusades. This strict separatist position keeps members from being tainted by "ecumenical evangelism." In 1955, the group began mandating that members affirm the premillennial return of Christ and the pretribulation rapture of the church.[15] The FBF has about 850 members who are affiliated with more than 400 churches located in 44 states.[16] At least one-fourth of the churches have ties to other fundamentalist organizations. To communicate with members, the FBF distributes *Frontline*, a journal published in Schaumburg, Illinois, since 1991. Maranatha Baptist Bible College of Watertown, Wisconsin; Denver Baptist Bible College; and San Francisco Baptist Seminary are supported by the FBF.[17]

The FBF has been hindered throughout its history due to a loss of significant membership on several occasions. The fellowship lost members to the BBU in 1923, to the General Association of Regular Baptist Churches in 1932, and to the Conservative Baptist Association of America, an evangelical organization that formed in 1947.[18]

In May 1965, more than 300 messengers from about 100 churches met at the Beth Eden Baptist Church in Denver and discussed forming a new separatist organization. The following year, messengers, meeting in Indianapolis, left the FBF and formally organized the New Testament Association of Independent Baptist Churches.[19] The founders of the NTAIBC opposed the neo-evangelical movement and its increasing influence upon their churches. They wanted strict separation from evangelicals who cooperated with non-evangelicals such as Billy Graham, and believed that the FBF had softened its separatist stance.[20] The association continues to practice what some Independents have

---

[15] Albert W. Wardin, ed., *Baptists around the World*, 386.

[16] Carol Logan, email to author, 18 August 2004.

[17] Ibid.

[18] Bill J. Leonard, *Baptist Ways* (Valley Forge: Judson Press, 2003) 404–405.

[19] George W. Dollar, *Fundamentalism in America* (Greenville SC: Bob Jones University Press, 1973) 248–49.

[20] Wardin, ed., *Baptists around the World*, 389.

referred to as second-degree separation. While first-degree separation involves a refusal to have any ties with theological liberals or ecumenical organizations such as the World Council of Churches, second-degree separation is the refusal to cooperate with Billy Graham and other neo-evangelicals who maintain relationships with theological liberals. The sole issue of second-degree separation, therefore, led to the formation of the NTAIBC. No new theological formulations resulted from the schism.

The association began with twenty-seven churches, but by the 1970s that number had doubled.[21] Today, about 100 churches are associated with the NTAIBC. About one-third of the churches are located in Minnesota. Richard Clearwaters, who pastored the Fourth Baptist Church in Minneapolis for more than forty years and founded the Central Baptist Theological Seminary in 1956 in the same city, served as a leading though controversial figure in the association during its formative years.[22] Institutions supported by the association are the Central Baptist Theological Seminary in Minneapolis and the Pillsbury Baptist Bible College in Owatonna, Minnesota. The organization publishes a small paper called *Testimonies*.[23]

Northern, Southern, and Canadian fundamentalists formed the BBU in 1923 after experiencing frustration over failed attempts to impose their dogma upon the Northern Baptist Convention. Convinced that Baptist schools had abandoned historic Christian doctrines and had embraced liberalism, fundamentalists began as early as 1915 to call for the NBC to investigate the schools.[24] Due to the agitation of fundamentalists, the NBC appointed a committee in 1920 to investigate a host of Baptist seminaries, colleges, and training schools for alleged

---

[21] Dollar, *Fundamentalism in America*, 249.

[22] George W. Dollar, *The Fight for Fundamentalism* (Sarasota FL: self-published, 1983) 82. For more details of Clearwater's life, see his autobiography, *On the Upward Road* (Minneapolis: self-published, c. 1991).

[23] Wardin, ed., *Baptists around the World*, 389.

[24] William H. Brackney, *The Baptists* (Westport CT: Praeger, 1994) 30.

liberal teaching.[25] The committee found only limited evidence of liberalism and issued a general statement of support for the schools.[26] The report proved to be divisive as delegates at the 1921 meeting greeted it with "shouting, hissing, applauding bedlam."[27]

Believing that orthodoxy in schools could be secured by way of a creedal formulation, fundamentalists attempted in 1922 to move the NBC to adopt a confessional statement that would be binding upon the schools. At the annual meeting, William B. Riley moved for the individual churches of the NBC to adopt a modified New Hampshire Confession of 1833 as its statement of faith.[28] The altered confession reflected a premillennial understanding of Christ's return.[29] The NBC refused to adopt the confessional statement. Instead, the group overwhelmingly approved a motion affirming the New Testament as its basis of faith and practice and declared that "we need no other statement."[30] Rigid fundamentalists were stung by this action. To them this action proved that modernists controlled the NBC.

Among the key players in the founding of the BBU were the leading fundamentalists in America: J. Frank Norris, volatile pastor of the First Baptist Church of Fort Worth, Texas;[31] Amzi C. Dixon, Baptist pastor,

---

[25] *Annual of the Northern Baptist Convention, 1921* (Philadelphia: American Baptist Publication Society, 1921) 48–50. Fundamentalists held that many Baptist professors denied fundamental Christian doctrines and were teaching evolution, higher-critical methodologies of Bible study, and socialist political theory.

[26] *Annual of the Northern Baptist Convention, 1921*, 93.

[27] *Watchman-Examiner*, 1 July 1920, 845. See also Russell, *Voices of American Fundamentalism*, 121.

[28] Russell, *Voices of American Fundamentalism*, 124.

[29] McBeth, *Baptist Heritage,* 576.

[30] *Annual of the Northern Baptist Convention, 1923,* 133. The motion, presented by Cornelius Woelfkin, pastor of Park Avenue Baptist Church in New York, passed by a vote of 1,264 to 637.

[31] Russell, *Voices of American Fundamentalism*, 20–46, 224. Although Norris is best known as agitator of Baptists in the South, he also served as a prominent fundamentalist figure in the North. Not only did he pastor the Fort Worth church from 1909 until his death in 1952, but he also pastored the Temple Baptist Church in Detroit,

revivalist, and editor of the first six volumes of *The Fundamentals*;[32] William B. Riley, pastor of the First Baptist Church of Minneapolis and founder of the World's Christian Fundamentals Association (1919);[33] and Thomas Todhunter Shields, the first president of the BBU. Shields, who pastored the largest Baptist church in Canada, Jarvis Street in Toronto and was called the "Canadian Spurgeon," greatly advanced the fundamentalist cause in Canada.[34]

Meeting in Kansas City, Missouri, the leaders of the BBU openly committed themselves to driving their opponents out of the NBC.[35] They passed a resolution calling for the removal of every professor who taught the "God-dishonouring, Bible-denying, man-degrading doctrine" of evolution, and named prominent pastors Cornelius Woelfkin and Harry Emerson Fosdick as modernists who must be purged from the NBC.[36] The BBU vowed to walk together with other Baptist churches that subscribed to "essential and clearly revealed doctrines" and to oppose any convention or church that "discredits the Bible and

---

Michigan, from 1935 to 1951. Norris traveled by train and plane between his two congregations.

[32] Leonard, *Baptist Ways*, 400.

[33] B. L. Shelley, "Riley, William Bell," *Dictionary of Baptists in America,* ed. Bill J. Leonard (Downers Grove IL: InterVarsity Press, 1994) 237. Riley formed the association in 1919 in order to carry the battle for the fundamentals across the continent mainly through Bible conferences held in large cities. He also formed several fundamentalist schools during his lifetime. Although a leader in the separatist movement, Riley stayed in the NBC until his death in 1947.

[34] William H. Brackney, ed., *Baptist Life and Thought: A Source Book* (Valley Forge: Judson Press, 1998) 503–504. Shields led in an investigation of alleged liberalism at McMaster University. The source book contains a brief document in which Shields attacks Modernism.

[35] W. B. Riley, "Why the Baptist Bible Union," *The Searchlight*, 4 May 1923, 1. Riley called the BBU a fellowship for true Baptists who would not fellowship with error.

[36] *A Call to Arms!* pamphlet issued by the executive committee of the Baptist Bible Union of North America (n.p., n.d. [1924]) 14–15, 17–18, in Brackney, ed., *Baptist Life and Thought: A Source Book*, 356–59. Much to the chagrin of fundamentalists, Fosdick succeeded Woelfkin as pastor of Park Avenue Baptist Church.

dishonors the Lord Jesus Christ."[37] The organization adopted the New Hampshire Confession as its doctrinal statement and added that a prerequisite to membership involved acceptance of a premillennial view of eschatology.[38]

Members of the BBU claimed initially that they did not desire to withdraw from denominational life nor did they intend to erect a denominational structure.[39] They referred to the group as "simply a gathering together of a fellowship of brethren of like faith and order and spirit within the denomination."[40] Nonetheless, soon after the creation of the BBU, its leaders began constructing powerful denominational machinery. By 1925, the BBU began making plans to send out its own missionaries. Leaders purchased a school in Des Moines, Iowa.[41] In 1928, the union passed a resolution acknowledging that complete separation "must be effected between those who believe and accept the authority of the Bible, and those who deny and reject it."[42] The attempt to put together a pan-fundamentalist Baptist organization failed, however. In the end the BBU crumbled due to internal strife and a growing disrepute of militant fundamentalists such as Norris, who shot and killed an unarmed man in his church office in 1926.[43] The Des Moines University debacle, however, was the final blow to the BBU.

---

[37] "Call and Manifesto," *The Baptist*, 7 October 1922, 1132, in *A Sourcebook for Baptist Heritage,* ed. H. Leon McBeth (Nashville: Broadman Press, 1990) 567–70.

[38] Ibid. See also *The Searchlight*, 17 November 1922, 2. Norris listed premillennialism as one of eight fundamental articles of faith of the BBU.

[39] Robert G. Delnay, "A History of the Baptist Bible Union" (Th.D. diss., Dallas Theological Seminary, 1963) 275. In appendix A, Delnay recorded the "By-laws and Aims" of the BBU, in which it is stated that leaders had no intention of creating a new convention or association.

[40] *The Searchlight*, 17 November 1922, 2.

[41] Delnay, "A History of the Baptist Bible Union of America," 196, 312–15.

[42] Ibid., 315–19. In appendix G, Delnay recorded the "Baptist Bible Union Resolution of 1928."

[43] Russell, *Voices of American Fundamentalism*, 35–36. Although Norris was acquitted of the murder of D. E. Chipps, a Fort Worth lumberman, his actions and the succeeding trial did nothing to enhance his reputation.

In 1927, the BBU took over a Baptist university in Des Moines that had only been in existence since 1916. Shields became president and made sweeping changes at the school. He banned intercollegiate athletics, disbanded all fraternities, fired faculty members he believed to be liberal, and was absent from the campus for extended periods of time.[44] The school experienced continual strife until it completely unraveled in May 1929. During a meeting of the board of trustees, a campus riot that involved faculty, students, and trustees brought police to the campus and the school to a shameful end. This well-publicized affair essentially ended the BBU as well, since many people who witnessed the Des Moines incident retreated from the group.[45] Only thirty-five delegates attended the annual meeting in Chicago in 1930.[46]

Although the BBU failed to be a viable organization, it can be viewed as the spiritual mother of the General Association of Regular Baptist Churches. Many of the pastors who supported the BBU reorganized their efforts in 1932 and formed this separatist association because they became convinced that they were not going to accomplish their goal of purging the NBC. Thirty-four delegates from eight states gathered at Belden Avenue Baptist Church in Chicago in May 1932 for the final meeting of the BBU and the first of the GARBC. Howard C. Fulton, pastor at Belden Avenue, set the tone for the new organization by telling delegates that we cannot "cooperate with and support those who deny the great verities of the historic Baptist faith."[47] The founders drew up a constitution requiring that all Baptist churches coming into the association must cease all affiliation and cooperation with the NBC

---

[44] Billy Vick Bartlett, *A History of Baptist Separatism* (Springfield MO: Temple Press, 1972) 16–17.

[45] Ibid.

[46] William H. Brackney, *Historical Dictionary of the Baptists* (Lanham MD: The Scarecrow Press, Inc., 1999) 43–44. Billy Vick Bartlett claimed that by 1927, the BBU had a membership of about 50,000 people. See Bartlett's *History of Baptist Separatism,* 13. Brackney notes that the claim of 50,000 members for the BBU is a dubious one.

[47] Howard Fulton, "What Old-Fashioned Baptists Stand For," *Baptist Bulletin* (May 1988): 22.

or any other organization that tolerated Modernism.[48] The name "Regular" differentiated orthodox churches in the association from heterodox churches of the NBC.[49] Delegates acted to restrict membership to churches rather than to individuals because individualism had been one of the primary weaknesses of the BBU.[50]

Robert Ketcham, an influential pastor who had withdrawn from the NBC in 1928 to form an association of independent Baptist churches in Ohio, emerged as the leading figure in the GARBC.[51] After serving four terms as president, Ketcham led in the effort to overhaul the organizational structure of the association. He felt that the few elected officers had too much power and responsibility. In 1938 the churches voted to abolish all offices, including the office of president, and elected a council of fourteen men to oversee the work of the association. The Council of Fourteen, elected to two-year terms at the annual meeting, was expanded to a Council of Eighteen in 1972. The association created the position of national representative in 1944 to handle increasing administrative demands.[52]

The GARBC also had a strong desire to protect the autonomy of the local church and serve as an alternative organization to the NBC while avoiding conventionism. Thus, the association began supporting existing independent missions organizations. These agencies sent funds directly from the local churches to missionaries on the field. Baptist

---

[48] Robert Ketcham, *The Answer* (Chicago: General Association of Regular Baptists, 1950) 47.

[49] Stowell, *Background and History of the General Association of Regular Baptist Churches*, 28–34. The term "Regular" had been used as early as the 1740s to describe mostly urban Baptist churches whose members did not enthusiastically embrace the emotional revivals of the first Great Awakening.

[50] Stowell, *Background and History*, 28–34.

[51] J. Murray Murdoch, *Portrait of Obedience: The Biography of Robert T. Ketcham* (Schaumburg IL: Regular Baptist Press, 1979) 298–99. Although Murdoch's work is a devotional biography, significant information about Ketcham is presented. Ketcham served as president for several years in the GARBC and also edited the *Baptist Bulletin* for a time.

[52] Paul N. Tassell, *Quest for Faithfulness: The Account of a Unique Fellowship of Churches* (Schaumburg IL: Regular Baptist Press, 1991) 42–43, 90, 280.

Mid-Missions, founded in 1920, is now the largest approved agency.[53] The GARBC has placed a heavy emphasis on missions throughout its existence.

Even with its anti-convention emphasis, over the years the GARBC has evolved into a complex body that supports multiple ministries, which include the production of Sunday school literature, chaplaincy endorsement, financial services, and an international literature distribution network that reaches 109 countries.[54] Several colleges and theological seminaries enjoy the support of the association.[55] Although the GARBC approves each agency and school annually, none of the groups has any organic connection with the association. The association endorses schools and agencies but does not own or control any of them.[56] An entity may be dropped from approved status if it does not maintain its separatist position. At the 1985 annual conference messengers voted to drop the Los Angeles Baptist College as an approved college because it came under the control of John MacArthur, a non-Baptist, who renamed it The Master's College.[57]

The GARBC is fundamentalist in theology, emphasizing biblical inerrancy and premillennialism.[58] The association also holds to Baptist distinctives that include individual soul liberty and separation of church and state.[59] As a socially conservative group, GARBC pastors unanimously oppose abortion and the ordination of women, while the

---

[53] William J. Hopewell, Jr., *The Missionary Emphasis of the General Association of Regular Baptist Churches* (Chicago: Regular Baptist Press, 1963) 33–44, 152.

[54] General Association of Regular Baptists; information available online at http://www.garbc.org.

[55] Jerry Falwell, ed., *The Fundamentalist Phenomenon* (Garden City NY: Doubleday, 1981) 114. Some of the key schools approved by the GARBC include Grand Rapids Baptist Bible College & Seminary, Michigan; Faith Baptist Bible College, Iowa; Cedarville College, Ohio; and Baptist Bible College, Pennsylvania.

[56] Tassell, *Quest for Faithfulness*, 43, 343–46, 366, 391.

[57] General Association of Regular Baptists, http://www.garbc.org (accessed 23 May 2005).

[58] Tassell, *Quest for Faithfulness*, 345–46.

[59] Ibid., 387–97. Appendix B of Tassell's book contains the Constitution and Articles of Faith of the GARBC.

vast majority is not in favor of women having careers of their own.[60] This conservatism has created tension in the GARBC as some individuals and churches have cooperated with other like-minded "non-Baptist" Christians to promote conservative social and political causes.[61] Even with this recent erosion in the separatist emphasis, the association is an intensely separatist organization, practicing both first- and second-degree separation.

The association, headquartered in Schaumburg, Illinois, since 1976, communicates with its churches through its official periodical, the *Baptist Bulletin*, which has been published since 1933.[62] According to the *Yearbook of American and Canadian Churches, 2004*, 1,415 independent congregations with 129,407 members make up the GARBC.[63] Although GARBC churches can be found in forty-six states, Saipan, and one Canadian province, most churches are located in the Northern and Western states and in Florida.[64]

Despite the fierce separatism of the GARBC, an organization arose from within its ranks solely over the issue of second-degree separation. The Independent Baptist Fellowship of North America came into existence in October 1990 when some GARBC members who believed the association had been straying from its strict separatist position for some time met in Oshkosh, Wisconsin, and created the Independent Baptist Fellowship in order to restore the strict separatist position. In order to protect and maintain the purity of their assembly, individuals, not churches, hold membership in this organization. Individuals must

---

[60] Tassell, *Quest for Faithfulness*, 412–13, 416–17. A 1988 survey of GARBC pastors revealed that these pastors were socially and politically conservative. Only 1 percent of pastors identified themselves as Democrats.

[61] Tassell, *Quest for Faithfulness*, 357–61.

[62] Certain sections of the most current edition of the *Baptist Bulletin* can be accessed online at the GARBC Web site, http://www.garbc.org.

[63] Eileen W. Lindner, ed., *Yearbook of American and Canadian Churches, 2004* (New York: National Council of Churches of Christ in the United States of America, 2004) 371.

[64] General Association of Regular Baptists, "Annual Conference 2004," http://www.garbc.org (accessed 23 May 2005).

renew their membership annually by providing a monetary payment and reaffirming the doctrinal stand of the IBF.[65] In contrast to the GARBC, the IBF has no perpetuating board and no approval system. The IBF touts itself as a fellowship of equal members that acts as a vehicle for cooperation without encroaching upon individual or local church autonomy.[66] Theologically, the IBF mirrors the GARBC except that it holds the King James Version to be the word of God in English and prefers that all conference preachers utilize it.[67] The IBF publishes *The Review* four to six times a year in order to communicate with members.[68] In 1993–1994, the group listed 250 members who represented 106 churches.[69] Currently, 423 individual members and 113 churches in the United States support the work of the IBF. Another three or four international churches belong to the group. About half of IBF members still have some ties to the GARBC.[70] The strongest area for the group is Pennsylvania.[71]

Southern Independent Baptists

In the same way that independent Baptist organizations initially arose in the North because of failed efforts to take over the NBC, Southern independent groups emerged because they were unable to purify the SBC of alleged liberal tendencies. Yet, one could hardly characterize the SBC as modernist. Modernism, as one prominent Baptist historian

---

[65] Independent Baptist Fellowship of North America, "Our Beginnings," http://www.ibfna.org (accessed 23 May 2005). See also L. Duane Brown et al., *What Happened to the GARBC at Niagara Falls?* (Sellersville PA: Bethel Baptist Press, n.d.).

[66] Independent Baptist Fellowship of North America, "Our Mission," http://www.ibfna.org (accessed 23 May 2005).

[67] Independent Baptist Fellowship of North America, "Articles of Faith," http://www.ibfna.org (accessed 23 May 2005).

[68] Independent Baptist Fellowship of North America, "The Review," http://www.ibfna.org (accessed 23 May 2005).

[69] Wardin, ed., *Baptists around the World*, 388–89.

[70] Richard Harris, moderator of IBFNA, email to author, 24 August 2004.

[71] Wardin, ed., *Baptists Around the World*, 389.

stated, "never strutted in the South as it had in the North."[72] Nevertheless, fundamentalists harassed SBC agencies and schools continually in the early decades of the twentieth century.

The undisputed leading figure among Southern Independents, J. Frank Norris, could easily be considered the father of the independent Baptist movement due to his strong presence in both the North and South. Norris, described as a "violent fundamentalist" by one scholar, made a name for himself by building one of the largest churches in the world—First Baptist Church in Fort Worth.[73] Once a loyal denominationalist, around 1917 Norris began using the pulpit and the pen to attack "all forms of wickedness."[74] In that year he founded a paper called *The Fence Rail*, which in 1921 became *The Searchlight* and finally in 1927 became *The Fundamentalist*.[75] In his flamboyant sermons and his widely circulated weekly paper with its sensationalist headlines and indecorous stories, Norris criticized the SBC for the same reasons that fundamentalists attacked the NBC. Norris opposed the SBC due to his belief in the extreme independence of the local church and because he believed Modernism had made inroads into the SBC, especially among its leaders. Norris became convinced that the SBC was a money-grabbing "ecclesiastical machine" that encouraged theological compromise.[76]

Of particular concern to Norris was the teaching of evolution in Baptist schools. He especially targeted his alma mater, Baylor University, in this regard. Norris charged several Baylor professors,

---

[72] Walter B. Shurden, *Not a Silent People: Controversies that Have Shaped Southern Baptists* (Nashville: Broadman Press, 1972) 89.

[73] Russell, *Voices of American Fundamentalism*, 21, 30. By 1928, Norris's Fort Worth church boasted an average attendance of 5,200. By 1943, his Detroit church counted 8,597.

[74] *The Fence Rail*, 26 January 1917.

[75] From 1921–1923, circulation of *The Searchlight* increased from 10,000 to 60,000. See Russell Theodore Newman, "Texas Baptists and the Evolution Controversy: 1920–1923," unpublished paper presented for Texas History Seminar 410, Baylor University, May 1953, 14–17. See also Cole, *History of Fundamentalism*, 287.

[76] *The Searchlight*, 19 September 1922.

primarily Samuel Grove Dow, a professor of sociology, with teaching Darwinian evolution in the classroom and in a book he had written. Norris fanned the flames of controversy by writing numerous heated editorials against Dow and Baylor president Samuel P. Brooks.[77] One issue of *The Searchlight* carried a cartoon depicting a large rattlesnake wrapped around the main building at Baylor, with the word "evolution" written in large letters across the body of the snake.[78] Dow disputed the idea that he adhered to strict Darwinian doctrine in which people are said to come from some distant species.[79] He agreed to clarify passages in his book. Norris editorialized in December 1921 that "it is not the ape in the book I am after but the ape in the professor's chair."[80] Dow resigned his position a week later while a victorious Norris gloated.[81]

Emboldened by such a victory, Norris and his faction took the evolution battle to national convention meetings. From 1922 to 1926, controversy over evolution beset the SBC annual meetings. To calm the waters, Southern Baptists did in 1925 what Northern Baptists refused to do in 1922. Messengers adopted a modified version of the New Hampshire Confession of Faith. An important alteration read, "Man was created by a special act of God, as recorded in Genesis."[82] Norris and his company of followers wanted a more explicit denial of evolution. A year later fundamentalists got what they wanted when they led the SBC to adopt the so-called McDaniel statement as the sentiment of the Convention. In his presidential address, George W. McDaniel had stated that the SBC "rejects every theory, evolution or other, which

[77] *The Searchlight*, 11 November 1921, 1; 9 December 1921, 1–2.

[78] *The Searchlight*, 13 April 1923, 1.

[79] Letter from Samuel P. Brooks to the Special Investigating Committee appointed by the State Baptist Convention of 1921, 10 December 1921, Brooks Papers, Pat M. Neff Division, Texas Collection, Baylor University, Waco TX.

[80] *The Searchlight*, 2 December 1921, 2.

[81] *The Searchlight*, 16 December 1921, 1. Norris took credit for forcing seven "evolution" professors at Baylor to resign. See J. Frank Norris, *Inside History of First Baptist Church, Fort Worth and Temple Baptist Church, Detroit* (Toronto: Jarvis Street Church, 1938) 112.

[82] *SBC Annual*, 1925, 72, 76.

teaches that man originated in, or came by way of, a lower animal ancestry."[83] Messengers at the same meeting also adopted a resolution calling upon all employees of Southern Baptist agencies and institutions to subscribe to the McDaniel statement.[84] After the dust settled, Norris wired the president of the Baptist Bible Union the following message: "Unprecedented victory in Southern Convention will tremendously help the Northern Baptist Convention."[85]

Having won these victories, a number of fundamentalists stayed put in the Convention. Norris's days with the SBC were numbered, however. Due to his bellicose attacks on Southern Baptist leaders and institutions, his local association excluded him and his church from fellowship in 1922 for being a threat to the unity of that body. In 1924 the Baptist General Convention of Texas permanently excluded him and his church.[86] Although Norris continued to maintain membership in the Southern Baptist Convention until the 1940s by contributing the annual minimum sum to the Cooperative Program and by leading demonstrations outside the meetings of each annual session, for all practical purposes Norris left the SBC in 1934 when he formed his own organization.[87]

Although many Southern Baptists believed Norris to be a destructive critic, a group of young preachers, mainly in Texas, came under his influence. By 1932, nineteen churches in Texas supported Norris's efforts either to purify Southern Baptists or leave to form their own organization. Two years later, Norris, along with Clarence P. Stealey, editor of the *Baptist Messenger*, the Baptist state paper of Oklahoma, founded the Premillennial Baptist Missionary Fellowship in Fort Worth.[88] Stealey became the first president.[89] The creed of this new

---

[83] *SBC Annual*, 1926, 18.

[84] Ibid., 98.

[85] *Gospel Witness*, 20 May 1926, 19, cited in Bartlett, *History of Baptist Separatism*, 12.

[86] Russell, *Voices of American Fundamentalism*, 39–40.

[87] Dollar, *History of Fundamentalism in America*, 129.

[88] Wilburn S. Taylor, "World Baptist Fellowship," *Quarterly Review*(Apr/June 1959): 38.

fellowship mirrored that of the former BBU, with a militant opposition to modernism and conventionism. The fellowship supported several mission stations in China, claiming that every cent raised went directly to the missionaries while only about three cents of every SBC Cooperative Program dollar made it to the mission field.[90]

In 1938, the organization took the name World Fundamental Baptist Missionary Fellowship. Norris claimed at that time that 300 pastors supported this organization. In 1939 Norris opened the Fundamental Baptist Bible Institute in Fort Worth with sixteen students. Since Norris had no use for a liberal arts education or formal theological study, he created the school to teach his uncritical approach to the English Bible.[91] He believed the integrity of the school to be guaranteed because it was founded by a local church and funded by local churches. For Norris, this fit the New Testament pattern.[92] He trained fundamentalist young people who wanted to enter Christian ministry by teaching them the Bible and nothing else. Norris believed the Bible was the only book worth studying, saying that "every Baptist preacher ought to be imprisoned for forty days with nothing but his Bible and a diet of bread and water."[93] The school became the Bible Baptist Seminary in 1945 in order to give it more credibility. By 1953 the school announced that 386 students were enrolled.[94] Earl K. Oldham, a Texas pastor, assumed the presidency of the school in 1953, and two years later, relocated it to Arlington, Texas, renaming it Arlington Baptist College. Under Oldham's leadership, the school became a four-year undergraduate institution.[95]

---

[89] Bartlett, *History of Baptist Separatism*, 26.

[90] Taylor, "World Baptist Fellowship," 38.

[91] Ibid.

[92] Leonard, *Baptist Ways*, 403.

[93] Quoted in James J. Thompson, *Tried as by Fire: Southern Baptists and the Religious Controversies of the 1920s* (Atlanta: Mercer University Press, 1982) 85.

[94] Taylor, "World Baptist Fellowship," 38.

[95] Arlington Baptist College; information available online at http://www.abconline.edu (accessed 23 May 2005).

Since 1950, Norris's organization has been called the World Baptist Fellowship (WBF) to distinguish it from the Baptist Bible Fellowship International, an organization formed the same year by a large number of pastors who grew tired of Norris's dictatorial and belligerent ways.[96] The WBF eventually formed its own mission agencies and currently supports 135 missionaries serving in more than 20 countries. There are about 1,000 churches affiliated with the WBF, and that number has remained constant for at least 20 years.[97] Half of the churches cooperate with other fellowships. About half of the churches are located in Texas, Florida, and Ohio.[98] The WBF continues to publish Norris's old paper, *The Fundamentalist*. Because Norris completely dominated the WBF until his death in 1952, the movement has struggled without his colorful leadership. The fellowship has also suffered due to the 1950 schism and another that occurred in 1984.

The first rupture in Norris's organization centered on the Bible Baptist Seminary. Norris always believed the school to be his, even after he turned it over to the WBF. In 1948, Norris installed George B. Vick as the new president. Vick had been successful as co-pastor with Norris at Detroit's Temple Baptist Church, one of two churches that Norris pastored simultaneously for years. Despite having little educational background, Vick made improvements in the troubled school, reducing the debt in half.[99]

Concerned that trustees had given Vick full authority, the "Texas Tornado," as Norris was sometimes called, swept in, and after a general housecleaning he resumed control of the seminary. After a severe struggle for control of the school that involved Norris's dismissing Vick as president and expelling about ninety students from the Temple Baptist Church in Detroit, a number of pastors could no longer accept

---

[96] Ibid.

[97] William H. Brackney, "World Baptist Fellowship," *Historical Dictionary of the Baptists* (Lanham MD: The Scarecrow Press, Inc, 1999) 457–58.

[98] Wardin, ed., *Baptists around the World*, 406.

[99] Mike Randall, *G. Beauchamp: A Concise Biography* (Milford OH: self-published, 1987) 8–15.

Norris's autocratic ways. Since Norris had won the battle for the school, about 100 pastors met in Fort Worth on 24 May 1950, intending to found a new school. Instead they founded a rival organization to the WBF.[100] No new doctrinal statement arose, but the Baptist Bible Fellowship International (BBFI) did make immediate plans to establish a newspaper, a missions agency, and a college.

The BBFI called its new paper the *Baptist Bible Tribune*. The group essentially took over the missions work of the WBF.[101] The BBFI has developed a strong missions program over the years. By 1973, the BBFI supported 450 missionaries.[102] Currently, the group sponsors more than 800 missionaries who serve in 107 countries.[103] The Baptist Bible College in Springfield, Missouri, described by one BBFI historian as the symbol and substance of the group, opened in summer 1950, with George B. Vick as president. During the first decade, enrollment grew from 107 to 565. By 1971, 2,207 students were enrolled.[104] Currently, the school has less than 1,000 students. In addition to the Springfield school, there are now six approved institutions. Although great emphasis is placed upon local church autonomy, a Committee of Forty-Five governs the national fellowship.[105] Some might suggest that the BBFI has in effect become a denomination, even though its leaders resist that designation.

According to the *Yearbook of American and Canadian Churches, 2004*, the BBFI has a membership of 1,200,000. Its churches, a few of which are the largest in the nation, number 4,500.[106] About 400 churches still associate with the WBF. BBFI churches appear in all fifty states, but the group's greatest strength has been in the urban centers in the South, the

---

[100] Combs, ed., *Roots and Origins of Baptist Fundamentalism*, 91–94.

[101] Ibid., 97–99, 102–104.

[102] Ibid., 103.

[103] Brackney, "Baptist Bible Fellowship," *Historical Dictionary of the Baptists*, 43.

[104] Bartlett, *History of Baptist Separatism*, 60–69.

[105] Brackney, "Baptist Bible Fellowship," *Historical Dictionary of the Baptists*, 43.

[106] Lindner, ed., *Yearbook of American and Canadian Churches, 2004*, 366.

Great Lakes region, and in the states of Florida, Kansas, and California.[107]

The second schism afflicting the WBF occurred in 1984. Although not as significant as the 1950 division, this conflict did siphon off more churches from the WBF. Raymond W. Barber, a professor at Arlington Baptist College and a former president of the WBF, became embroiled in a serious dispute with others at the school. He withdrew from the college and the WBF and led in the founding of the Independent Baptist Fellowship International (IBFI) and the Norris Bible Baptist Institute. Barber also opened a missions office and revived *The Searchlight*.[108] Now called the Norris Bible Baptist Seminary (NBBS), the Fort Worth, Texas, school has an enrollment of only twenty students. The IBFI missions agency currently supports twenty-six missionaries in thirteen mission fields. There are approximately 500 churches associated with the IBFI, the vast majority of which cooperate with other independent fellowships. Barber, who pastored the Worth Baptist Church in Fort Worth for thirty-five years and now serves as pastor emeritus, continues to exercise leadership in the IBFI as chancellor of NBBS and as a member of the IBFI executive board.[109]

The most noteworthy graduate of Baptist Bible College in Springfield, Missouri, is Jerry Falwell of Lynchburg, Virginia, who founded a school of his own, Liberty Baptist University, which claims to have more than 10,000 students. Falwell, often called the leading fundamentalist pastor/evangelist in America, has led the 21,000-member Thomas Road Baptist Church since its organization 1956. The church has maintained relationships with the BBFI, the Southwide Baptist Fellowship, and other independent Baptist groups.[110] Falwell gained

---

[107] Wardin, ed., *Baptists around the World*, 406.

[108] Ibid. For an account of the formation of the IBFI from the perspective of members of the WBF, see Mr. and Mrs. Earl K. Oldham, *USS-WBF: Sail On* (Grand Prairie TX: self-published, c. 1992) 338–46.

[109] Independent Baptist Fellowship International; information available online at http://www.ibfi-nbbi.org (accessed 23 May 2005).

[110] Leonard, *Baptist Ways*, 405.

national attention when he founded the Moral Majority in 1979, a political organization that provided numerous conservatives with a vehicle to oppose abortion, pornography, drug use, the breakdown of the traditional family, homosexuality as an alternative lifestyle, and the general disintegration of American moral culture. Members of the Moral Majority came together not out of any common theological commitments, but because they were socially and politically conservative.[111]

Falwell also sought to galvanize Americans who shared his moral values through the publication of the *Fundamentalist Journal* beginning in 1982[112] and through the sponsorship of a fundamentalist rally in Washington, D.C., in 1984.[113] Even with these unification efforts, which strict separatists have resisted, Falwell is spiritual father to a small independent fellowship he organized in 1977—Liberty Baptist Fellowship. The organization provides fellowship and accountability for approximately 100 pastors, most of whom are alumni of Liberty Baptist University. The fellowship also supports church-planting efforts and endorses chaplains. A periodical, the *Liberty Baptist Fellowship*, has been published since 1977.[114] The Liberty Baptist Mission, a related agency founded in 1978, supports twenty missionaries serving in seven countries.[115]

Lee Roberson began as pastor of the Highland Park Baptist Church of Chattanooga, Tennessee, in 1942, and over a forty-year period he led it to become one of the largest Baptist congregations in the nation. By

---

111 Jerry Falwell, *Fundamentalist Phenomenon*, 188–92. Falwell announced in 1989 that the Moral Majority had achieved its goals; thus, he disbanded the organization.

112 Jerry Falwell, "Editor's Note," *Fundamentalist Journal* (September 1982): 1. In this first issue of the monthly periodical, Falwell expressed his excitement about Fundamentalism and its influence on American society.

113 Edward Dobson, *In Search of Unity* (Nashville: Thomas Nelson Publishers, 1985) 101–103.

114 Brackney, "Liberty Baptist Fellowship," *Historical Dictionary of the Baptists*, 259.

115 Wardin, ed., *Baptists around the World*, 406.

1983 it claimed more than 57,000 members with about 60 chapels.[116] Roberson also established Tennessee Temple Schools, a system of schools that included a seminary, a college, and an elementary school.[117]

Roberson, one of the leaders in founding a premillennial fellowship in Chattanooga in 1948, founded the Southern Baptist Fellowship, now the Southwide Baptist Fellowship, in 1956 after leaving the SBC in 1955. Roberson left the SBC stung by criticism from leaders of the local association who resented his lack of support and cooperation in Southern Baptist endeavors.[118] About 150 pastors from 8 states met at the Highland Park church, where they formed a doctrinal fellowship for like-minded Baptists. The fellowship declared itself to be independent of the SBC. The pastors adopted a conservative statement of faith that emphasized the autonomy of each local Baptist church and cited premillennialism as a test of fellowship. They elected Roberson as president. By November 1956, 424 pastors subscribed to the Articles of Faith.[119] The Southwide Baptist Fellowship has grown slowly over the years. The names of 1,193 pastors and staff members, representing approximately 500 churches, appear in the 2003 directory.[120]

The SBF also has ties to Baptist International Missions, Inc., which Roberson founded in 1960. This organization supports more than 500 missionaries around the world.[121] The corporate headquarters of the SBF is located in Garland, Texas. The SBF often associates with other independent fellowships, particularly in joint rallies or conferences. It

---

[116] John N. Vaughan, *The World's Twenty Largest Churches* (Grand Rapids: Baker Book House, 1984) 109–16.

[117] Elmer Towns, *The Ten Largest Sunday Schools* (Grand Rapids: Baker Book House, 1969) 27. Roberson is currently chancellor at Tennessee Temple University.

[118] Wardin, ed., *Baptists around the World*, 407.

[119] Kenneth C. Hubbard, "Anti-conventionism in the SBC, 1940–1962" (Ph.D. diss., Southwestern Baptist Theological Seminary, 1963) 252.

[120] *Directory*, Southwide Baptist Fellowship, 2003. Since individuals, not churches, are members of the group, its leaders can only estimate the number of churches that support the SBF.

[121] Wardin, ed., *Baptists around the World*, 407.

has also established ties with evangelicals and fundamentalist SBC pastors, a move that strict separatists have roundly criticized.[122]

An important figure in the Independent movement who helped establish the Southwide Baptist Fellowship was John R. Rice. Rice was a member of the Highland Park Church and a staunch ally to Roberson.[123] A former Southern Baptist, Rice never joined any of the fellowships but cooperated extensively with many Independent Baptist groups. In 1934 Rice founded one of the most influential Independent Baptist papers in the nation. Under his direction, *The Sword of the Lord* became the most widely distributed fundamentalist paper in America. The circulation grew from 7,200 weekly readers in 1934 to more than 100,000 by 1956.[124] Rice connected with many fundamentalists who resonated with his numerous articles dealing with organizational separation from modernists and personal separation from such evils as gambling, dancing, drinking, and card games. Rice's premillennial emphases also appealed to readers. Rice teased his readers with headlines such as "SIGNS OF THE SOON COMING OF CHRIST," then in his articles interpreted world events such as the rise of Fascism, Communism, and Nazism in such a way as to suggest that the parousia could occur at any moment.[125]

Although most independent Baptists associate with one or more of the fellowships or associations, some pastors and churches stand alone, refusing to join any of the fundamentalist organizations. While pastors

---

[122] Dollar, *History of Fundamentalism in America*, 243–44; Dollar, *The Fight for Fundamentalism* (Sarasota, Fl.: self-published, 1983) 122–23. Gary Coleman, executive treasurer of the SBF, in a personal phone conversation with the author on 24 August 2004, stated that about twenty or thirty pastors had left the SBF in the past few years because the SBF did not adhere to a strict separatist stance.

[123] Hubbard, "Anti-conventionism in the SBC, 1940–1962," 253.

[124] Falwell, *Fundamentalist Phenomenon*, 120.

[125] See John R. Rice, "Dallas Fair a Place of Gambling, Drunkenness and Lewdness," *The Sword of the Lord*, 5 October 1934, 1; "The Dance! Child of the Brothel, Sister of Gambling and Drunkenness, Mother of Lust—A Road to Hell," *The Sword of the Lord*, 7 June 1935, 1; "Signs of the Soon Coming of Christ," *The Sword of the Lord*, 28 June 1935, 1.

of these distinctive churches may be friendly or inimical toward the fundamentalist fellowships, they believe that a truly independent church does not affiliate or identify with any organized convention, association, or fellowship. They insist that the only organization established and commissioned in the New Testament is the local church.[126] Perhaps the most significant of these churches is the First Baptist Church of Hammond, Indiana, which, like Highland Park in Chattanooga, has become a denomination in miniature.

In 1957, the Dallas Baptist Association in Dallas, Texas, excluded from fellowship the Miller Road Baptist Church of Garland where Jack Hyles was pastor. Local church leaders determined that Hyles not only failed to support SBC programs, but he also established rival ministries. Hyles formed a Bible college, a bookstore, and a missions program that sponsored almost thirty missionaries. Miller Road also did not use SBC literature in its Sunday school classes. In response to the dismissal by the Dallas Baptist Association, Hyles indicated that jealous pastors in the area had caused it.[127]

In 1959, after increasing the membership at Miller Road from 44 to 4,128 in six and a half years, Jack Hyles became pastor of the First Baptist Church in Hammond, Indiana.[128] He led the church out of the American Baptist Convention and established it as the world's third largest congregation. The church grew from 3,000 members in 1960 to 74,373 members in 1982. At its peak, Hyles's Sunday school had an average attendance of about 18,504 people, making it the largest Sunday school in the world. Hyles's recipe for growth included aggressive witnessing campaigns, publicity schemes, an extensive bus ministry, dynamic fundamentalist preaching, creative ministries, numerous publications, and the establishment of a system of Christian schools, which included Hyles-Anderson College at Crown Point, Indiana.[129]

---

[126] M. L. Moser, "What is an Independent Baptist Church," http://www.pbministries.org (accessed 23 May 2005).

[127] Hubbard, "Anti-conventionism in the SBC, 1940–1962," 174–80.

[128] Vaughan, *World's Twenty Largest Churches*, 102.

[129] Ibid., 102–108.

In 1989, an article by fundamentalist evangelist Robert L. Sumner appeared in a fundamentalist Baptist newspaper named *The Biblical Evangelist*. In it, he charged Hyles with sexual misconduct with a church secretary, financial mismanagement, and doctrinal deviation. In 1990 a lawyer who had attended Hyles's church for twenty years wrote a lengthy book detailing Hyles's alleged indiscretions. Although Hyles survived the storm, his reputation became tarnished and the Hammond Church lost many members.[130] Upon his death in 2001, the leadership of Hyles's empire fell to his son-in-law, Jack Schaap. Despite the loss of the colorful and controversial Hyles, the church should continue to thrive as long as a charismatic leader pastors it.

Independent Baptist Distinctives: Summary and Analysis

The term *anti-conventionist* describes independent Baptists well. One cannot understand Independents without examining this aversion to conventionism. Several factors account for their opposition to denominations. Their inability to capture and control the major Baptist conventions in the early part of the twentieth century soured Independents on denominational connections. They concluded that centralization weakened local church autonomy.

Further, Independents followed a strict literal hermeneutic allowing only for that which Scripture explicitly revealed. Independents could not find conventions and mission boards in the New Testament, so they surmised that these modern innovations must be scrapped. These unbiblical organizations were most dangerous because they fostered centralization of power. independent Baptists came to believe that the New Testament pattern of doing the Lord's work is through local autonomous congregations. Richard Clearwaters criticized the National Council of Churches, the Roman Catholic Church, and Protestant denominations as "man-made and unbiblical systems" and concluded

---

[130] Voyle A. Glover, *Fundamental Seduction: The Jack Hyles Case* (Schererville IN: Brevia Publication Company, 1990) 1–8. Glover claimed that First Hammond had about 50,000 members.

that the "only Biblical system is the Local Church as a Pure Democracy; Self-owned, Sovereign, and Autonomous."[131]

Although Independents resist denominationalism, most favor joining fellowships or associations where like-minded individuals and churches can cooperate together in ventures such as missions, Bible conferences, and publications. Most Independents do not view such cooperation as a threat to local church autonomy since theoretically there is no organic connection between the fellowships. Each local church can choose which agency, school, or missionaries it will support. This approach to ministry is no innovation. It is, in effect, a return to the society approach popular among Baptists in the North in the nineteenth century.

Although local church autonomy seems to be protected in this system, such an arrangement has often led to the exercising of doctrinal control over related agencies and local churches by fellowships and associations, at times with little financial investment. The GARBC, for instance, approves only those agencies they deem orthodox, but since the association has no official connection to any of them, it assumes little administrative and financial burden. One might conclude that independent organizations, although called fellowships or associations, are actually quasi-denominations.

In fact, more often than not, less freedom exists for local churches in the Independent system than for congregations that are part of a convention. Even in the conservative SBC, local churches are not mandated to adopt the *Baptist Faith and Message* in order to maintain membership in the Convention. Salaried missionaries and seminary professors might have to sign the confessional statement, but not local churches. To be a part of a fundamentalist fellowship, one must subscribe to a creed. The IBFNA dictates that any individual desiring to join the group must pay a fee and agree to its creedal statement on an annual basis.

---

[131] Richard V. Clearwaters, *The Local Church of the New Testament* (Chicago: Conservative Baptist Fellowship, 1954) 38.

Local churches must also stay in line with the aims of the leaders of their organizations. Despite the fact that Independents rail against hierarchical denominational machines, frequently referring to denominational leaders as bishops, their own organizations are led by powerful personalities. There seems to be little difference between the national representative of the GARBC and the director of the executive committee of the SBC. Since Independent entities frequently center on charismatic individuals who exercise a great deal of authority over churches, pastors and churches must comply or leave the organization. Personality conflicts and power struggles between leaders have resulted in more than a few schisms among Independents, a fact that their own historians lament.[132]

A further reason Independents have opposed conventionism is the desire to be theologically pure. They believe that in a denominational system, individuals and churches sacrifice theological integrity for the sake of organizational unity, and that such compromise is unacceptable because it dilutes the true faith. They refuse to associate with liberals or moderates or any bodies they deem to be doctrinally impure. They have been harsh critics not only of Protestant denominations, but also of the Roman Catholic Church and the National and World Council of Churches for promoting heterodoxy. Cooperating in any way with those they consider heterodox is tantamount to supporting apostasy. It is not enough to reject liberalism; liberals themselves must be avoided. In an article titled "Should Baptists Unite?" John R. Rice stated, "Instead of building even larger organizations and joining in with infidels and doubters who deny the Bible, let all true Christians simply love each other, pray for each other, and help hold revival meetings to win souls. That is the unity or 'unification' taught in the Bible. And not one verse in the Bible urges organic union into denominations, and the Bible explicitly forbids joining in with unbelievers and infidels on any basis."[133]

---

[132] Dobson, *In Search of Unity*, 136.

[133] John R. Rice, "Should Baptists Unite?" *The Sword of the Lord*, 5 October 1934, 3.

Many Independents also refuse to cooperate in any way with conservatives who work with theological liberals, moderates, Charismatics, Roman Catholics, and others that are considered heretical. Northern groups seem to be stricter in this regard than those in the South. Independents have largely resisted the evangelical movement because its leaders, such as Billy Graham, have engaged in cooperative ventures with Christians from a variety of communions. When Graham stated in 1979 that the Pope was a great spiritual and moral leader, Bob Jones, Jr., whose father founded the school that bears his name, called Graham "a servant of apostasy."[134]

Those who are ultra-strict separatists also practice what has been referred to as third-degree separation.[135] That is, they refuse to cooperate with another Independent who has maintained ties with an evangelical or a conventionist who may have been tolerant of some liberals. George Dollar packed one of his books with numerous criticisms of fellow fundamentalists who had relaxed their separatist practices. He condemned Jerry Falwell for working with non-fundamentalist accommodationists. He even expressed his disapproval of John R. Rice's practice of including fundamentalist Southern Baptists on his conference programs and publishing their sermons in his paper.[136]

Independents also emphasize the importance of personal separation from worldliness. Although some diversity exists, Independents have embraced a remarkably uniform moral code that they believe to be biblically based but that also appears to be a reaction to cultural trends. Some of their more visible rules are short hair for men, modest attire for women, and no smoking, drinking, dancing, divorce, or listening to rock music. In Jack Hyles's sermon titled "Jesus Had Short Hair!" he indicated that subversive cultural revolutionaries were using modern art, music, new dress, and hairstyles as a way to bring about a new radical

---

[134] Dollar, *Fight for Fundamentalism*, 98.

[135] Dobson, *In Search of Unity*, 63.

[136] Dollar, *Fight for Fundamentalism*, 126–27.

social order.[137] Separation from any hint of worldliness is necessary, or one runs the risk of sliding down the slippery slope into rampant sin. In *The Sword of the Lord*, the headline to an article warning of the dangers of dancing read, "The Dance! Child of the Brothel, Sister of Gambling and Drunkenness, Mother of Lust—A ROAD TO HELL!"[138]

The most important issue facing Independents today centers upon the issue of separation. The conundrum facing Independents in the past has been that a strict separatist position has resulted in withdrawal from society. Yet, to have a significant voice in the political and social realm in recent years, they have had to cooperate with others who are outside their theological boundaries. This cooperation brought strife and division as arguments arose concerning the appropriate degree of separation one should practice. New independent groups have been formed solely over the separation issue as they have charged parent organizations with compromise and accommodation. A new independent strategy has emerged in recent days, however, that could enable Independents to have a measure of power in the social and political realm without cooperating with the doctrinally impure.

In 2003 fundamentalists formed the International Baptist Network, a group that is seeking to unite, not merge, various associations of independent Baptists, including the BBFI, the SBF, and the WBF. John Rawlings, who is spearheading the movement, stated that he envisions an international movement of independent Baptists that will rival and perhaps even obtain more influence than the Baptist World Alliance.[139] This latest attempt to unite Independents, however, has already met criticism from strict separatists.[140] Some Independents hold that a unity

---

[137] Jack Hyles, "Jesus Had Short Hair!" http://www.baptist-city.com (accessed 23 May 2005).

[138] John R. Rice, "The Dance! Child of the Brothel, Sister of Gambling and Drunkenness, Mother of Lust—A Road to Hell," *The Sword of the Lord*, 7 June 1935, 1.

[139] "International Baptist Network Meeting Makes History," *Baptist Bible Tribune*, http://www.tribune.org/modules.php?op=modload&name=news&file=article&sid=94 (accessed 23 May 2005).

[140] David Cloud, "Should Independent Baptists Unite?" 31 December 2003, http://www.wayoflife.org/fbns/should-ifb-unite.html (accessed 23 May 2005).

movement that involves the creation of entities beyond the local church, even if restricted to fundamentalists, will result in doctrinal compromise. It is difficult at this stage to measure if opposition to the unity movement will be abundant. If the International Baptist Network is eventually successful, new independent organizations are likely to be created in protest to the effort to build a pan-fundamentalist Baptist organization.

Another key independent element is fundamentalist theology. Independent churches, fellowships, or associations are fundamentalist in doctrine across the board. Fundamentalists may hold to some of the same doctrines that non-fundamentalists espouse. The fundamentalist, however, wants to impose his own system of doctrine upon the entire group. The fundamentalist worldview is absolute. A fundamentalist is on God's side of the argument.

At the center of fundamentalist theology is a particular understanding of Scripture. Independents esteem the Bible so highly that they have encountered accusations of bibliolatry.[141] For the fundamentalist, the Bible so far outstrips other books in providing instruction for every area of one's life that it is the only book worthy of serious study. Of course, the biblical text forms the basis of belief and practice for many mainstream Christian denominations. Yet, Independents tend to utilize restrictive interpretive methodologies, refusing to take advantage of higher critical approaches to biblical study.

This understanding of Scripture explains why Independents have resisted the use of Sunday school literature and have formed Bible schools instead of liberal arts colleges. Their schools follow a pedagogical approach that assumes that truth is not to be discovered but has already been clearly revealed in Scripture. The ministerial student, in order to be competent in his vocation, need not dialogue with modernist theologians such as Barth or Bonhoeffer; instead, he needs to prepare to refute them. All that is required for success in ministry is to be a student of the Bible, read conservative books that address biblical texts, and study practical aspects of ministry. Jack Hyles stated proudly, "We may

---

[141] Brackney, *The Baptists*, 31.

have been too dumb to learn theology, but we were smart enough not to take graduate study under Niebuhr, Brunner, Kierkegaard and Barth. We may have said, 'I have did,' instead of 'I have done,' but what we 'had did' was faithful to the Word of God!"[142]

Independents assert that the Bible is a unified document containing consistent propositional truths. They accept the supernatural elements of the Bible, affirm that it is infallible in every area of reality, and contend that it is to be interpreted literally in the vast majority of cases. Ultimately, they hold not merely to the inerrancy of Scripture, but to the infallibility of their interpretation of Scripture. The doctrine of premillennialism serves as a case in point.

Early on in the movement, Independents embraced premillennialism as the only acceptable eschatological view. The BBU made the doctrine a test of fellowship. When Norris formed his Premillennial Missionary Baptist Fellowship (1933), he made premillennialism a requirement for membership. He held this doctrine to be the only acceptable biblical position, charging conventionism with being postmillennial in orientation.[143] These actions set the tone for future independent organizations. All Independent organizations today have articles of faith that reflect some form of premillennial doctrine. It has become *the* Independent eschatological position to which members must subscribe, although on occasion a person may not comply. The heavy emphasis on the soon and unexpected Second Coming of Christ has fostered an intense interest in Bible prophecy. The Independent Baptists read their Scofield Bibles with an eye upon the skies. This heightened expectation of the Second Coming makes evangelism all the more urgent. Frequently preachers remind their hearers that there would be disastrous consequences for those who are caught in an unregenerate state if Jesus were to appear suddenly.

---

[142] Jack Hyles, "Jack Hyles Speaks on Biblical Separation," 44, http://www.baptist-city.com/books1/biblicalseparation.html (accessed 23 May 2005).

[143] J. Frank Norris, *Inside History of the First Baptist Church, Fort Worth and Temple Baptist Church, Detroit,* 112.

One can readily see that Independents place a high value on orthodoxy. Such an exalted emphasis upon holding to correct doctrine has encouraged controversy and fragmentation as independent Baptist pastors, who dominate their churches, and have been unable to agree on every sub-point. The doctrinal boundaries drawn by Independents are exclusive rather than inclusive. This narrowness may mean the movement will plateau or steadily decline over the long haul. The higher one builds the walls, the less likely it is that people will want to climb them. On the other hand, Independents articulate their beliefs uncompromisingly and with little or no ambiguity. The movement will continue to be attractive to those who see life in black and white and who desire certainty over doubt. The sense of certainty found in independent circles helps explain why the membership is highly committed to the program. It also explains why Independents can often appear strident to people outside their realm.

Since independent entities frequently center upon magnetic individuals who exercise a great deal of authority over the churches, the movement also appeals to people who enjoy charismatic, pastor-centered associations and churches. Independent pastors generally exercise tremendous authority over their churches. The basis of this power is rooted in the fundamentalist understanding of independent churches. Independents believe that the fundamentalist church, as the protector and sustainer of true Christianity, holds the only key to saving the American nation from certain moral disaster.

Independent pastors believe the fundamentalist church is the only hope for America. A leading pastor expressed his desire to build a fundamentalist church that could be reproduced across America "to help save our nation."[144] It is not difficult to see how independent pastors, who serve the most important churches in the world, hold such an exalted position. The independent pastor is the real keeper of the keys to the kingdom, possessing authority that many bishops would envy. Often the identity of the church is embodied in the pastor. Possessing this sort

---

[144] Vaughan, *World's Twenty Largest Churches*, 104.

of power enables the pastor to control the direction of the church but often leads to power struggles and church splits.[145] Although many independent churches rejoice that the pastor has a great deal of power, some question it. As one disillusioned fundamentalist lamented concerning powerful pastors of large independent churches, "we've made them idols. We've made them superstars.... They...walk like gods in our midst."[146]

The independent movement has further distinguished itself as a place where many souls are won to Christ. Independent churches are highly evangelistic because they believe it to be biblical and because they are convinced that the key to saving the nation and the world is through winning souls for Christ. Independent pastors are noted for their dynamic, evangelistic preaching and their "soul-winning" programs. Churches often utilize busing, a weekly visitation program, and publicity gimmicks as evangelistic methods. Independent churches stress missions as well. Local congregations, often through fellowships, support international missionaries. Social ministries may exist in independent churches, but they take a back seat to evangelism and missions. Independent pastors have also used radio and television broadcasts effectively to reach people beyond the walls of their churches. Jerry Falwell has utilized media more effectively than any independent fundamentalist in the last half of the twentieth century. Broadcasts of his morning worship service at Thomas Road, called the *Old Time Gospel Hour*, could be seen weekly on 297 television stations and heard on approximately 500 radio stations by the early 1980s.[147]

Independent churches also attract the politically and socially conservative. Jerry Falwell's Moral Majority gained many supporters from fundamentalist circles because he championed a socially and

---

[145] Ammerman, *Bible Believers: Fundamentalists in the Modern World*, 122–26. Ammerman's fine study of a particular independent congregation, a revision of her Ph.D. dissertation, discusses the tremendous authority the local congregation gives its pastor and the consequences therein.

[146] Voyle A. Glover, *Fundamental Seduction*, 10.

[147] Vaughan, *World's Twenty Largest Churches*, 119.

politically conservative agenda with which they agreed. Some fundamentalists have been willing to modify their separatist stance and cooperate with non-fundamentalists because they are in agreement in opposing abortion, homosexuality, the ordination of women, and the like.

Fundamentalists all concur that a pastor must be male. The churches reflect a patriarchal leadership in which women cannot exercise authority over a man. On the home front, women are encouraged to be submissive to their husbands and are discouraged from having their own careers. Their primary role is to maintain the home.[148] Women generally accept their secondary status and find ways to gain power, but their diminished voice does not serve the movement well. In the end, the greatest issue facing Independents today is separatism. J. Frank Norris named his first newspaper *The Fence Rail.* This name reflects the Independent quandary—who belongs inside the fence and who should be shut outside the fence and who should be shut outside. Ecumenical Independents have been roundly criticized by strict separationists who accuse them of being spiritually contaminated. Such internecine conflicts have definitely injured the movement and may in the end cripple it.

---

[148] Tassell, *Quest for Faithfulness*, 416–17. A recent survey of GARBC pastors revealed their patriarchal views, which undoubtedly parallels fundamentalist understandings in general.

Chapter 6

The National Association of Free Will Baptists

William F. Davidson

Origins

Until the middle of the twentieth century, Free Will Baptists trusted their tradition as they sought answers to questions of origin. Earlier, it was assumed that Benjamin Randall and the Freewill Baptists of New England were responsible, either directly or indirectly, for all the people, churches, and conferences that make up the present denomination. After 1950, a new tradition traced the beginnings of the movement in America back to Paul Palmer and the General Baptists of North Carolina in the early eighteenth century. Recent research has substantiated the denomination's claim that Palmer formally organized the first American Free Will Baptist Church in eastern North Carolina in 1727. Churches and leaders from the earlier movement had adopted the newer name and identity by 1807. But that was just the beginning of the story. It also became evident that other groups of like faith had sprung from entirely different sources in other parts of the country. The final mix would include remnants of Randall's New England group,[1] remnants of an Arminian Separate Baptist movement in Tennessee, and Palmer's

---

[1] Randall's followers identified themselves as "Freewill Baptists," while the group in the South more often used "Free Will Baptists." Throughout chapter 6, this pattern will be used to identify the two groups.

heritage in the Southeast. It would be a number of years before the various groups would come together in a cooperative organization.

By 1609, John Smyth completed a spiritual metamorphosis that led him from the Anglican priesthood (1594) to Puritanism, then to Puritan Separatism, and finally to a new Baptist faith. In 1608 or 1609, he adopted the idea of believer's baptism and broke with the Church of England. First in England and later in exile in Holland, he served as pastor of a small group that agreed with his new dogma. Failing to locate an acceptable administrator for believer's baptism, Smyth baptized himself and then his followers. The little band's final break with England came in the publication of Smyth's *Character of the Beast* in 1609. There he boldly defended his rejection of the infant baptism of the larger church: "...al that shal in tyme to come Separate [sic] from England must Seperate from the baptisme of Englan, and if they wil not Seperate from baptisme their is no reason why they should seperate from England as from a false church...."[2]

Soon, Smyth began to question his "se-baptism" (self-baptism) and petitioned the Waterlander Mennonites in Holland for membership and for baptism. Two of his church leaders, Thomas Helwys and John Murton, refused to follow Smyth and attempted to discourage the Waterlanders from accepting him. Smyth died before his request could be honored. After his death, Helwys and Murton returned to England to found the first Baptist church on English soil at Spitalfield just outside London in 1612.

In his "A Declaration of Faith of English People Remaining at Amsterdam Holland,"[3] written in 1611, Thomas Helwys set the boundaries for the new Baptist faith—general atonement, prevenient grace, believer's baptism, and the possibility of apostasy for believers. It was to this original General Baptist faith that the Free Will Baptists in

---

[2] W. T. Whitley, "The Character of the Beast," *The Works of John Smyth, Fellow of Christ's College, 1594–1598* (Cambridge: University Press, 1915) 567.

[3] Thomas Helwys, "A Declaration of Faith of English People Remaining at Amsterdam Holland, 1611," in H. Leon McBeth, ed., *A Sourcebook for Baptist Heritage* (Nashville: Broadman Press, 1990) 38–41.

the southeastern United States would later point as the beginning of their heritage. Though in America the movement would continue to be identified as General Baptist until 1812, the newer name had been suggested much earlier in England. Champlin Burrage noted that a non-Calvinistic congregation existed as "free-willers" as early as 1551.[4] In 1611, Thomas Helwys used the alternate name in the title of his article, "An advertisement or admonition, unto the congregation, which men called the New Frylers [Freewillers], in the lowe Countries written in Dutche," and by 1659, the newer title was being used both by the General Baptists and their opponents.[5]

General Baptists in America

Choosing eastern North Carolina as the birthplace of the Free Will Baptists in the South has been complicated by the fact that General Baptists were to be found in other Southern states as well. Virginia noted their presence as early as 1699, and the movement there could be linked directly to the General Baptists in England through the arrival of Robert Norden in 1714. He came to Virginia from England at the request of a congregation in Isle of Wight County. Norden served as pastor of a

---

[4] Though Burrage simply referred to this congregation as anti-Calvinistic or separating non-conformists, Barry R. White would later clearly identify them as "free-willers." See Champlin Burrage, *The Early English Dissenters in the Light of Recent Research,* vol. 1. (New York: Russell and Russell, 1967 [1912]) 236, and B. R. White, *The English Separatist Tradition from the Marian Martyrs to the Pilgrim Fathers* (London: Oxford University Press, 1971) xii–xiii.

[5] In 1983, the author discovered two documents relating to early English General Baptist history that referred to the group as "freewillers." The first, from 1659 and written by General Baptist authors, was titled "A declaration of a small society of baptised believers, undergoing the name of Free-Willers, about the city of London." The document evidently was intended to serve as an apologetic for the General Baptist faith. The second was the work of an opponent, I. Beevan, who had once been General Baptist but now had adopted a Calvinistic theology. His work, "A Loving Salutation to all People Who Have Any Desires After the Living God: but especially to the Free-Will-Anabaptists," was designed as an evangelistic tool and encouraged the General Baptists to return to the Calvinistic fold.

church at Burley, across the James River from Jamestown, until his death in 1725. Two years later, two other General Baptist elders arrived from England to continue Norden's work. Richard Jones was installed as pastor of the Burley church, and Casper Mintz was commissioned by the church to establish a new work in Surry.[6] Sometime after 1727, Virginia and North Carolina General Baptists joined forces in the establishment of a formal Yearly Meeting. Paul Palmer, a General Baptist in North Carolina, confirmed the new level of organization in a 1729 letter to John Comer in New England: "There is a comely little church in the Isle of Wight county, of about thirty or forty members, the Elder of which is one Richard Jones, a very sensible old gentleman, whom I have great love for. We see each other at every Yearly Meeting, and sometime more often. There is another church in Surry County, where my brother Jones lives, I suppose of about thirty more."[7]

But the Virginia churches would not survive. Apart from sparse reports regarding its birth, the Surry church did not appear again in General Baptist records, and the Burley church had been lost to the denomination by 1756. A devastating plague in 1742 caused a portion of the congregation to flee to North Carolina under the leadership of William Sojourner. There Sojourner founded the Kehukee General Baptist Church and, through its influence, three other churches in Pitt County, North Carolina—Great Cohara, Upper Fishing Creek, and Tar River Falls. The remaining remnant in Virginia joined the Philadelphia Baptist Association, a Calvinist body, in 1756. Though Sojourner's churches predated Paul Palmer's eastern North Carolina work by more than thirteen years, they cannot be included in the list of resources for

---

[6] John Hamerstley to Nicholas Eyres, 1742, quoted in Robert B. Semple, *A History of the Rise and Progress of the Baptists in Virginia* (Richmond: John Lynch, Printer, 1810) 444–45. Norden's death in America has been questioned since the General Baptist minutes recorded permission for him to return to England in 1725. Virginia records, however, have recorded the inventory of the estate of "Robert Norden, Dec'd." See W. T. Whitley, "General Baptists in Carolina and Virginia," *Crozer Quarterly* 13 (January 1936): 26–27.

[7] David Benedict, *A General History of the Baptist Denomination in America and Other Parts of the World*, 2 vols. (Boston: Lincoln & Edmands, 1813) 11, 24.

the birth of the Free Will Baptists. By the middle of the eighteenth century, these churches, along with Toisnot and Bertie, had become the nucleus of the Kehukee Baptist Association, an association based on the Particular (Regular, Calvinistic) Baptist plan. The reorganization of the Great Cohara church as a Calvinistic church in 1759 ended the possibility of any influence of the Virginia churches on the continuing General Baptist movement.[8]

This story was repeated in South Carolina. Two churches, Stono and Rocky River, began as General Baptist churches, but both appeared on the scene after the beginning of Palmer's ministry and were destined for short life. The Stono church began as a split from the Calvinistic Baptist church in Charleston, now First Baptist Church, in 1733. Rocky River, under the leadership of Jeremiah Walker, applied for membership in the Georgia Baptist Association. The association, wary of the church's General Baptist leanings, reacted slowly to the request, and Rocky River soon ceased to exist under the old name. The General Baptist movement in Virginia and South Carolina was officially dead.

Three General Baptist leaders demand special attention in the story of the denomination's life in eastern North Carolina—Paul Palmer, Joseph Parker, and William Parker. Palmer's early life in the area is something of a mystery. Though some historians have attempted to trace his lineage back to the Palmers in England, there are no extant records that would affirm that heritage. He first appeared on the American scene in 1717 in York County, Virginia, when his marriage to Martha Hansford Hill was listed in county records.[9] Unfortunately, Martha died in their first year of marriage and Palmer was next to be found in North Carolina, where, in 1719, the minutes of the Perquimans Precinct Monthly Meeting of Friends (Quaker) recorded his request for

---

[8] See William F. Davidson, *The Free Will Baptists in History* (Nashville: Randall House Publications, 2001) 19–22, for a more detailed study of the Virginia churches.

[9] George Stevenson, "Paul Palmer," in William S. Powell, ed., *Dictionary of North Carolina Biography*, vol. 5 (Chapel Hill and London: University of North Carolina Press, 1994) 10.

dismissal from the monthly meeting.[10] By 1727, Palmer evidently was converted to a General Baptist faith. He married Johanna Peterson sometime after 1720, and her father, Benjamin Laker, probably influenced him toward this new spiritual position. In any case, in 1727 Palmer founded a church in Chowan County, North Carolina. The small congregation near the village of Cisco was the first formally organized General Baptist church in North Carolina.

A second church also can be traced to Palmer's ministry. On 5 September 1729, Palmer and seven others petitioned the Pasquotank Precinct Court for a license to worship as dissenters in the home of William Burgess.[11] By now, Palmer had established a pattern. His ministry was to be that of a church planter rather than pastor. Joseph Parker soon assumed pastoral leadership at Chowan, and William Burgess became the settled pastor at Pasquotank. Though Palmer probably gathered a number of other churches in the area,[12] none of them, including the first two, remained General Baptist for more than a few years. The Chowan church ceased to exist by 1732, and the congregation at Pasquotank converted to a Calvinistic dogma by 1757. Most of his other churches followed Pasquotank's lead. Finally, Palmer himself disappeared from the records by 1742—his latter years remaining as much a mystery as his early ones.

Though Palmer gained a place of special importance in the early movement, it was the work of the pastors of the early churches that became more vital to the group's continuing history and to final development into the Free Will Baptist denomination. Elder Joseph Parker served as pastor of the first church at Chowan and later founded a church at Meherrin. The latter location became a mission point for

---

[10] "Minutes of the Perquimans Monthly Meeting, 1680–1762," vol. 1, indexed by Dorothy Lloyd, Gilbert and Mildred Marlette, microfilmed from the original by Charles E. Rush, librarian for the University of North Carolina Library, 1942, old page 19/new page 32.

[11] J. R. B. Hathaway, *The North Carolina Genealogical* Register, 3 vols. (January 1900–July 1903) 1:293.

[12] See Davidson, *Free Will Baptists*, 27–32 for an extended discussion of Palmer's impact on the General Baptist movement in North Carolina.

other churches, as the Parkers became instrumental in establishing churches in other parts of eastern North Carolina.[13] Joseph Parker, following the popular Baptist "preacher-farmer" method of church growth, purchased property at Meherrin, donated a plot of land for a church, built the church, served as its pastor for a number of years, and then moved on to Little Contentnea Creek in Green County. William Parker, his successor, served the church for the rest of his life and during that time kept the church true to its General Baptist heritage. It was finally lost to the denomination when it was reorganized as a Calvinistic Baptist church by Lemuel Burkitt and Jesse Read in 1794.[14]

Joseph Parker purchased land on Little Contentnea Creek in Green County in 1756.[15] True to pattern, he donated land for a church and soon was preaching to his new congregation. In a few years a number of General Baptist churches were found in the near vicinity—Conetoe (Gum Swamp), Wheat Swamp, Grimsley, Pungo—all attributed to the ministry of the Parkers. These churches functioned as the nucleus for a new Free Will Baptist movement.

Three events serve as incontrovertible evidence that the present National Association of Free Will Baptists must be traced back to the General Baptist work of Paul Palmer and the two Parkers. First, James Roach succeeded Joseph Parker at Little Contentnea Creek and probably at his other churches as well. Roach later, in 1812, signed the first Free Will Baptist declaration of faith along with Jesse Heath. The

---

[13] Shortly before the middle of the eighteenth century, the General Baptists boasted of some fifteen churches and as many ministers, but by 1761, all but four churches and three ministers had been converted to a Calvinistic theology through the ministry of John Gano, Benjamin Miller, and Peter Vanhorn, envoys from the Philadelphia Baptist Association sent to "...rescue their Carolina brethren from error" (Davidson, *Free Will Baptists*, 58–68).

[14] Lemuel Burkitt and Jesse Read, *A Concise History of the Kehukee Baptist Association From Its Original Rise to the Present Time* (Halifax NC: A. Hodge, 1803) 209.

[15] North Carolina, *Craven County Deed Books*, deed recording the sale of property on Little Contentnea Creek to Joseph Parker by Jacob Blount (deed book 10, 25 December 1756).

two championed the new movement during the first few decades of the nineteenth century. Second, the statement of faith signed by Roach and Heath served as both the last apology for the General Baptists and the first for the evolved group using the new name. By this time, 1812, the two names were used interchangeably by the members themselves and by their enemies. Writing at the beginning of the new century, Lemuel Burkitt and Jesse Read, two Calvinist pastors and clear opponents of the Arminian Baptists, spoke of the Parker descendants as "Free-will Baptists," reminding their readers that most of the churches in their own Kehukee (Calvinistic) Baptist Association were first gathered by the "Free-will Baptists."[16] Rufus K. Hearn, a nineteenth-century Free Will Baptist pastor, grew up during the time when the General Baptists gave way to the new Free Will Baptists. He concluded, "We bear the same name, we have the same book of discipline, we preach the old doctrine, we receive members the same way without an experience of Grace, we commemorate the Lord's supper the same way, we wash the saints feet the same way, we are the same persecuted old Free Will Baptists that was organized in 1727 by Elder Paul Palmer."[17]

Finally, both the eighteenth-century General Baptists and the nineteenth-century Free Will Baptists used the same statement of faith, an almost verbatim copy of the General Baptist "Standard or Brief Confession of Faith" drawn up by the General Baptists in England in 1660.[18] Therefore, the National Association of Free Will Baptists of the twenty-first century can be traced back at least as far as the work of Palmer and the Parkers in eastern North Carolina in 1727 and probably

---

[16] Burkitt and Read, *Concise History of the Kehukee Baptist Association*, 232.

[17] Rufus K. Hearn, *Origins of the Free Will Baptist Church of North Carolina*, in D. B. Montgomery, *General Baptist History* (Evansville IN: Courier Company, Book and Job Printers, 1882) 176–77. Hearn loaned his manuscript to Montgomery to be included in his larger text. The Hearn article was not published separately.

[18] *A Brief Confession of Faith*, quoted in William L. Lumpkin, *Baptist Confessions of Faith* (Valley Forge: The Judson Press, 1969) 224–35; *An Abstract of the Former Articles of Faith Confessed by the Original Baptist Church Holding the Doctrine of General Provision with Proper Code of Discipline* (Newbern NC: Salmon Hall, 1814 [1812]).

beyond that to the General Baptist movement in England in the seventeenth century.

The tradition mentioned earlier cannot be ignored. Though it has been proven that Palmer's group in North Carolina preceded that of Benjamin Randall in New England, the latter group did play an important role in the history of the present-day National Association of Free Will Baptists.

The First Great Awakening in America gave rise to a number of new Christian movements in the mid-eighteenth century, so it is not surprising that an Arminian splinter also would emerge. By the time Randall organized the first Freewill Baptist church in New England, he had passed through a relatively rapid spiritual evolution—a period of unconverted piety in his Congregationalist family's home, a time as a Congregationalist believer, a rather radical move to the Separate Baptists (a Calvinistic Baptist group that was given birth by the Awakening), and finally, the larger part of his life that was spent as a Freewill Baptist pastor. While his move to the Separate Baptist faith was not totally unexpected since he still retained his Calvinistic theology except for the substitution of believer's baptism for that of infants, his adoption of General Atonement and an Arminian theology was indeed radical. Though both Calvinistic and Arminian Baptists were present in the new world since New England was first founded, the Calvinists gained the upper hand by the beginning of the eighteenth century. So, while the General Baptists already enjoyed a long history in the South, Arminianism was something of a novelty in the far North. But Randall's conversion to his new faith had little to do with influence from North Carolina. It seemed to have grown out of his own conversion experience: "I saw an universal atonement—an universal love—an universal call—and that none would ever perish, only those who refused to accept.... O what love too I felt for all mankind, and wanted that they all might share in that all fullness, which I saw so extensive, and so free to all...."[19]

Randall founded the first Freewill Baptist church in New England in New Durham, New Hampshire. On 30 June 1780, four men and three women signed a confession of faith, the "Church Covenant and Articles of Faith," that was drafted by Randall. This document set the new Arminian tone for the fledgling group. Growth came slowly at first, and Randall had to turn to other Arminian Baptists for fellowship and encouragement. But within ten years the denomination was enjoying phenomenal growth. In 1790, the movement could point to twenty churches, eight ministers, nine elders, and seven unordained ministers.[20] By the middle of the nineteenth century, they developed a strong organizational structure based on quarterly and yearly meetings and a general conference, created colleges and seminaries from Maine to Michigan, and instituted an effective missions program that supported missionaries overseas and on the Western frontier in America. By 1888, the general conference represented more than fifty yearly meetings and 148,082 members.[21]

But growth was short lived as declining membership and an increasingly popular ecumenical spirit moved the group toward new alliances. As early as 1834, Randall's group was involved in a "union meeting" that included Presbyterian, Baptist, Methodist, and Free Baptist churches. Additional but unsuccessful negotiations with the Disciples of Christ were pursued by the latter part of the century. At least two assumptions gave credence to the possibility of union: (1) more effective mission involvement could be achieved through the combining of resources of the various denominations, and (2) the theology taught

---

[19] John Buzzell, "An Extract of the Experience of Elder Benjamin Randall (taken from a manuscript), Written by Himself, Corrected by the Editor," *A Religious Magazine* 6 (February 1822): 206.

[20] I. D. Stewart, *The History of the Freewill Baptists for Half a Century* (Dover NH: Freewill Baptist Printing Establishment, 1862) 95.

[21] G. A. Burgess and J. T. Ward, *Free Baptist Cyclopaedia* (Chicago: Free Baptist Cyclopaedia Co., 1889) 211.

by the denomination's founders "...had been so far adopted by other Christian churches as to make the separate testimony of Free Baptists less important, if indeed necessary at all as in former years."[22] This latter conclusion was assumed to be especially true of the Northern Baptists, making that denomination an especially attractive choice for merger. A pamphlet published by the Freewill Baptists in 1908 reminded its readers that the Northern Baptists had modified their rigid Calvinism in the 1832 Confession of Faith adopted by the New Hampshire State Convention and that the Philadelphia Baptist Confession had been so revised as to "have little, if any more sense of restrictions in their Calvinism than Benjamin Randall had in 1780."[23]

The merger between the Northern Baptists and the New England Freewill Baptists affected in 1910–1911 saw the smaller denomination swallowed up by the larger. Though earlier agreements had guaranteed that the smaller body would be allowed to retain its identity, its membership, and its property, it quickly became evident that this was not possible. In a few short years, the Freewill Baptists disbanded their home missionary society and made their mission funds available to the their new parent body; the *Morning Star*, the weekly paper published by the Freewill Baptists for seventy-five years, was incorporated into *The Examiner*, a Northern Baptist periodical, under the new title of *The Watchman-Examiner*; the Bible schools and seminaries of the smaller body became the responsibility of the larger group; and Sunday school literature and publishing endeavors were reassigned to the American Baptist Publication Society.[24]

While the merger carried the day, there were at least three other factions within the denomination that pleaded for alternative measures:

---

[22] Alfred Williams Anthony, "Twenty Years After: The Story of the Union of Baptists and Free Baptists During the Period of Negotiation and Realization, 1904–1924," reprint from *Christian Work*, 18 October 1924, 1.

[23] "The General Conference of Free Will Baptists: Information Respecting the Basis of Union and Proceedings Thereto," pamphlet, American Baptist Historical Society, Rochester NY, 1908, 4–5.

[24] For a more thorough account of the Northern/Freewill Baptist merger, see Davidson, *Free Will Baptists*, 251–56.

(1) continued negotiations with the Disciples of Christ; (2) a return to the even older heritage found in the Congregational Church; and (3) maintenance of the status quo with the Freewill Baptists continuing as a denomination. The latter group was the most vocal and boasted the most resources. When the smoke cleared and the negotiations were complete, a significant remnant resisted the merger, including congregations in Ohio, Kentucky, West Virginia, Nebraska, Missouri, and Texas. These survivors retained their identity as Freewill Baptists and later played a significant role in the birth of the National Association of Free Will Baptists.

The National Association of Free Will Baptists

Lessons learned from the merger continued to guide the various groups of Free Will Baptists that remained after 1911—the Cooperative General Association in the West (1916), the Tri-State Association in Appalachia (1919), and the Second General Conference in the South (1921). The first two were established to sustain the New England remnant, while the latter conference was a revival of an earlier Eastern Conference that ceased to exist in 1910.[25] The merger set the Northern remnant adrift without a central organization, and the group in the South never enjoyed a close relationship with Free Will Baptists in other

---

[25] The Cooperative General Association included membership from Nebraska, Kansas, Missouri, and Texas. It was organized officially on 27 December 1916 at the Philadelphia Church of Pattonsburg, Missouri. The Tri-State included churches from Ohio, West Virginia, and Kentucky. The organizational structure of yearly meetings followed the pattern set by Benjamin Randall in New England. The association dates from 4 October 1919. The Second General Conference of the South succeeded an older conference that had disbanded in 1910. This conference could be traced back as far as Paul Palmer's ministry in eastern North Carolina in 1727. This Second General Conference of the South drafted organizational papers on 26 May 1921 at Cofer's Chapel Church in Nashville. At first the new conference was limited in scope to the Southeast, but by 1935 it represented churches and associations in Alabama, Florida, Georgia, North Carolina, Tennessee, Nebraska, and Texas.

parts of the country.[26] Though "merger" now carried a somewhat frightening connotation, concern for survival seemed to dictate a joining of forces for Free Will Baptists east and west.

A first attempt at union occurred in 1918 as representatives from the South and East visited the Cooperative General Association meeting in Paintsville, Kentucky. J. L. Welch of Tennessee and F. H. Styron and P. E. Beaman of North Carolina were warmly welcomed by the association and were invited to sit on various working committees. The fellowship was so warm that the Western group was invited to meet in Nashville the next year so that discussion between the two bodies could continue. But any expectations for merger were soon shattered when disagreement surfaced over the question of foot-washing as an official ordinance of the faith. John L. Welch, the host pastor for the 1919 conference in Nashville, remembered the results of that meeting.

> When we met at Nashville, we found that the Cooperative Association would not take a definite stand on the matter of feet washing. John H. Wolfe, you know about him from Nebraska. He was a part of the old Northern Free Will Baptists. He refused to join in with the others. He fought the whole movement. He was at the head of this Cooperative Association and he didn't practice feet washing, the Free Wills of the North didn't. Well he had a man named Samuel (Samra) Smith. He was his right-hand or left-hand man in the movement and Smith wouldn't agree. And they had another man named Waterman, Ira Waterman. He didn't go along with it so they wouldn't agree to take a stand on it. They wanted to leave it an open question. The North Carolina and Tennessee people wanted it as an ordinance you see. Well, the result of the argument was that the North Carolina group and our group (Tennessee) pulled out from the Cooperative because we had been accepted in this 1919

---

[26] Some leaders of the New England Freewill Baptists seemed to assume that the General Conference in the South was officially linked with them during the nineteenth century. Statistics for the southern group often were included in New England reports, and North Carolina actually petitioned for membership in the New England General Conference in 1880, but formal contacts between the two groups were limited and delegates were seldom exchanged.

meeting at Cofers, but we pulled out over this question of feetwashing.[27]

Welch was an eyewitness to the 1919 event, and his account is valuable in documenting the cause for failure of the new merger. But Wolfe went through the merger between the Randallites and the Northern Baptists and was credited with almost single-handedly rescuing the Nebraska yearly meeting from that attempt at union. He came to the 1919 meeting with a strong suspicion of such negotiations, and it is possible that the ordinance of foot-washing was just the vehicle used to prevent another perceived disaster.

In any case, the failure of the two groups to come to terms in 1919 generated three positive responses in the Southeast: (1) the birth of the Second General Conference of the Original Free Will Baptists of the South;[28] (2) a reaffirmation of foot-washing as a third ordinance; and (3) a new determination to find suitable alliances with groups of like faith.

Initially, the new conference contained fewer churches and associations than had been true of the old. However, by 1935,[29] the body included twenty conferences in nine states—the Alabama State Convention, the Alabama-Florida State Line Association, the Southeastern Conference of Alabama, the Liberty Association of West Florida, the Salem Association of West Florida, the Martin Association (GA), the Midway Association (GA), the Union Georgia Association, the Nebraska/Northern Kansas Association, the Cape Fear Conference (NC), the Central North Carolina State Convention, the Eastern North Carolina Conference, the North Carolina State Convention, the Ohio River Association, the South Carolina Conference, the Cumberland

---

[27] John L. Welch, interview by Robert Picirilli, 25 April 1971, transcript, Free Will Baptist Historical Collection, Free Will Baptist Bible College, Nashville TN, p. 11.

[28] The new conference intended to recover the heritage of the earlier Triennial General Conference and adopted as its name, "The Second General Conference of the Original Free Will Baptists of the United States." Subsequent references will refer to the newer body as the "General Conference."

[29] The National Association of Free Will Baptists organized in 1935.

Association (TN), the Union Association (TN), and the Texas State Convention.[30]

E. C. Morris, pastor of the Free Will Baptist Church in Bryan, Texas, from 1929 until 1932, claimed to have drafted and delivered the first formal proposals for merger of Free Will Baptists east and west.[31] In 1932, after leading the Texas State Convention into the Eastern General Conference, Morris, along with M. L. Sutton and J. L. Bounds, attended the Cooperative General Association meeting and invited the delegates there to send representatives to the next general conference meeting at the Bryan church in June 1932. This was the first of a number of visits between the two groups over the next few years.

But if Morris was the first to offer formal proposals for merger, he was not the first to consider a joining of forces of the Free Will Baptists in the United States. In spite of the failures of earlier negotiations, the General Conference had not given up hope. In 1930, R. F. Pittman, moderator of the conference, chose national union as the topic for his keynote address. In his message, he appealed to the delegates to "lay

---

[30] *Minutes of the Fifteenth Annual Session of the General Conference of the Original Free Will Baptists of the United States* (Ayden NC: Free Will Baptist Press, 1935) 2. By this time, the membership of the Tri-State Association seems to have been embraced by the both the Second General Conference and the Cooperative Association. The Tri-State was not mentioned by name during the organizational negotiations that gave birth to the national association, and it was not included in the new association's agreement that East and West would be allowed to maintain their identities within the new organization. At the same time, however, churches and organizations from the Tri-State were represented at the first national meeting through the merger's larger parties.

[31] Upon accepting the pastorate at the Bryan Church in 1929, Morris discovered that leaders of the church had mistakenly assumed it was a part of the 1910–1911 merger with the Northern Baptists. Once they understood that they were not formally related to the Calvinistic Baptists, Morris was able to lead them into membership in the General Conference of Free Will Baptists in the East (E. C. Morris to the editors of "The History Corner," *Contact* [18 December 1971]: 2). For a more detailed account of Morris's role in the merger negotiations, see Davidson, *Free Will Baptists*, 275.

aside selfishness and look beyond our Association and conferences, into a National view."[32]

By 1933, an appointed planning committee was ready to present a plan of union to the two groups. The committee included J. L. Welch, J. W. Alford, K. V. Shutes, Henry Melvin, A. D. Ivey, and M. L. Morse from the General Conference and G. W. Scott, Jr., B. F. Brown, Selph Jones, Melvin Bingham, Noel Turner, and Winford Davis from the Cooperative General Association. Both bodies approved the proposal, though it required two full years before it was implemented into a full union.

> We the Joint Committee of the General Conference and the Cooperative Association, agree to the following.
>
> We agree to accept the Articles of Faith of the *1901 Treatise*, also the Church Covenant contained in the same Treatise, together with all the forms and usages set forth in same, with such amendments as may be made and approved by the body when perfected into one organization.
>
> We heartily agree to the merging of the General Conference and Cooperative General Association into one body, and we urge that steps be taken immediately for the final consummation of such a union.[33]

Only two other articles were added to the agreement before the actual organizational meeting took place in 1935: (1) that the two bodies would retain their individual identities without accepting responsibility for one another's continuing obligations and (2) that the terms of union would not suggest jurisdiction of one conference over the other.[34]

The first official session of the National Association of Free Will Baptists met at Cofer's Chapel Church in Nashville on Tuesday evening,

---

[32] *Minutes of the Tenth Annual Session of the General Conference of the Original Free Will Baptists of the United States* (Ayden NC: Free Will Baptist Press, 1930) 5.

[33] *Minutes—General Conference* (1933)12.

[34] *Minutes of the Seventh Triennial Session of the General Cooperative Association of the Freewill Baptists* (Wanette OK: Wanette Printing Co., 1934) 6.

5 November 1935. The next day, I. J. Blackwelder, secretary pro tem, seated delegates from six state conventions and fourteen local associations. Representatives seated were from Alabama, North Carolina, Georgia, Mississippi, Oklahoma, Missouri, Texas, Nebraska, Tennessee, Kentucky, West Virginia, and Ohio. Arkansas also sent official observers to the meeting, though churches in that state were not yet ready to commit to the union. The first slate of officers for the new national association reflected the concern for equal representation from east and west. J. L. Welch (moderator) and I. J. Blackwelder (secretary-treasurer) were from the General Conference, while Winford Davis (assistant moderator) and B. P. F. Rogers (assistant secretary-treasurer) were from the Cooperative General Association.

A newly drafted constitution declared the combined bodies to be the National Association of Free Will Baptists, with the eastern group being renamed the Eastern Association and the western becoming the Western Association. The new parent body was to be advisory in nature but claimed the right to settle questions of discipline, doctrine, and usage that member organizations brought before it. A system of boards was designed to plan and implement programs related to home and foreign missions, to youth and women's work, and to Sunday school.[35]

For the first time since Randall's New England group had merged with the Northern Baptists, the Free Will Baptists were actively involved in an international mission project. As early as 1901, appeals for foreign missions were presented to the delegates of the Eastern General Conference. In that year, the missions committee declared that "The Spirit of the triune God is manifestly missionary. God's children having his nature and spirit are missionaries."[36] But the business of the committee was limited to a yearly message of exhortation and encouragement until 1930 when it was replaced by a general secretary who was to raise funds and identify personnel for a new foreign missions program. I. J. Blackwelder served in that position until 1935, when he

---

[35] Davidson, *Free Will Baptists*, 278.

[36] *Thirty-First Session of the Free Will Baptist Triennial General Conference, 1901*, 5.

was appointed as secretary-treasurer of foreign missions for the new national association.

In 1938, the national association approved support for three missionaries already on the field—Thomas Willey (Panama—$150.00 per month), Laura Belle Barnard (Kotagiri, South India—$50.00 per month), and Bessie Yeley (Venezuela—$50.00 per month). Miss Barnard, often considered the first official missionary for the new denomination, was commissioned by the Eastern General Conference in 1935 shortly before the national association convened for the first time. Miss Yeley was serving under the auspices of Free Will Baptists in Ohio. The entire income for the denomination between its first meeting in 1935 and its second in 1938 was $7,228.03, which was divided among the three missionaries according to the policy mentioned earlier. Five years later, in 1943, the new program was officially organized as the Board of Foreign Missions, and Winford Davis was appointed as chairman-treasurer of the board with the task of supervising the denomination's mission activity.

Attention to foreign missions did not create neglect for home missions. The Eastern General Conference boasted a Home Missions Society as early as 1904, and less formal church-planting ministries had been in place since the early eighteenth century.[37] The Home Missions Board was appointed in 1938 when the national association met for its second session in Nashville, and it included M. L. Hollis, chairman; J. K. Warkentin; Mrs. J. E. Frazier; Rev. Lizzie McAdams; and George Dunbar.[38]

Earlier attempts at education were less than successful for the Free Will Baptists. Those institutions that prospered—Bates College and

---

[37] In the eighteenth century, Joseph and William Parker had pioneered a missions activity that the next century would dub the "Baptist preacher-farmer" approach. In contrast to the Methodist "circuit-rider," the Baptist preachers would purchase a farm, donate a portion of the land for a church, serve the church as pastor, train new preachers, and finally send them out to repeat the pattern. The two Parkers were responsible for the gathering of churches at Little Contentney Creek, Grimsley, Wheat Swamp, Louson Swamp, and Meherrin in eastern North Carolina.

[38] Davidson, *Free Will Baptists*, 302.

Cobb Divinity School (Maine), Hillsdale (Michigan), Geauga and Rio Grande (Ohio)—had all been New England projects and were lost in the 1910–1911 merger. The Cooperative General Association sponsored a college in Tecumseh, Oklahoma, to meet the needs of Free Will Baptists in the West, but the school survived for just a few years. Begun on 12 September 1917 amid high expectations and much excitement, the school offered seven different programs of study—classical, philosophical and scientific, literary, classical theology, English theology, expression, and a normal school curriculum. Led by President John H. Wolfe, Tecumseh opened its first semester with six resident faculty members and three more on contract for later in the first year of operation. A School of Correspondence offered three courses—Systematic Theology and History of the Bible, Church History and Evidences of Christianity, and Pastoral and Practical Theology—to students who were unable to attend resident courses or who were not qualified for campus classes. The school was an early example of a Christian liberal arts college. By offering free tuition and a total student fee base of $6.75, the school was able to draw twelve students for its first year of training. By 1927, faculty numbered fourteen and the school offered the Bachelor of Arts, the Bachelor of Christian Letters, and the Bachelor of Letters. In that year, unfortunately, the campus was demolished by fire after serving Free Will Baptists in the West and the Midwest for a decade.[39]

Three schools—Eureka College, Ayden Seminary, and Zion Bible School—met similar denominational needs in the East. In 1890, the Annual Conference in North Carolina appointed an educational committee and assigned its members the task of making recommendations for a school in that state, but it was years later before plans were completed for a seminary in Ayden, North Carolina. The

---

[39] *Minutes of the First Triennial Session of the Cooperative General Association of Freewill Baptists, 1916*. (Weatherford TX: *The New Morning Star*, 1917) 3–7; *Minutes of the First Adjourned Session of the Cooperative General Association of Freewill Baptists, 1917* (Tecumseh OK: New Morning Star Publishing House, 1918) 14–21; *Tecumseh College Catalogue and Announcements, 1921–1922*, 11.

idea for the school was conceived in 1896, and a two-year program of planning, fundraising, and property acquisition allowed for the first students to enroll in 1898. Under the leadership of its first president, J. E. B. Davis, the Free Will Baptist Theological Seminary offered training for primary and high school students as well as for pastors already on the field. The theological curriculum was rigorous, offering Theology, Free Will Baptist Faith (Doctrine), Church History, Luke in Greek, and Homiletics.[40] The seminary prospered in its early years but fell victim to declining denominational support and to the growing convenience of public education. As the size of the student body decreased, the school board became more convinced that a college-level program was needed.

The seminary closed in 1920 as the denomination turned its full attention to the establishment of Eureka College. The school opened its doors to students on its own campus on 26 September 1926 but quickly found itself in difficulty when too few students enrolled to plan for a sophomore class and budget shortfalls promised a difficult future. During the 1928–1929 school year, services were reduced, and in 1929 Eureka suspended operations. In 1931, the school plant suffered the same fate as Tecumseh when fire destroyed the administration-classroom building.

In Georgia, T. L. Mellette sponsored the final attempt at denominational education in the East. Coming to Georgia via South Carolina first and Duke University later, Mellette offered expertise both in teaching and in educational administration. He purchased land in Southwest Georgia and founded a new school designed to prepare young people for vocational Christian ministry. A number of denominational leaders were trained in Bible and theology during the school's existence from 1935 to 1942.[41]

Finally, after the birth of the national association, Free Will Baptists came together to establish a national Bible college that would serve the educational needs of the entire denomination. Free Will Baptist Bible

---

[40] Michael Pelt, *A History of Ayden Seminary and Eureka College* (Mount Olive NC: 1983) 4–5.

[41] Steven R. Hasty, "Zion Bible School," *The Time Machine* 1/1 (1982): 2–3.

College was founded in 1942 in Nashville, Tennessee, and offered a two-year pastoral curriculum under the leadership of its new president, L. C. Johnson. The first class consisted of nine students, with four of those constituting the first graduating class in 1943. In 1946, growing enrollment and growing interest in biblical education allowed the school to add the Evangelical Teacher Training Association Diploma as a supplement to the two-year degree already offered. In 1949, a third year of study was approved, and by 1950, the board approved a full four-year baccalaureate with a focus on biblical studies. Enrollment in that year reached 100, and faculty and staff totaled 10 (7 faculty and 3 staff members). For the next few years, this institution was the only denominational source for pastoral training, and Free Will Baptists continue to appreciate the school's long and productive heritage.[42]

Free Will Baptist Distinctives

In outline, Free Will Baptist distinctives include biblical authority, a conservative and Arminian theology, believer's baptism, autonomy of the local church, foot-washing as a third ordinance, and a conservative lifestyle.

In a recent theological text, Leroy Forlines has defended "Classical Arminianism" as the defining characteristic of Free Will Baptist theology:

> My treatment of Arminian theology is what I have chosen to call Classical Arminianism. This is in distinction from Wesleyan Arminianism. The term "classical" is used because I think this view is in essential agreement with James Arminius. I believe that there are some important distinctions between my view and Wesleyan Arminianism besides that Wesleyan Arminians believe in a second work of grace. Wesleyan Arminians, for the most part, believe in the governmental view of atonement or some modification of that view.

[42] Davidson, *Free Will Baptists*, 303–305.

> Classical Arminianism, in agreement with Arminius, is strongly committed to the satisfaction view of atonement.[43]

Following Forlines's lead, two other Free Will Baptist theologians, Matthew Pinson and Stephen Ashby, have inferred that Classical Arminianism might even be considered, at least in part, as "Reformed Arminianism."[44] The focus here, of course, is on the two elements of Free Will Baptist faith mentioned in Forlines's definition—rejection of the Wesleyan second work of grace and adoption of the satisfaction view of atonement that is also held by followers of John Calvin. In addition, Free Will Baptists defend the doctrine of total depravity as vehemently as would a Reformed theologian: "We teach that man is so totally depraved that he is unable to save himself—to get to God on his own."[45] Even so, the name "Free Will Baptist" demands that the definition of total depravity be revisited. In Forlines's Classical Arminianism, the original creation of humans included the constitutional likeness of God, which denotes personhood, and the functional likeness of God, which denotes personality. Where the Reformed view of the biblical fall infers the destruction of God's image in humanity, the view of Classical Arminianism would argue that part of the image that denotes personhood, though damaged, remains. "This damage reflects itself in man's personality. Man lost his functional likeness of God in the fall. He no longer thinks, feels, and acts in the likeness of God."[46] While lost humanity then is incapable of contributing anything to God that would incur God's favor and result in salvation—humans are indeed depraved—they do retain personhood and still have the ability to think, feel, and act, even though they can no longer be holy and please God. This allows for options. They can respond to the word of God and to

---

[43] F. Leroy Forlines. *The Quest for Truth: Answering Life's Inescapable Questions* (Nashville: Randall House Publication, 2001) xvii.

[44] Ibid., foreword, x.

[45] J. Matthew Pinson, *A Free Will Baptist Handbook* (Nashville: Randall House Publications, 1998) 47.

[46] Forlines, *Quest for Truth*, 223.

the wooing of the Holy Spirit and say "yes" or "no" to the Spirit's appeal.

The key question for any theological system is that of the scope of the atonement. Free Will Baptists contend that Christ died for all humans and that everyone has the capacity to respond to the gospel in faith.[47] This position contrasts sharply with the Reformed assumption that faith is a gift that can be exercised only after regeneration has taken place. In this case, the ability is already present in the constitutional likeness that the individual retains after the fall. Though desperately depraved and unable to make any contribution toward salvation (the functional likeness is inoperative), humans are capable of responding to the word and to the wooing of the Holy Spirit. "For whom did Christ die?" is the question that finally separates any Arminian theology from that of the Reformed church.

Southern, American, and some independent Baptists often are termed "moderate Calvinists" because they defend the one Reformed dogma of the perseverance of the saints. Free Will Baptists carry their Arminianism full circle by defending the possibility of apostasy for believers. Working from such passages as 1 Peter 1:5, Hebrews 6:1–6, and Hebrews 10:26–29 and assuming that the individual's ability to think and make decisions remains after salvation, denominational doctrine warns that apostasy is possible at the point when a believer totally rejects Christ. The National Treatise states, "There are strong grounds to hope that the truly regenerate will persevere unto the end, and be saved, through the power of divine grace which is pledged for their support; but their future obedience and final salvation are neither determined nor certain, since through infirmity and manifold temptations they are in

---

[47] General Baptists in North Carolina (the Palmer/Parker heritage) were often called "free willers" by their Regular (Reformed) Baptist neighbors. The name was becoming popular by the beginning of the nineteenth century, and in 1828 the group there adopted the name "Free Will Baptists." The reference, of course, was to the doctrine of General Atonement taught by the General Baptists. See Davidson, *Free Will Baptists*, 151; R. K. Hearn, *Origin of the Free Will Baptist Church in North Carolina*, quoted in D. B. Montgomery, *General Baptist History* (Evansville: Courier Company, 1927) 167–68.

danger of falling; and they ought, therefore, to watch and pray lest they make shipwreck of their faith and be lost."[48]

From their earliest history, Free Will Baptists have jealously guarded the autonomy of the local church. Members of the General Conference in New England said it best in 1841 when they resolved "that the strict independence of the churches in all matters related to the transaction of their own business, is indispensably necessary in order to promote the uninterrupted enjoyment of religious liberty in our denomination."[49] Though local churches quite early delegated some responsibilities to the district association—ordination of ministers and deacons and counsel in difficult church conflicts—and some to the national association—missions and educational literature—the larger bodies functioned only in an advisory capacity. Final decisions in all matters were made at the local level. The denomination continues to be firmly committed to a congregational model in church government.

The denomination defends three ordinances—believer's baptism, the Lord's Supper, and the washing of the saints' feet. Use of the term "ordinance" affirms the group's conviction that the practices are symbolic rather than sacramental. In the *Confession of Faith* published in 1855 in North Carolina, the General Conference affirmed its belief that the foot-washing service should stand alongside the other two ordinances. "We believe, as touching Gospel ordinances, in believers' Baptism,...receiving of the sacrament in bread and wine, washing the saint's feet...."[50] Actually, the confession included the laying on of hands,

---

[48] *A Treatise of the Faith and Practices of the National Association of Free Will Baptists, Inc.* (Nashville: Executive Office of the National Association of Free Will Baptists, Inc., 1935 [2001]) 12. Arminius retained the Reformed doctrine of perseverance, but the General Baptists in England rejected the doctrine early in the seventeenth century. See Thomas Helwys, *A Declaration of Faith of English People*, in McBeth, ed., *A Sourcebook*, 40.

[49] *Minutes of the General Conference of the Freewill Baptist Connection, 1841* (Dover NH: Freewill Baptist Printing Establishment, 1859) 335.

[50] *An Abstract of the Former Articles of Faith, Confessed by the Original Baptist Church, Holding the Doc-trine of General Provision, With a Proper code of Discipline* (New York: D. Fanshaw, 1855) 8.

anointing the sick with oil, fasting, prayer, singing praises to God, and the public ministry of the word as ordinances, but these soon disappeared from the literature. The 2001 revision of the National Treatise acknowledges only the former three. Footwashing ordinarily is celebrated in conjunction with the Lord's Supper. Men and women are separated, but both follow the same pattern of service—hymns or choruses, prayer, and the act itself. In a solemn ceremony, one individual wraps a long towel around his waist, holds the foot of another member over a basin, and gently washes and wipes it. As laymen and leaders wash one another's feet, they are reminded of the humility of Christ as he washed the feet of his disciples, and they are also made aware of their need for daily cleansing.

The phenomenal growth that the Southern Baptists and some independent Baptists have enjoyed has eluded the National Association of Free Will Baptists. Though recent statistics have given cause for optimism, the movement continues to grow at a leisurely pace. A number of factors come to bear here. First, the denomination finds it difficult to shed its rural character and its country-crossroads mentality. At the end of the first quarter of the twentieth century, only 4 of 1,024 churches were reported as ministering in an urban setting. Until the middle of the twentieth century, the majority of Free Will Baptist churches were more likely to number 100 or less in membership and to be found in smaller communities or rural areas. The smaller churches tend to dictate the need for part-time pastors who find it necessary to serve more than one church. Even as late as 2002, more than half of the Free Will Baptist pastors reporting to the state association in Oklahoma were listed as part-time ministers. But in the same records, a new trend seemed to be emerging as 155 pastors were reported to serve urban churches as opposed to 73 in rural settings.[51] Large urban churches in Nashville (Tennessee), Norfolk (Virginia), and Tulsa (Oklahoma) also would suggest that the denomination has found a way to minister to the city.

---

[51] *The Ninety-Fourth Annual Session of the Oklahoma State Association of Free Will Baptists* (14–17 October 2002) 15.

Second, a lack of focus on the training of ministers has tended to limit the denomination's ministry to blue-collar workers and the lower classes. But, here again, change is evident. As the shift from rural to urban has continued to accelerate, pastors find their congregations peopled by professionals from every discipline, and the new mix demands a well-prepared clergy. In response, the denomination now boasts four colleges—Free Will Baptist Bible College (Nashville), Hillsdale Free Will Baptist College (Oklahoma), California Christian College, and Southeastern Free Will Baptist College (North Carolina)—as well as seminaries in Mexico and Oklahoma; reports a growing number of advanced degrees among the clergy; and finds numbers of young men and women applying to institutions of higher learning in search of graduate degrees. A Higher Education Task Force was appointed by the national association in 1999 and given the task of preparing a "long range, comprehensive plan for Christian education among Free Will Baptists."[52]

Finally, a rigidly conservative theology and lifestyle has made the denomination less than attractive to a postmodern world. Here, however, little change has occurred and little should be expected. The twenty-first-century Free Will Baptist could still be described as having a conservative Arminian theology, a focus on holy living, and a tendency toward separation from a world that denies the existence of objective truth. Even so, however, the denomination attempts, short of compromise, to reach the changing culture in which it ministers.

Free Will Baptists have consistently supported and encouraged both home and foreign mission programs since the birth of the national association in 1935. From three missionaries and a monthly budget of $300.00 in that first year, the Board of Foreign Missions now oversees a

---

[52] "Resolutions to the National Association of Free Will Baptists: Georgia and Arkansas," presented to the General Board by the Arkansas and Georgia delegations, approved and presented to the national association as item 3 of the General Board Report, 21 July 1999. (Unpublished copy of the 1999 National Association minutes faxed to William F. Davidson from the Office of the Executive Secretary, 20 January 2000, p. 3.)

budget of $5,933,090.83 and the ministry of 97 missionaries in 14 countries.[53] In 2002, the Board of Home Missions reported the commissioning of 8 new missionary couples, the graduation of 6 mission projects to full church status, military chaplain ministries in 6 countries (oversight of the chaplaincy resides in the Home Mission Department), and gift income of $4,181,871.89.[54]

Free Will Baptist Bible College in Nashville announced a 5-percent growth in student enrollment in 2003, following a 13-percent increase the year before. Hillsdale Free Will Baptist College in Oklahoma introduced a new graduate degree program in 2003, and the first cohort of students has already begun their studies. At the moment, this constitutes the only graduate-level curriculum for the denomination, but it expresses the movement's concern for expanded training for pastors, for missionaries, and for potential denominational leaders. The Higher Educational Task Force continues its attempts to draft a long-range planning instrument that will serve as a guide for the denomination as it continues its efforts to meet the educational needs of its people.

The new millennium began with clear evidence of a changing of the guard. An entire generation of leadership was giving way to a new and younger phalanx of national leaders, college presidents and professors, and major board directors. Keith Burden, executive secretary for the denomination; Matthew Pinson, president of Free Will Baptist Bible College; and James Forlines, general director of the Board of Foreign Missions, represent a new and youthful leadership for the denomination, and expectations are high as their vision for the future is implemented over the next few years. Jack Williams, editor of *Contact*, the official publication for the denomination, has expressed well the confidence with which Free Will Baptists face the future.

---

[53] "Foreign Missions," in *Digest of Reports: National Association of Free Will Baptists, 67th Annual Convention, July 20–24, 2003*, 45–70. The report lists statistics for the year 2002; *The 2004 Free Will Baptist Yearbook*, A-10.

[54] "Home Missions," in *Digest of Reports*, 113.

> The twenty-first century holds the brightest promise for Free Will Baptists since the days of Paul Palmer and Benjamin Randall.... New mission fields are opening in Korea, China, Russia and all over Asia. Doors closed to the gospel during the twentieth century are swinging open.
>
> New leadership is taking hold at local, state and national levels.... Who are these new leaders? God bless them—they're our children!
>
> They sat in our Sunday schools, watched us conduct the Lord's business in our meetings and graduated from our colleges. They set their sails by the sure compass of the Almighty.
>
> Look around. They're everywhere. They're in their 20s and 30s, some in their 40s and 50s. They're ready to take the reins of responsibility. They believe they can pay the bills and build a better future. Their motive is holy, their faith strong, their vision contagious.
>
> ...I can hardly wait to see what God does through Free Will Baptists as new hands touch the helm in the twenty-first century.[55]

The National Association of Free Will Baptists can trace its heritage back at least to 1727 and Paul Palmer's church-planting ministry in eastern North Carolina and probably beyond that to the General Baptists in England at the beginning of the seventeenth century. Descendants of this heritage later joined with the remnant of Benjamin Randall's New England Freewill Baptists and the offspring of the Arminian Separate Baptists in Tennessee to form a national union in 1935. The movement has grown now to embrace a total of 294,237 members in 2,458 churches,[56] to support 97 foreign missionaries in 14 countries, to publish its own literature through Randall House Publications, and to oversee 4 colleges. *The Free Will Baptists in History*, a recent text chronicling the denomination's unique history, closes with this analysis:

---

[55] Jack Williams, "What a Century!" in "Briefcase," *Contact* (February 2000).

[56] "The Executive Secretary's Report, 2002," in *Digest of Reports*, 4; *2004 Yearbook*, A-227.

In many ways—basic theology, commitment to separation, mission concern—the denomination has remained the same. But in others, it has seen significant change. Of those changes, the most evident and noteworthy is the evolution from a purely rural character to a more flexible nature that has allowed ministry to a broader spectrum of the society. Beginning with innovative mission strategies, specifically in South America, the denomination found itself capable of reaching the cities and of ministering vertically across social barriers. ...it is too early to determine the degree of impact this change will have on the denomination, but it does, without question, offer the most promising potential for growth that the denomination has known in its long history.[57]

[57] Davidson, *Free Will Baptists*, 354–55.

Chapter 7

THE PRIMITIVE OR OLD SCHOOL BAPTISTS

John G. Crowley

The Primitive or Old School Baptists are known in the United States by a variety of frequently derogatory nicknames: Hardshells, Footwashing Baptists, Old Baptists, Anti-Missionary Baptists, Anti-Effort Baptists, Mossybacks, Broadbrims, Ironjackets, Hardsided Baptists, etc. As is the case with most epithets of this nature, the Primitives sometimes use them but resent their use by outsiders. Primitive Baptists, Old Baptists, and Old School Baptists are the most widely accepted and generally approved titles for their order, with primitive being used in the sense of original.

One cognomen nearly all present-day American Old Baptists disavow is Calvinist or Hyper-Calvinist, although formerly they would use the term "Calvinistic" to describe their doctrine.[1] While they mostly agree with the early Calvinists on the desirability of eliminating all "popish dregs" from worship, and they preach the five points with a consistency that would have made Calvin himself blink, they disagree with the Genevan reformer on many issues both doctrinal and practical. Unlike Calvin, Primitive Baptists oppose all union of church and state, infant baptism, baptism by aspersion, ecclesiastical hierarchy, and the necessity of a formally trained, professional ministry. Doctrinally, they differ from most professed Calvinists in denying the so-called free offer of the gospel and the belief that the preaching of the gospel is

[1] William McElvey to *Primitive Baptist*, 15 June 1839.

instrumental in regeneration.[2] They also feel that a title such as "Calvinist" implies that they follow Calvin rather than the Apostles. Ironically, they heap such founder-derived titles on other denominations and factions of their own order with which they disagree: Jackite, Crawfordite, Bennettite, Battleite, Coonite, etc.[3] I use the term "Calvinist" solely as a convenient title for one who believes in the five points.

Most Primitive Baptists, like the Landmarker Baptists, believe in a literal Baptist "apostolic succession" from the beginnings of Christianity, considering the Waldensians and other such groups to have been of their belief and practice.[4] However, the Primitive Baptists as a distinctive group emerged in the second and third decades of the nineteenth century. Their parent body was the Regular Baptist denomination, which emerged from the union of the Separate and Regular Baptists in 1787–1801. From the Regulars they derived a fierce adherence to the "Abstract of Principles" derived from the Philadelphia Confession and to its attendant high view of predestination. While few American Baptists of that period completely denied the doctrine of the "free offer of the gospel," their perpetual conflicts with the rising Methodists made them take ever higher ground in regard to predestination. English Baptists and allied traditions also played a role in heightening predestinarian emphasis. The writings of such staunch British predestinarians as John Gill and William Huntington circulated among the Regular Baptists. From the Regular tradition also came strong associations of churches, modeled on the Philadelphia and Charleston associations, and strict discipline both in churches toward individual members and in associations toward churches.[5]

---

[2] Cushing Biggs and Sylvester Hassell, *History of the Church of God, from the Creation to A.D. 1885; Including Especially the History of the Kehukee Primitive Baptist Association* (Middletown NY: Gilbert Beebe's Sons, 1886) 269–356.

[3] John Crowley, *Primitive Baptists of the Wiregrass South: 1815 to the Present* (Gainesville: University of Florida Press, 1998) 118.

[4] Suwannee River Baptist Association, minutes, 1838.

[5] Crowley, *Primitive Baptists*, 1–5.

From the Separate tradition, steeped in the more radical phases of the Great Awakening, came an emphasis on simplicity of dress, worship, and meetinghouse design, together with reliance on unlearned, bi-vocational preachers who often sang or chanted their extemporaneous sermons and prayers in a manner believed to result from direct divine inspiration. Also prominent in their worship was a powerful congregational musical tradition based on the slow, unaccompanied "lined out" singing of the hymns of Isaac Watts and others.[6]

In the first decades of the nineteenth century, the Great Revival spread from the Kentucky frontier across the nation, resulting in vast ingatherings into the Baptist churches as well as others. It also generated a mania for reform and improvement that soon collided head on with the Calvinistic pessimism and suspicion of moneyed hierarchical institutions that was endemic among the Baptists. The conversion of Adoniram Judson and Luther Rice, and the subsequent drive to organize missionary societies and state and national conventions to coordinate them, tapped into both these growing energies and resulted in major schisms among the Baptists in many areas. The English Baptists fragmented about the same time over similar issues, resulting in the formation of the Gospel Standard Strict Baptists and related groups. A small Covenanted Baptist Church appeared in Canada, impelled by similar forces.[7] Doctrine played a more prominent role in England and the Northeastern United States, and practice was the rallying point of the opposed parties in the Southern and Western states.

Practically all American Baptists were initially enthusiastic over missions. But five years after the conversion of Judson and Rice in 1812, some Baptist associations were demonstrating reserve toward missions, which soon hardened to active hostility. In 1819, the Hephzibah and Piedmont associations in eastern Georgia decided to "have nothing to do with missions," and in 1823, the minister who invited Hephzibah to join the fledgling Georgia Baptist Convention narrowly escaped physical

---

[6] Ibid., 5–12.

[7] Ibid., 16–17; Hassell and Hassell, *History of the Church of God*, 616–20, 880–85.

assault.[8] In 1827, the Kehukee Association in North Carolina, the fourth oldest Baptist association in the United States, declared a complete non-fellowship with missions and related enterprises. Joshua Lawrence expressed its members' views in the *Declaration of the Reformed Baptists of North Carolina*, an indictment of the entire "benevolent empire" and one that circulated widely in the South.[9] In 1832, churches of the Baltimore Association held a convention at Black Rock Church in Maryland and drafted the Black Rock Address, still regarded by most Primitive Baptists as one of the best expressions of their stand on the issues then in question. The Black Rock meeting received a warm endorsement from the aging John Leland in Massachusetts, a Baptist hero of the Great Awakening in Virginia and as opposed to modern Baptist money-based organizations as he had been to the Anglican establishment in colonial Virginia. It also endorsed Gilbert Beebe's *Signs of the Times*, a periodical that commenced the same year and was dedicated from its inception to "the absolute predestination of all things" and "waging war with Arminianism the mother and her whole brood of institutions."[10] Three years later, *The Primitive Baptist* commenced publication in Tarboro, North Carolina, under the auspices of Joshua Lawrence and the Kehukee Association. More popular in the South than *Signs*, this periodical bore on its masthead the call "Come ye out from among them." These two periodicals threw into high relief the issues dividing liberal and conservative Baptists, and the *Primitive Baptist* especially was credited in many areas with leading to open schism.[11]

Almost all associations lined up on one side or the other by 1845. In that year, the "Missionaries" organized the Southern Baptist Convention in Augusta, Georgia, an institution anathema to the Old School. Also in

---

[8] Crowley, *Primitive Baptists*, 57; Hephzibah Baptist Association, minutes, 1819; Piedmont Baptist Association, minutes, 1819; W. L. Kilpatrick, *Hephzibah Baptist Centennial 1794–1894* (Augusta GA: Richards and Shaver, 1894) 43.

[9] Joshua Lawrence, "Declaration of the Reformed Baptist Churches in the State of North Carolina" [1827], *Primitive Baptist* 7 (14 May 1842): 129–31.

[10] *Signs of the Times* 1 (28 November 1832).

[11] Crowley, *Primitive Baptists*, 75–76.

1845, the Primitive Baptists in Georgia and other areas adopted their version of *Apostolicae Curae* declaring the baptisms and other "official work" of the missions party to be utterly null and absolutely void.[12] By the early 1800s, many Baptists in the South had adopted the idea of church successionism, that there had been a continuous, unbroken succession of Baptist churches, ordinations, and baptisms from the days of John the Baptist until the present.[13] This view became all but universal among the Primitive Baptists, and it fueled their disdain for other denominations. Unlike the Roman Catholic version of the apostolic succession, however, among the Primitive Baptists heresy or even disciplinary laxity resulted in the invalidation of any official work conferred after the commencement of the disorder. The remainder of the nineteenth century saw a few defections back and forth, but essentially the division and its issues were set in stone by 1850.

Some Baptists reacted strongly against the benevolent movements for a number of reasons. In America, the most frequently expressed concern was that missionary societies, Sunday schools, theological seminaries, and the like were not part of the life of the early church as described in the New Testament. The major Baptist distinctive was their repudiation of infant baptism and baptism by aspersion because these were unscriptural, purely traditionary practices. Thus Baptists were sensitive on the issue of direct biblical authority for practices as well as doctrine. The renowned Primitive Baptist preacher Wilson Thompson is a case in point. As a young minister he met Isaac McCoy and was inspired to join him in his work among Native Americans. However, after a doubt assailed him as to the scriptural propriety of moneyed, hierarchical mission societies, a study of the Bible on the subject

---

[12] Ochlocknee Primitive Baptist Association, minutes, 1844; Alabaha River Primitive Baptist Association, minutes, 1845; Suwannee River Primitive Baptist Association, minutes, 1845.

[13] Suwannee River Baptist Association, minutes, 1838.

convinced him that modern missions were unscriptural, and he became one of their staunchest opponents in Missouri and the Ohio Valley.[14]

Along with fears of departure from scriptural norms, many Baptists feared the concentration of money and power in large religious conventions and societies. This concern was common in the Jeffersonian political and social philosophy of the day. Many Primitive Baptists suspected the missions party of trying to lay the groundwork for an established church and religious taxation.[15] Old School Baptists even opposed as an establishment of religion the hiring of chaplains for Congress and the armed services.[16] They especially detested emphasis on money both because of the biblical admonitions against the love of it and because they had so little to give in many cases and were made to feel inferior on that account. Missions money also went in many cases to supercilious young college and seminary graduates who made a poor job of hiding their contempt for the rough, unlettered, and highly Calvinistic frontier Baptists. In the frontier areas in particular, seminaries seemed likely to produce a breed of idle, privileged parsons, demanding elaborate dwellings and salaries and too much like the colonial Anglican priesthood.[17]

In a society where whiskey was as much medicine as beverage and both its manufacture and retail were frequently in the hands of ministers and churchmen, the marriage of the temperance movement to the missions cause further alienated many rural and frontier Baptists. Although Baptist churches disciplined members guilty of drunkenness,

---

[14] Wilson Thompson, *The Autobiography of Elder Wilson Thompson, His Life, Travels, and Ministerial Labors* (Conley GA: Old School Hymnal Co., 1978; reprint of 1867 ed.) 198–205.

[15] Bertram Wyatt-Brown, "The Antimissionary Movement in the Jacksonian South: A Study in Southern Folk Religion," *Journal of Southern History* 36 (November 1970): 501–29.

[16] Hassell and Hassell, *Church of God*, 787–91.

[17] Joshua Lawrence, "Declaration of the Reformed Baptist Churches in the State of North Carolina [1827]," *Primitive Baptist* 7 (14 May 1842): 130.

they regarded it as venial sin in most cases.[18] The redoubtable Isham Peacock, a native of North Carolina and the first Baptist evangelist to preach in Florida, so despised temperance societies that he would not preach in a church that harbored a member who had taken the pledge. When he was nearly 100 years old, he would drink from a hollow cane full of whiskey in front of his congregations, both to recruit his flagging energy and also to demonstrate the bounds of Christian liberty in regard to the "creature."[19] The Old School condemned early prohibition drives as the entering wedge for more legislation on religious and moral issues, culminating in an established church.[20]

Doctrinal issues played a major role in the establishment of the Primitive Baptists. An inevitable tension exists in most theological systems between the sovereignty of God and the freedom, or at least responsibility, of humankind. In the eighteenth century, many leading English Baptists and others, such as John Gill, denied the "free offer" of the gospel—that is, that the benefits of the atonement should be offered indiscriminately to all hearers—as a denial of the doctrine of particular redemption, that Christ died for the elect only. They also condemned the belief that every rational human being had a duty to exercise saving faith and repentance since it implied that the will of fallen man was not totally depraved and was capable of good.[21] Few American Baptist preachers held such high ground on predestination. John Leland spoke for most of them when he proclaimed that the most effective preaching was that which mixed the doctrine of sovereignty with a little tincture of

---

[18] J. H. Campbell, *Georgia Baptists: Historical and Biographical* (Richmond: H. K. Ellyson, 1847) 242; Union Primitive Baptist Church, minutes, October & December 1835, January 1836, March & December 1838, June 1839, May 1841, April 1842.

[19] *History of the Baptist Denomination in Georgia, Christian Index* (Atlanta: James P. Harrison and Company, 1881) 166.

[20] Prior Lewis to *Primitive Baptist*, 29 December 1839.

[21] John Gill, *A Body of Doctrinal and Practical Divinity; or, A System of Practical Truths Deduced from the Sacred Scriptures* (London: Button and Son, and Whittingham and Arliss, 1815; reprint, Streamwood IL: Primitive Baptist Library, 1977; originally pub. 1771).

Arminianism.[22] However, the English high Calvinists, like John Gill, were respected by American Baptists, and as conflicts with the rising Methodists increased, some of them began to take ever higher ground on the doctrine of the divine decrees, such as Jeptha Vining of South Carolina and Georgia who dwelt almost exclusively on election in his sermons, although he was a most successful evangelist.[23]

Andrew Fuller, a young English Baptist, published in 1785 a seminal work titled *The Gospel Worthy of All Acceptation*, in which he challenged the high Calvinist opposition to free offers and reinterpreted the Calvinist doctrine of the atonement in a more indefinite direction. Fuller and his friend William Carey were also instrumental in launching the missionary movement among English Baptists.[24]

The arrival of these new doctrines, bringing with them a train of new practices and institutions, provoked the conservatives to separation in both England and America at about the same time.[25] Although stated here in a few words, it is difficult to conceive of the bitterness and acrimony that attended these divisions in both England and America. Only present-day conflicts within churches over biblical inerrancy, abortion, and gay rights give any conception of the ferocity of the dispute that was carried on with not only the greatest verbal and printed acrimony but also not infrequently with fistfights in the churchyards.[26]

---

[22] John Leland, "A Letter of Valediction, on Leaving Virginia, in 1791," in L. F. Greene, ed., *The Writings of Elder John Leland, Including Some Events in His Life, Written by Himself, With Additional Sketches* (Religion in America, ed. Edwin S. Gaustad [New York: G.W. Wood, 1845; reprint, New York: Arno Press and the New York Times, 1969] 172).

[23] Gill, *Body of Doctrinal and Practical Divinity*, 387–88; Hassell and Hassell, *Church of God*, 569–70; Jesse Mercer, *History of the Georgia Baptist Association, Compiled at the Request of that Body*, With an Introduction by Waldo P. Harris, and Appendix "Early Baptist Churches in Georgia," by Robert G. Gardner, and an Index by Anne F. Gardner and Robert F. Gardner, (Washington GA: n.p., 1838; reprint, Washington GA: Georgia Baptist Association Executive Committee, 1970) 385–86.

[24] Hassell and Hassell, *Church of God*, 337–41.

[25] Ibid., 356, 616–18.

[26] The late Judge Folks Huxford of Homerville, Georgia, FASG and the foremost historian and genealogist of southern Georgia, informed me that many of

With no centralization above associations and occasional councils, periodicals played a large role in Primitive Baptist history. As discussed earlier, the first such paper was the *Signs of the Times*, edited for its first fifty years by Gilbert Beebe, a native of Connecticut and later a resident of Virginia and New York. *Signs* circulated widely throughout the United States. As with all Primitive Baptist periodicals, the decided views of its editors coupled with their editorial policy of providing a forum for debate on many issues both united the denomination and perpetuated several ongoing internal controversies.

The *Primitive Baptist*, published in North Carolina from 1835 until 1879, led the way in calling for total separation between the advocates of missions, and the periodical also seems to have provided the title for the denomination in most of North America. The *Primitive Baptist* ceased publication in 1879 and is not to be confused with an influential periodical of the same name started several years later. Subsequently, other periodicals exerted great influence, particularly in hands of able editors. The *Pilgrim's Banner*, initially edited by Allen V. Simms and later by William H. Crouse as the *Banner-Herald*, became the organ of the Progressive Primitive Baptists.[27] Another periodical that gave its name to a faction of Primitive Baptists was the *Trumpet of Truth*, whose supporters became known as the trumpet Baptists. Winiford J. Berry exerted tremendous influence during the twentieth century through the *Old Faith Contender*, possibly the best religious periodical ever published by a Primitive Baptist and one of the few to enjoy a significant readership throughout the denomination and beyond its borders.[28] Periodicals still play an important role among some Primitive Baptists, as witnessed by the wide circulation of the *Remnant*, edited by elders James Poole and C. C. Morris in the interest of the Absolute Predestinarian Primitive Baptists. However, many Primitive Baptists have exhibited

---

the children of the pioneers insisted the missions controversy in south Georgia was frequently carried on by means of fists.

[27] Crowley, *Primitive Baptists*, 75–76, 134–35.

[28] As a teenager and a young man, I subscribed to the *Contender* and regarded it as one of the few Old Baptist publications worth reading.

suspicion of periodicals devoted to their cause as something outside the New Testament pattern, or at least a thing superfluous. A prominent preacher in Georgia, O. J. Rives, once remarked that he had a Bible as well as the writers in a popular periodical and preferred to get his doctrine from that source.[29] A suspicion of non-biblical reading is certainly evident among many Primitive Baptists. Elder Lamar Carter of Georgia once threw away an expensive copy of Sylvester and Cushing Biggs Hassell's *History of the Church of God*, a massive history of the Primitive Baptists, because he found it both confusing and taking time away from his study of Scripture.[30] Believing that the natural mind is unable to comprehend divine truth unaided, some Primitive Baptists even look askance at systematic reading of the Bible. As one elderly minister remarked, "As long as that Bible will leave me alone, I leave it alone."[31] Elder Mahue Young once remarked to me that he had never read the entire Bible from cover to cover, during a ministry of several decades.

After the division from the Missionary Baptists, the Primitives underwent a long series of schisms, sometimes over doctrinal issues, more frequently over practice, and quite frequently over disciplinary issues. As a result, by 1970, there were more than a dozen subvarieties of Primitive Baptists in the lower half of the state of Georgia alone.[32]

The earlier disputes tended to be over doctrinal issues. Although all Primitive Baptists took high ground on predestination, some of them took positions during the missions controversy that even some other

---

[29] As related to me by his wife, Nora Waters Rives.

[30] As related to me by Elder W. Lamar Carter.

[31] A remark made to me by Elder Robert Register, then the moderator of the Original Union Primitive Baptist Association in Georgia.

[32] When I was twenty years old (1975), between the Atlantic Ocean and the Chattahoochee River there were Progressive Primitive Baptists, Absolute Predestinarian Primitive Baptists, three factions of Crawfordites, the African American Old Line Primitive Baptists, the "Peace Move" PBs, the independent PBs, the 'Shepherdites," the "Jackites," the "Josh Davis Side," the "Charley Vickers Folks," the "Nell Purvis Side," and a scattering of Progressive African American PBs. For the most part, none of them would have anything to do with the others.

Primitive Baptists regarded as extreme. Most Primitive Baptists eventually denied that the preaching of the gospel is instrumental in regeneration or that the unregenerate are in any sense the subjects of gospel address.[33] Several groups in different parts of the United States did not agree with this position. Prior to the Civil War, Primitive Baptists in Ohio and South Georgia and Florida withdrew from communion with the rest of the denomination because they maintained the older position that preaching was instrumental in the salvation of the elect and that sinners in general at least ought to be warned of their perilous state, leaving the results of the warning in the hands of God. The latter nineteenth century saw a fresh series of controversies and divisions over this issue.[34]

The Two Seed controversy was a more widespread doctrinal dispute that led to the formation of an entirely separate denomination. Daniel Parker of Illinois, a fervent and early opponent of missions, developed a Manichean interpretation of election in response to his critics, although he claimed that he did not originate the doctrine. The most developed form of Two Seedism held that Satan was an eternal, self-existent being, that the souls of the elect were literally emanations from the being of God, and that the souls of the wicked were emanations from the being of Satan himself. Thus, in effect, God did not create the entire human race, or at least not every human soul, and the damnation of the wicked was even more certain than in traditional Calvinism. Since the souls of the elect and the reprobates were emanations from the actual substance of two eternal beings, souls were seen as preexistent and eternal, hence another name, "eternal children," that was sometimes applied to the doctrine.[35] Although Parker himself never went so far, some of his followers adopted a belief common in Alabama and other areas that the physical body of Christ had nothing human about it and came down from heaven into the Virgin Mary. The bodies of all others

---

[33] Hassell and Hassell, *Church of God*, 337, 633–34.

[34] Thompson, *Autobiography*, 325–27; Alabaha River Primitive Baptist Association, minutes, 1860, 1862, [Crawford Faction], 1884.

[35] Hassell and Hassell, *Church of God*, 636.

were not subject to redemption or resurrection. Eventually, this wing of the Two Seed movement developed a belief that the souls of the elect and the wicked lacked personal identity, so that at death it was Christ only who returned to heaven and Satan only who returned to hell, hence earning them the title "No-Hell" Baptists in some areas. Controversy and division flared up over this complex of beliefs in many areas between the 1840s and 1870s, usually resulting in the formation of separate Two Seed Baptist churches and associations, although the Two Seeders seldom called themselves by this name and frequently retained the title Predestinarian or Primitive Baptist, making it difficult to distinguish them in surviving records from the orthodox Primitive Baptists. Although most Primitive Baptists repudiated the dualism of classical Two Seedism, the non-resurrection, no-hell aspects of the doctrine found lodging in many Primitive Baptist groups, usually in areas where some phase of Two Seedism existed. As a young man, I still occasionally heard the ancient Two Seed *shadada* whispered: "Nothing is going to heaven but what first came down from there." Both giving rise to and supporting these ideas was a highly allegorical reading of Scripture that, eventually in the case of some, reached a point where almost nothing in the Bible was taken in its literal sense and a divine guidance was assumed necessary to understand anything in Scripture. Among the Two Seeders especially, their ministers were regarded as divinely inspired, and some of their views practically constituted a supplemental revelation. This view of inspired interpretation has found a good deal of support among Primitive Baptists, though it reached its apotheosis in the Two Seed movement.[36]

A bitter dispute raged during the middle of the nineteenth century over Trinitarian doctrine. With their naturally argumentative nature, leading Primitive Baptist spokesmen could not resist venturing into the Great Serbonian Bog of the relationship of the three persons of the Trinity. While some put forward views that approached Arianism and others veered toward Sabellianism, it is doubtful that any of those

[36] Crowley, *Primitive Baptists*, 118–33.

concerned actually departed far from orthodoxy. However, they waged fierce war in the columns of the denominational periodicals, and some actual divisions took place over these matters.[37]

The Civil War illustrates as nothing else the detachment of the Primitive Baptists from the world around them. Primitive Baptists both North and South usually found no fault with slavery and some, though not many, Southern Primitives owned slaves. Since the Bible did not forbid slavery, neither would they. Curiously, they were willing in some cases to apply their extremely non-literal hermeneutic to doctrinal issues, but they quickly returned to an extreme literalism on social issues. To a remarkable extent, the Primitive Baptists tried to ignore the looming conflict between the free and slave states and only took positions as the war actually erupted. Even then, references to the war among Southern Primitive Baptists are extremely rare. Northern Primitive Baptists were usually democrats and Confederate sympathizers, but they also tried to remain above the elements of this world as much as possible. Except for the interruption of travel during the war, there was no significant division between the Primitives North and South as there was among several other denominations.[38]

After the war, relatively little changed in the denomination. Southern Primitive churches had had relatively few black members. In areas where they were sufficiently numerous, black Primitive Baptists organized churches and associations of their own in the 1860s, although blacks continued to join predominately white Primitive Baptist churches for the remainder of the nineteenth century, and visitation by blacks continued well into the mid-1900s. Although white and black churches and associations had little or no official dealings with one another, black Primitive Baptists were generally as conservative as their white counterparts, with no differences in doctrine and little in practice, save that their singing is in a more traditional African American style. In

---

[37] Hassell and Hassell, *Church of God*, 633, 636–37.

[38] Ibid., 800; Crowley, *Primitive Baptists*, 86–98; Julietta Haynes, *A History of the Primitive Baptists* (Ph.D. diss., University of Texas, 1959; reprint, Ann Arbor: University Microfilms International, 1989) 157–65.

Florida, a progressive black Primitive Baptist movement arose during Reconstruction, in which it appears that numerous freedmen adopted the title Primitive Baptist mainly to distance themselves from the denomination of their former masters, most of whom were Missionary Baptists.[39] At that time and subsequently, racial attitudes of white Primitive Baptists were usually indistinguishable from the Southern generality, that is to say, ranging from indifference at best to a racist "gall of bitterness and bond of iniquity" probably inconsistent with the presence of sanctifying grace in the soul. I once asked a venerable Primitive Baptist deacon how his denomination compared with others in the white South in regard to treatment of blacks. After sinking the chin of reflection upon the breast of doubt for a moment, he weakly replied, "Pretty well."[40] To their credit, it should be remembered that while one popular preacher in Middle Georgia argued that blacks had no souls, two deacons at a South Georgia church banned him from their pulpit.[41]

The Reconstruction era saw several more controversies erupt among Primitive Baptists, together with a decline in membership and standards in some places. Georgia Primitives were rent with a bitter controversy over whether church members should take advantage of the new homestead law, which allowed debtors to declare bankruptcy and secure part of their estate from their creditors. Divisions resulting from this controversy are perpetuated to this day in some areas. The Crawfordite Primitive Baptists of Georgia, perhaps the most conservative of all the denomination, who had earlier ceased communion with most other Primitives over the denial of the role of the gospel in salvation, now had their final rupture with the rest of the denomination over this issue.[42]

---

[39] Crowley, *Primitive Baptists*, 99–104.

[40] Deacon L. B. Bennett of Adel, Georgia, told me this in the late 1980s.

[41] Deacon Tommy Driggers of Zion's Rest Church, Waycross, Georgia, related this to me. He and Deacon Stonewall J. Raulerson were the deacons involved in the incident.

[42] Crowley, *Primitive Baptists*, 106–10.

Also in the 1870s, controversy arose in Georgia and Florida over the reception of members from the Missionary Baptists without rebaptism. The majority of the churches were totally opposed to this practice, holding that the reception of Missionary baptism would imply endorsement of that group's doctrines and practices.[43]

The Progressive Era saw a new range of conflicts and divisions. Primitive Baptist churches in some areas began to grow at a rate phenomenal for them. With increased growth, and increased competition from Methodists and Missionary Baptists in rural areas, some Primitive Baptists began to advocate a series of new practices that they hoped would close the increasing gap between them and their competitors. While in most cases the so-called "Progressives" remained true to Primitive Baptist doctrine, their practical departures from the tradition provoked widespread opposition and resulted in the formation of separate Progressive Primitive Baptist organizations.

Initially, the reform program called for a greater degree of financial support of the ministry and the curtailing of inter-church and inter-associational correspondence, a practice they thought often led to the erection of bars to fellowship whenever correspondence was dropped for some cause or another. The more radical Progressives wished to abolish associations totally, since Primitive Baptist associations tended to adopt a degree of oversight of their constituent churches which some felt gravely compromised their sovereignty. After actual schism with the "Old Line" began around 1900, the Progressives added musical instruments in worship and much later Sunday schools and Bible studies to their program.[44]

---

[43] Hassell and Hassell, *Church of God*, 894; Beulah Primitive Baptist Association, minutes, 1874; T. W. Stallings, Lowndes Co. GA, to W. M. Mitchell, Opelika AL, 1 January 1876, in "Voices of the Past," *Signs of the Times* 146 (July 1978): 161–65.

[44] I. J. Taylor to Lee Hanks, *Pilgrim's Banner* 4 (1 September 1897): 7–12; "Basis of Agreement," Ibid. (1 January 1898): 1–2; Ochlocknee Primitive Baptist Association [Simms-Barwick Faction], minutes, 1899; Valdosta [GA] Primitive Baptist Church, minutes (manuscript in possession of the church) 1900, October 1901, February 1906, July 1907.

The "organ" became the rallying cry of the conservative party and the symbol of progressivism. Like their Baptist forbears, most Primitive Baptists had never even considered the use of musical instruments in their worship. In a story told so often and set in so many different places it almost surely never happened anywhere, a conservative church member called upon to pronounce the benediction in the first service using an organ growled, "Let the machinery do it. If it can sing to God, let it pray to him as well." By 1910, the Progressive Primitive Baptists were essentially a separate subdenomination, and their practices in worship and organization became more like those of conservative Southern Baptists. Doctrinally, they usually remained essentially the same as the Old Line.

Coeval with the Progressive controversy, and helping to fuel it in some places, came a dispute over the extent of predestination and a new doctrine called conditional time salvation. Although belief that the elect and they alone are absolutely predestined to salvation is a principal distinguishing mark of a Primitive Baptist, some of them had long expressed discomfort over the expression "the absolute predestination of all things," which had figured in the prospectus of the *Signs of the Times*. Some Primitives felt that this expression logically made God the author of sin. Beginning in Texas in the 1880s, actual divisions began to occur over the extent of the divine predestination, with some arguing that predestination applied to the salvation of the elect but not to all things without exception.[45]

The conditional time salvation doctrine seems to have appeared almost simultaneously in several places, and it quickly spread through the medium of periodicals and traveling preachers. "Conditionalists" held that the salvation of the elect and the time of their regeneration were entirely in God's hands and were predestined. However, between regeneration and death, believers might earn or lose a "time salvation," consisting of a quiet conscience and the joys attendant on obedience to the divine commands. This also gave preachers a platform from which to

[45] Crowley, *Primitive Baptists*, 135–36.

exhort those they supposed to show some sign of regeneration to join the church and to remain active after doing so. In scriptural interpretation, Conditionalists classified every reference to salvation as either being "in time" or "in eternity." This doctrine eventually played much the same role among the Primitive Baptists that the shallow and formal "acceptance of Christ" played among the Southern Baptists. Eternal salvation was taken for granted in most instances, and the disobedient no longer manifested reprobation but were reclassified as "disobedient children of God." Preachers were now able to preach Saul, Judas, and equally unlikely characters into heaven as having missed the "joys of their salvation" and not eternal salvation itself. This gave rise during the twentieth century to a creeping universalism in which the sting of Calvinism was drawn by supposing that the great majority of the human race would be saved.[46] In some parts of Appalachia, this tendency went even further into full-blown universalism, with every human soul saved in eternity but not all enjoying timely salvation in this life.[47] In one extreme example of Conditionalist exegesis, I once heard an earnest old sister of that way critique a funeral sermon by saying the preacher had put the "many mansions" of John 14:2 in the wrong place. Since Christ had said "there ye *may be* also," the promise was conditional and therefore the mansions referred to a home in the churches in time.[48] By about 1930, most Old Line Primitive Baptists were either firmly in the absolute predestinarian, "Absoluter," or conditional time salvation, "Conditionalist," camps. The Absoluters tended to have their greatest strength in the Northern states, and their ministers had more literary talent as well as being closer to traditional Calvinist orthodoxy.

---

[46] I have heard all these positions advocated *ad nauseam* and have heard several Primitive Baptist ministers try to save Judas in the pulpit.

[47] See Howard Dorgan, *In the Hands of a Happy God: The "No-Hellers" of Central Appalachia* (Knoxville: University of Tennessee Press, 1997). All of Dorgan's books on the "Old Baptist" traditions are highly recommended.

[48] Related to me by the Primitive Baptist in question after a funeral at Sharon Primitive Baptist Church, Greenville, Florida.

One more great upheaval in the twentieth century was the Towaliga controversy. In the 1860s, the Towaliga Primitive Baptist Association in Georgia had been dropped from fellowship by other Primitive Baptists for receiving Missionary Baptists without rebaptism and for retaining in fellowship members who belonged to "secret orders," especially the Masons. In the 1930s, a movement emerged to reintegrate the Towaliga association into the mainstream of Primitive Baptist life, resulting in a spectacular upheaval. Related to the Towaliga controversy was increasing discomfort among Southern Primitive Baptists with Northern brethren who did not wash feet as part of their Communion service. During the 1930s, numerous associations in the Southeast set up bars of fellowship against the Towaliga association and its supporters and also against the practice of so-called "optional foot-washing." While the foot-washing issue has at last subsided somewhat, the "secret orders" issue is still a hot-button topic among many Primitives, although most have adopted a "don't ask, don't tell" policy in regard to fraternal orders such as the Masons.[49]

The divisive tendency of Calvinists, mocked as early as Butler's *Hudibras*, remains a prominent feature of the Primitive Baptist tradition, causing ever shifting realignments of fellowship among churches, associations, and individuals. The Towaliga controversy was the last major "split" to be based on a general principle. Recently, however, the Internet has provided a route for almost every ancient dispute to be resurrected for fresh debate.[50]

Progressive Primitive Baptists, both African American and white, so resemble other denominations in their worship that there is little point in describing them. The Statesboro, Georgia, Primitive Baptist Church is a vast Greek revival edifice, complete with stained glass and spire. It has a robed choir, organ, etc., and the only observable difference from a Southern Baptist church is that what emanates from the pulpit is not

---

[49] Crowley, *Primitive Baptists*, 152–67, 175–76.

[50] There are now several Primitive Baptist message boards, where zealous young ministers and brethren seek to rehash ancient controversies that once left whole fellowships in ruin.

what one Primitive charitably referred to as "Arminian free-will goat fodder."[51]

Among Old Line Primitive Baptists, the setting of worship is often distinctive. Most of their churches, still often called meetinghouses, are largely in rural settings of often great natural beauty, though seldom landscaped. The buildings are plain and functional, seldom with even tinted windows, and virtually never with a spire or steeple unless acquired from another denomination. Since many congregations are small and elderly, it is not unusual for the buildings to be somewhat dilapidated. During the course of the last century, Primitives slowly began to paint, ceil, and install glass windows in their churches, along with wood-burning heaters and later space heaters, indoor plumbing, and finally air conditioning. Usually, each of these improvements had to triumph over bitter opposition. The Crawfordites rejected the entire program and still meet in roofless, unheated, unpainted frame buildings.[52]

Many Primitive Baptist churches still meet only once a month, usually on the preceding Saturday also to hold their church conference in addition to their worship service. They sing for about half an hour before preaching, and their singing has always been one of their great distinctives. A few groups still "line out" hymns and sing in a slow unison, but that practice has ceased in most churches. A variety of hymnbooks have been used, nearly always edited by Primitive Baptists. One of the most characteristic and long-lived is Benjamin Lloyd's 1845 compilation *The Primitive Hymns*, a words-only hymnal containing 700 to 704 hymns depending on the edition. Most of its hymns are by Watts, Cowper, Newton, Leland, Toplady, and the other luminaries of the Great Awakening. The churches that use this book often have an almost

---

[51] Someone writing under the pseudonym "Z" in a late 1970s number of the *Signs of the Times*.

[52] Crowley, *Primitive Baptists*, 180–81.

canonical regard for it, although curiously, its hymns are often more evangelical than their preaching.[53]

Traditionally, Primitive Baptists sing *a cappella* rather slowly, in a highly ornamented style, often influenced by the *Sacred Harp* and other shape-note hymnals. They are also usually the backbone of the shape-note singing tradition wherever it exists. African American Old Line Primitive Baptists sing in a distinctive but equally old and powerful style. Sung in the old manner, Primitive hymns have an overwhelming melancholy power. Older and more traditional Primitive Baptists dislike bright, fast tunes. As one of their preachers once remarked, "There are tunes that go to your heart and others that only go to your feet."[54] Regrettably, there is an increasing tendency to "borrow" tunes and hymns from other traditions and to sing faster, which is gradually eroding much of the beauty and power of Old Line Primitive Baptist worship. This is not as prevalent in places where the *Sacred Harp* and Lloyd's hymnbook still exert an influence.

After the singing service, the ministers present go into the pulpit, called the "stand," a long affair with a bench in it to accommodate several ministers. If more than one minister is present, arrangements are made for the order of preaching, usually with three ministers to preach and the pastor closing the service. The ministers are all male since Primitive Baptists do not accept the validity of women preachers. Primitive Baptist preachers have no seminary training or any formal training in ministry other than what they acquire by grace, experience, and the guidance of older preachers. In recent years, as the general level of education has increased, so has the educational level of the Primitive ministry. However, as one Primitive minister with a collegiate degree

[53] See Joyce Cauthen, ed., *Benjamin Lloyd's Hymn Book: A Primitive Baptist Song Tradition* (Montgomery: Alabama Folklife Association, 1999). The accompanying CD gives examples of White and African American singing in the Primitive Baptist tradition. Of especial interest are the first three selections, sung by the Lee family of Hoboken, Georgia, who are among the greatest living Primitive Baptists and Sacred Harp singers.

[54] A comment of the late elder Marcus Peavey, Ray City GA, related to me by the late deacon Clem Mikell, also of Ray City.

remarked, “an education might prevent you from embarrassing yourself in public, but it would not teach anyone how to preach.”[55] Primitive Baptist ministers have traditionally been either older, retired men or bi-vocational, serving several churches on different weekends. This practice is so sanctified in some areas that an appeal has been made to the tree of life in Revelation that bore twelve crops of fruit a year to justify the practice as a divine institution.[56] In principle, a Primitive Baptist church is a strict democracy with the minister very much in the servant’s role. Throughout their history, however, Primitive Baptists have often submitted tamely for generations to the rule of charismatic authoritarian ministers.

The minister chosen to open the service begins by giving out a hymn and then offering prayer, always kneeling. The prayer is extemporaneous and is usually delivered in the same chanting style as the sermon. Both prayers and sermons were lengthy in the past, but this is not as true today.

Preaching is also extempore, frequently not even having a particular text as a basis. When a text is read, the sermon is often in no danger of any contagion from it. Highly allegorical “type and shadow” preaching has always been much in favor among Primitive Baptists, though perhaps not quite as much in the present. I once heard a minister take for his text Isaiah 6:1, where it is said that the Lord’s “train filled the temple.” He then delivered a long, lively, and entertaining sermon comparing the economy of salvation to the operation of a railway train. When he finished, a sister who had spent many years among the Southern Baptists warmly congratulated him and told him it was a wonderful sermon even though not one word of it was in the Bible.

One of the most striking features of traditional Primitive Baptist preaching is its delivery in a chanted or sung fashion, with the preacher scarcely aware of himself while preaching. It is difficult to understand for

---

[55] A remark by the late elder C. F. Wells, Irwinton GA, related to me by Elder I. B. Hall, Tifton GA.

[56] This summary of current Primitive Baptist practice is culled from my observations of them over thirty-five years, unless otherwise indicated.

those not used to it, but older Primitive Baptists usually regarded it as a sign of divine inspiration. Preachers are often at a loss at the beginning of their sermons, waiting for the word to come through them. I heard a venerable elder remark that the Primitive Baptists were criticized because they had nothing to offer young people. He added, "If the Lord doesn't come on the scene, I'll have nothing to offer the old people either."[57] Some preachers today preach in a more polished manner, especially among the Progressives, but the majority of Primitive Baptist preachers still preach in this manner. Such sermons often possess great beauty and power as the minister is swept out of himself with the power of his message. At its most magnificent, it is like the recitative of an opera. On the other hand, chanting, vulgarly known as "jumping the rabbit," also serves on occasion simply to kill time. The Primitive Baptists have always been burdened with a class of ministers they refer to as "empty wagons" since they make a great noise and carry no cargo.

The content of their sermons reflects devotion to their core doctrines and their almost total disassociation with the outer world. Primitive Baptists meet to worship in order to be "lifted above the weak and beggarly elements of this world,"[58] and preachers who insist on dragging social issues and news headlines into the pulpit often meet with a chilly reception. A friend of mine once wished to attend a Primitive Baptist service. At the conclusion, she told me, "These people care nothing about the world outside their meetinghouse." When the late Elder C. W. Vickers was invited to pray at the opening of the Georgia legislature, he curtly replied that he had better things to do.[59]

Primitive preaching heavily emphasizes predestination and election. Indeed, the core beliefs in the divine sovereignty cannot be expressed too starkly. I recall the late Elder Mayhew Young, a preacher of great power and eloquence, declaring from the pulpit, "Your ticket is punched, you are bound for heaven or hell, and there is nothing you or anyone else can

---

[57] Remark I heard from Elder I. B. Hall in the pulpit at Bethany Primitive Baptist Church, Clinch GA.

[58] A stock phrase in Primitive Baptist prayers.

[59] Related to me by Deacon Clem Mikell.

do about it." So strong is their belief in predestination that most Primitive Baptists see little point in addressing anyone on the subject of their conversion or frightening them with hell and damnation. In fact, they shy away from such preaching for fear it will introduce unconverted members into their churches with nothing but a "hell-scared religion." On occasion, reference may be made to abortion or some of the other controversies of the day, but such things are rare. Although sometimes quite active in the lives of their communities, Primitive Baptists at worship are truly strangers and pilgrims.

After preaching on Saturday, the church then sits in conferences. The pastor usually presides as moderator. Deacons act as the spokesmen for the church, and the clerk records the proceedings. Most members are received at church conferences. In contrast to the high-pressure techniques common in some Southern Baptist churches, the moderator simply announces an open door to the church and, if no one comes forward, quickly proceeds to other business. A candidate for membership is expected to relate his or her experience of conversion. In former times this was expected to be somewhat detailed and often featured the relation of dreams and visions. Today a simple expression of love for the church and belief in its doctrines are sufficient if the applicant is well known to the members, which is usually the case. In some churches, prospective members are sometimes questioned as to whether they have been divorced or remarried, belong to a secret society, or have declared bankruptcy or otherwise taken advantage of the law to avoid paying debts. The attitude on divorce has evolved perhaps more than any other aspect of church discipline. At the beginning of the twentieth century, no Primitive Baptist church would have received a divorced and remarried member or retained one in membership. Over the years this attitude has relaxed in some places to the point that divorced parties are evaluated on a case-by-case basis, with few hard-and-fast rules. However, in parts of Georgia, the Carolinas, and perhaps elsewhere, the old rules continue in their former rigor.

Conferences also handle church discipline, which has grown somewhat slack in recent years. At one time, dancing, drunkenness, failure to pay debts, membership in secret orders, and any sexual irregularities would bring swift action to exclude the offending members. Today, however, the disciplinary standards are more lax, though by no means forgotten. Gross sins will still bring one to the attention of a Primitive Baptist conference, and associational statistics still reveal a respectable number of excommunications from time to time.

All factions of the Primitive Baptist denomination have experienced a marked decline in membership during the last half of the twentieth century. Efforts to counteract this through the establishment of youth camps, Bible studies, and other techniques have called forth harsh criticism from conservative Primitive Baptists, who view the numerical decline of their church as part of the mysterious outworking of divine providence.

The absence of engagement and outreach in most Primitive Baptist churches, coupled with their usually intransigent doctrines and austere worship seem a recipe for extinction to most observers. Many of their critics have been preaching their funeral since the 1840s. But in many small Southern communities, where the oldest and largest cemeteries are often attached to their churches, those same critics lie with their mouths stopped with dust, while ancient, melancholy Hardshell hymns thunder over their graves.

Chapter 8

THE NORTH AMERICAN BAPTIST CONFERENCE

Philip E. Thompson

If we were to choose one word from the heritage of the German branch of the Baptist family in America by which to explore that branch, it would be *Gemeinde*. The sign that for years hung over the door of the oldest German Baptist church in America read "*Versammlungshaus der getauften Gemeinde*" (Meetinghouse of the Baptized Community). While often used for "church," *Gemeinde* means most basically "community." It is the life shared in and by the grace of God that the New Testament calls *koinonia*. The story of the shared life of German Baptists in North America is an important part of the Baptist story on these shores and one about which little is generally known.

Throughout the history of these Baptists, lives have been brought together in Christ, and in this union the lives of persons of varied circumstance and condition have joined; immigrants from Europe have found sisters and brothers in the United States and in Canada and in other Baptist communions. The North American Baptists are distinct in certain ways. Their ethnic and language background factors significantly in their history. The assimilation of the second and third generations of successive immigrant waves presented distinct challenges for much of their existence. North American Baptists are unique among Baptist denominations on this continent, being binational with congregations in the United States and Canada from their beginnings. While they have been theologically conservative and evangelistic from the beginning, they have not been doctrinaire or given to zealotry. Their orientation to

Christian life has been more pietistic and inward rather than revivalistic, more focused orthopraxis than strict orthodoxy. They have placed emphasis upon the cultivation of a deep relationship with Jesus Christ the Savior.[1] Conrad Moehlman noted that to live faith in Christ has been "the superlative fundamental of the German Baptists."[2] While their story deserves a fuller telling, what follows is an essential introduction.

Beginnings

Frank H. Woyke observed, "The history of any group, especially in its beginnings, is usually the extended story of its leaders."[3] This is certainly true of the German Baptists in North America. There was no early principal "mother church" to which large numbers of other German Baptist congregations could trace their lineage. Neither was there a central figure whose work gave rise to many Baptist congregations here—no figure corresponding to J. G. Oncken, to whom many Baptist churches in Germany and Eastern Europe trace their origins. Rather, within a matrix constituted by widespread spiritual awakening and a wave of sustained northern European immigration in the 1840s, Baptist life emerged in various German-speaking American communities under

---

[1] Albert John Ramaker, *The German Baptists in North America: An Outline of their History* (Cleveland: German Baptist Publication Society, 1924) 44–49; and Frank W. Woyke, *Heritage and Ministry of the North American Baptist Conference* (Oak Brook Terrace IL: North American Baptist Conference, 1979) 86–88. I wish to express sincere thanks to Rev. Ron Berg, Dr. John Binder, Dr. Marv Dewey, Rev. and Mrs. George W. Lang, Dr. Ed Link, Mrs. Kristi McLaughlin, Dr. David Priestly, Mr. Gordon Unger, and Dr. Ernie Zimbelman for their incalculable assistance in this project. I must express special thanks to Miss Berneice Westerman, associate archivist for the North American Baptist Conference Historical Commission, without whose help this project would have been far more difficult and far less accurate.

[2] Conrad Henry Moehlman, "Introduction," in Ramaker, *German Baptists in North America*, n.p.

[3] Woyke, *Heritage and Ministry*, 27. Woyke's text remains the most thorough study of the history of North American Baptists.

the leadership of several pioneers. Many of these pioneers were themselves not Baptist before coming to America.

A look at the lives of the founders of German Baptist life in North America shows rather clearly that this work was not transplanted from Germany. Though there have been occasional claims to the contrary over the years, it seems clear that German Baptist life in America did not grow from the work of J. G. Oncken's work in Germany. Indeed, when Oncken suggested a direct connection, the German Baptists in North America strongly asserted their independence.

In 1858, the editor of the denominational periodical *Der Sendbote des Evangeliums* (*The Gospel Messenger*), Konrad Anton Fleischmann, declared, "May it be mentioned here that the work of our German churches in America is not, as has often been stated, just an extension of the Baptist mission in Germany, under the leadership of Brother Oncken. It is the work of special divine providence and guidance. The oldest workers, before their arrival in America, have never been in contact with the churches in Germany.... Yet we maintain a mutual friendly relationship, since we agree in all points...."[4] While a few early leaders and members were associated with Oncken's work before their arrival on these shores, their influence in the founding and growth of Baptist life here was not significant.[5]

The relation seems to be similar to that of Baptist life in England and the American colonies in the 1600s. The movements were parallel and contemporaneous. The first Baptist church in Germany appeared in 1834. The first German Baptist church in North America was established in 1843, and its founder (Fleischmann) was Baptist neither when he came to America in 1839 nor when he established the church! Again, as in the 1600s, there were good relations between Baptists on

---

[4] Konrad Anton Fleischmann, "Unsere Stellung un Aufgabe," *Der Sendbote des Evangeliums* 6/1 (1858): 2, trans. Reinhold J. Kerstan, in Reinhold J. Kerstan, *Historical Factors in the Formation of the Ethnically Oriented North American Baptist General Conference* (unpublished Ph.D. diss., Northwestern University, Evansville IN, 1971) 79.

[5] Woyke, *Heritage and Ministry*, 86–88.

both sides of the Atlantic and even mutual influence. German Baptists in America contributed much to Baptist life in Germany. The seminary in Rochester, New York, was older than the Baptist seminary in Hamburg and exercised influence upon the German school. Sunday school work by German Baptists in America also helped shape similar work in Germany.[6]

There were two founding figures whose contributions stand above those of others and require special attention. These are Konrad Anton Fleischmann (1812–1867), founder of the oldest church and driving force behind the organization of German Baptist life in America, and August Rauschenbusch (1816–1899), founder of German Baptist life in Canada, founder of the German Baptist seminary, and whose impress was born by the theology and piety of several generations of German Baptist faithful.

Fleischmann was born in Nürnberg, Bavaria. At age nineteen, he had a profound conversion experience during a time of spiritual seeking and became a Separatist.[7] The Swiss Separatists were not identical to the English Separatists out of which the General Baptists arose.[8] They practiced the baptism of both believers and infants, observed open Communion, and placed little emphasis upon organization.[9] After wrestling with the question of baptism for two years, Fleischmann arrived at the conviction that believers' baptism was the scriptural pattern. He received believer's baptism in Basel, though he did not leave the Separatists.

In 1838, he was asked to undertake mission work among German immigrants in America. Arriving in New York in March 1839, he began work in New York City and Newark, New Jersey, with little success. He

---

[6] Albert John Ramaker, "The Seventy-Fifth Anniversary of the German Department," *The Rochester Theological Seminary Bulletin* 78/1 (October 1922): 41–42.

[7] Woyke, *Heritage and Ministry*, 27.

[8] Ibid., 4, notes that they were more similar to the Plymouth Brethren than to the English Separatists.

[9] Woyke, *Heritage and Ministry*, 4; Ramaker, *German Baptists in North America*, 15–18.

baptized three converts in October that year and directed them to join an English-speaking Baptist church. By the end of the year, though still a Separatist, he accepted an appointment from the American Baptist Home Mission Society (ABHMS) to serve the German population of eastern and middle Pennsylvania. He met with far greater success among Germans of Pietist, Mennonite, and Tunker background around Reading. A great revival broke out under his preaching in 1841. While he baptized more than 200, he did not organize them into churches, in keeping with separatist practices. In 1842, at the urging of Baptists in Philadelphia, he moved to pursue missionary work among the German population around that key city of Baptist life in America.

In March 1843, he baptized five converts. Others followed, and on 10 April he celebrated the Lord's Supper with a community of nineteen. On 9 July of that year, he presented a statement of principles for them to sign and so to be constituted "The German Church of the Lord that meets on Poplar Street." Fleischmann served the church, which came in later years to be known as Fleischmann Memorial Baptist Church, as pastor until his death. It is to these events that North American Baptists trace their formal beginning. Yet there was ambiguity, reflecting Fleischmann's own ambiguous ecclesial status and perhaps enduring reservation about being confused with the Anabaptists.[10] The church name did not say "Baptist." The sign over the door noted earlier also lacked explicit identification with Baptists. Reticence to use the name notwithstanding, the church joined the Philadelphia Association in 1848.[11]

August Rauschenbusch was born in Altena, Westphalia. A man of incredible intelligence, he was the sixth in an unbroken lineage of pastors, eventually succeeding his father as Lutheran pastor in Altena. A

---

[10] Woyke, *Heritage and Ministry*, 27, notes that the Baptist practice of closed Communion was perhaps the most difficult obstacle for Fleischmann to overcome in becoming Baptist. Indeed, the principles he drafted were silent on the matter, and the church practiced open Communion for a period of time. This may well have contributed to the hesitance to take the name "Baptist."

[11] Woyke, *Heritage and Ministry*, 27.

Pietist conversion experience in 1836 brought him to hold strong evangelical and conversionist emphases. A. H. Strong is reported as having once said that had Rauschenbusch been born in an earlier day in England, he would have been a Puritan of the strictest sort.[12] These emphases, however, were not well received by all in his church.

Between 1830 and 1850, approximately two and one half million Germans immigrated to America. Since few pastors came with them, the spiritual need of the German communities in America was great. Rauschenbusch came to America in 1846 to work as a missionary among German immigrants in the American Midwest, serving in St. Louis as a colporteur for the American Tract Society (ATS). The following year, he moved to New York to become the head of the German department of the ATS and editor of their German language publication. In that year he also began wrestling with the question of baptism, having witnessed a Baptist baptism that impressed him as being "New Testament baptism."[13]

In 1849, he suffered one of the several health breakdowns that would afflict him throughout his life. He returned to St. Louis, where he connected with a group of German Baptists. While there he decided to seek believer's baptism and sent for his friend, pastor Sigismund Küpfer of Newark. Rauschenbusch was baptized in the Mississippi River on 19 May 1850, on the Illinois side because he did not want to be baptized in a slaveholding state.[14] He continued to work for the ATS, returning to New York City and joining the First German Baptist Church. He was ordained into the Baptist ministry in 1851.

In June of that year, he traveled to Waterloo County, Ontario, at the behest of Heinrich Schneider, whom Rauschenbusch had sent as an ATS colporteur and whose ministry among Lutheran immigrants was meeting marked success. In this visit, Rauschenbusch won Schneider and

---

[12] Ramaker, "The Seventy-Fifth Anniversary of the German Department," 35.

[13] George W. Lang, "Glimpses of Selected North American Baptist Leaders (German Baptist Leaders in the United States & Canada)" unpublished paper, December 2001, 10.

[14] Ibid., and Woyke, *Heritage and Ministry*, 45.

others to Baptist views and administered believers' baptism to them. On 10 September 1851, he organized them into the Bridgeport Baptist Church, the first German Baptist church in Canada.[15] Rauschenbusch strengthened and shaped German Baptist life in Canada through lectures, articles, and debates with non-Baptists.[16] Because the ATS did not allow "denominational work," Rauschenbusch was unable to continue his ministry with them.

Rauschenbusch returned to Germany in 1853. En route, he assembled the first hymnal used by German Baptists in America, *Die Pilgerharfe* (Pilgrim's Harp). In 1854, he married and returned to America with his bride, settling with a community of German immigrants in Gasconade County, Missouri, forming a Baptist church there in early 1856.

While Rauschenbusch made many significant contributions to the life of the German Baptist communities in the United States and Canada, it was as an educator that he had his deepest and widest effect. The divinity school at the University of Rochester had from its beginning in 1850 included provision for a German department to provide qualified pastors for the German immigrant communities. This was part of the American Baptist mission to the German community. The first student came in 1851 and left the same year. In 1852, five more students came, largely at Rauschenbusch's encouragement. Four were highly gifted and made significant contributions to Baptist life in America and Germany. While Albert John Ramaker reckoned the school's beginning from this date, Rauschenbusch's arrival in 1858 to become the first German Baptist professor has become the more accepted date.[17]

---

[15] Edward B. Link, "North American (German) Baptists," in Jarold K. Zeman, ed., *Baptists in Canada: Search for Identity Amid Diversity* (Burlington ON: G. R. Welch Company, Limited, 1980) 88; Ramaker, *German Baptists in North America*, 33–35; and Woyke, *Heritage and Ministry*, 45–47.

[16] Link, "North American (German) Baptists," 89.

[17] Ramaker, "The Seventy-Fifth Anniversary of the German Department," 33–34.

The department had languished from its inception, and there had been repeated pleas for Rauschenbusch to take up the work. He was the only man in the denomination qualified for it. Until a second professor was added in 1877, he taught the entire curriculum: Latin, Greek, theology, ethics, homiletics, history, psychology, botany, zoology, and astronomy.[18] Of Rauschenbusch's wide range of expertise, Strong commented, "What he did, he did well."[19] He also did it selflessly. The department was not adequately funded. Yet he persevered even in the absence of funds. "I can never break faith with the men who came hither on my invitation," Rauschenbusch said.[20] Until his retirement in 1889, August Rauschenbusch supervised 199 students. Of these, 77 continued in pastoral service until their deaths.

There were other early leaders of the German Baptists in North America. While none had the degree of influence of Fleischmann and Rauschenbusch, many rendered faithful and fruitful service. Another notable contributor to the beginnings of German Baptist life was Johann Eschmann, who organized the second German Baptist church in North America in New York City in 1846. Additionally, Andreas Heinrich began a church in Rochester, New York, in 1848, and in the following year under the pastoral leadership of former Prussian military officer Alexander von Puttkamer, a church was organized in Buffalo, New York. The year 1849 also brought the founding of a German Baptist church in Springfield, Illinois, by people who had been baptized by Oncken in Oldenberg, Germany. In 1850, Christopher Schoemaker organized a German Baptist church in St. Louis, and Konrad Lesler constituted one in Chicago. In 1851, Jeremias Grimmel, who had been baptized by Oncken, organized a German Baptist church in Brooklyn, New York. The following year, J. H. Krueger, who had also been baptized by

[18] Ibid., 34. The curriculum included both college and theology courses.

[19] Ramaker, "The Seventy-Fifth Anniversary of the German Department," 34.

[20] Ibid., 35.

Oncken in Germany, began a German Baptist Church in Peoria, Illinois.[21]

Organizing Beyond the Local Level

In 1851, there were 635 German Baptist Christians in North America. There were eight churches with 405 members, and numerous smaller groups that had not yet been formally constituted as churches with just over half again as many adherents. They were spread from the Middle Atlantic westward into Wisconsin and Illinois and north into Canada. Fleischmann sensed the need for these widely scattered individuals and churches to be brought into a more inclusive *Gemeinde*. In order that they would have an opportunity to become better acquainted, to share their Christian experiences, to inspire and edify one another through sharing and consultation, he called for a gathering, a "conference" of those involved in the work.[22]

"The First Conference of Pastors and Co-workers of the German Churches of Baptized Christians, (usually called Baptist)" met at Fleischmann's church in Philadelphia 6–12 November 1851.[23] The principal matters of discussion focused on the development of a confession of faith and statement of church order, the compiling of a hymnal (*Die Pilgerharfe*), and the establishment of a periodical (*Der Sendbote des Evangeliums*, which began publication in 1853 with

---

[21] Ramaker, *German Baptists in North America*, 20–32; and Woyke, *Heritage and Ministry*, 30–56.

[22] Woyke, *Heritage and Ministry*, 3–11.

[23] Ibid., 3. Woyke notes that the last words were both in parentheses and in much smaller print. There was a marked reticence among German pastors in the early years to employ the designation "Baptist." The conference even recommended that the churches refer to themselves as "Churches of Baptized Christians." A variety of factors may have contributed to this. Those comprising the First Conference did not come from a Baptist background. Fleischmann and Eschmann shared a Swiss separatist background, which tended to eschew denominational names. Also frequently noted in this reticence is an abiding desire not to be associated with the Anabaptists.

Fleischmann as editor). The latter two especially were bold steps for such a small group and indicate that they anticipated continued growth. Discussion centered on the problem of training ministers for the German people of North America and questions concerning the Lord's Supper and membership in secret societies. A strong resolution against slavery and an equally strong resolution encouraging the instruction of children in the German language were adopted.[24]

The meeting of German Baptists beyond the local congregation has from the beginning been called a "conference" rather than an association or convention. Within the idea of a conference echoes the Pietist emphasis on a gathering of equals for the purpose of edification and mutual counsel.[25] Given this, the focus was decidedly away from centralization and control. Following the first conference, Eschmann composed a letter for the churches. In it he assured the churches that the conference had undertaken no action that would impinge upon the autonomy of the local congregations.[26] The conferences of the German Baptists in the early days more closely reflected the society model rather than that of the association.[27] It was not until 1858 that "and churches" was added to "Pastors and Co-workers," and representation of churches did not come until 1865. It was not until the 1870s that the conference structure became a "true association" of churches.[28]

There were annual conferences from 1851 through 1858. It was a time of significant growth, with a roughly fivefold increase in churches and members. This growth was widely spread and resulted in a larger proportion of German Baptists in the interior of the United States. Logistical problems occurred, making it difficult for people in the West

---

[24] Ibid., 4–9.

[25] Arthur A. Schade, "Milestones Across the Century," in *These Glorious Years: The Centenary History of German Baptists of North America 1843–1943* (Cleveland: Roger Williams Press, n.d.) 43–44.

[26] Woyke, *Heritage and Ministry*, 9.

[27] Ramaker, *German Baptists in North America*, 55, notes that the early organization resembled gatherings of Swiss Separatists more than any other ecclesial body.

[28] Ramaker, *German Baptists in North America*, 55.

to attend conferences in the East; and the conferences held in the West (St. Louis in 1857 and Cincinnati in 1858) had but a slight Eastern presence. The Cincinnati Conference, with only two from east of Ohio attending, recommended that Eastern and Western conferences be formed in order to facilitate communication and administration of cooperative ventures.[29]

While this division was not the result of disagreement and was not intended to create opposition within the German Baptist community, a kind of competitiveness did emerge during the years that the Eastern and Western conferences maintained distinct and independent existence (1859–1864). There were temperamental differences. The Westerners, more of whom had some association with Oncken, tended to maintain closer ties with Baptists in Germany. They were more careful in matters of doctrine and so were concerned to maintain oversight of the preparation of ministerial students in Rochester. The Western Conference was also more aggressive in its support of missions. Meeting in Springfield, Illinois, in 1859, the Western Conference formed a missionary society. The Eastern Conference did not follow suit until 1867.

There was also duplication of work between East and West. The first meeting of the Western Conference witnessed the launching of a periodical, *Die Biene auf dem Missionsfeld* (*The Bee on the Missionfield*), intended to be primarily a missionary journal. Philipp W. Bickel, pastor in Cincinnati, was elected editor. It was not intended as a replacement for, nor competitor with, *Der Sendbote*. Indeed, the Western Conference passed a resolution encouraging continued support of the older paper by the Western churches. Nonetheless, the papers did become the forums within which differences of opinion between the two sections were aired.[30]

---

[29] Schade, "Milestones Across the Century," 41–42; Ramaker, *German Baptists in North America*, 56–58; and Woyke, *Heritage and Ministry*, 91–92.

[30] Ramaker, *German Baptists in North America*, 56–58; and Woyke, *Heritage and Ministry*, 92–97.

Despite assurances from both sides that neither wished a permanent or deep division between East and West, the division continued to grow more pronounced during the time of separate meetings and threatened to become insurmountable. In 1863, the Eastern Conference proposed a general meeting of the two conferences and joining of publication work as a means by which to bring the two together. While the Western Conference was supportive, discussion of details revealed how deep the division had become. Perhaps at greatest risk in a permanent split was the seminary, but August Rauschenbusch encouraged both parties to stay in communication.

The first general conference was held in the unlikely venue of rural Wilmot, Ontario, from 14–20 September 1865. While none knew what to expect or hope from the meeting, it proved providential. Since less than 1 percent of German Baptists lived in Canada at the time, and Wilmot was equally inconvenient to people from both sections, it proved to be a truly neutral site. Its rural setting dictated a slow meeting pace and an environment free of distractions that enabled the fostering of personal relations among those present. A spirit of Christian charity prevailed. Fleischmann was elected moderator. A common Publication Society was chartered and planned to be headquartered in Cincinnati. *Die Biene* was discontinued, and Bickel became editor of *Der Sendbote* with Fleischmann as associate. An orphanage and fund to support retired ministers and the widows of ministers was discussed. A committee to examine graduates of the seminary was also established.[31]

Growth and Development

Ever since 1865, there has been a general meeting of the denomination held triennially.[32] As the German Baptist population has spread across

---

[31] Ramaker, *German Baptists in North America*, 58–69; and Woyke, *Heritage and Ministry*, 97–105.

[32] Because of the Second World War, there was a gap of four years between the meetings in Burlington, Iowa (1940) and Milwaukee, Wisconsin (1944). The General

North America, regional conferences have continued to be established. This growth was the result largely of the arrival of successive waves of German-speaking immigrants from Europe, each of which came from a different circumstance in the old country and settled farther westward. The Western Conference divided into Central, Northwestern, and Southwestern conferences in 1880, and a Texas Conference was added in 1884. In 1894, the Eastern Conference divided into Eastern and Atlantic conferences. The Pacific Conference was organized the following year. In 1902, the Northern Conference, comprised of churches in the provinces of Manitoba, Alberta, and Saskatchewan, was formed. The Dakotas Conference was established in 1909.[33] This would be the basic configuration of the denomination through the first two-thirds of the twentieth century. By the turn of the century, the churches were grouped into associations in smaller areas within the regional conferences for the purpose of fellowship and inspiration.[34] Also significant during this time was the founding in 1907 of *Der Allgemeine Schwesterbund Deutscher Baptisten von Nord Amerika* (similar to the Woman's Missionary Union among Southern Baptists), which through the years has lent inestimable support to German Baptist ministries.[35]

The greater part of immigration into Canada came somewhat later than immigration into the United States.[36] In 1875, ten years after the first general conference was hosted in Canada, still fewer than one of every ten German Baptists lived there.[37] Yet Canada experienced in that decade the beginnings of an influx of German speakers from Russia (*Russlanddeutsche*) into the western provinces that would last through the rest of the nineteenth century. In 1876, the German Baptists of Canada formed their own mission society. The Baptists were almost alone in

---

Conference met again in 1946 in Tacoma, Washington, putting the meeting back on schedule.

[33] Ramaker, *German Baptists in North America*, 70; and Woyke, *Heritage and Ministry*, 168, 259–60.

[34] Link, "North American (German) Baptists," 93.

[35] Woyke, *Heritage and Ministry*, 270.

[36] Ibid., 110.

[37] Link, "North American (German) Baptists," 88.

providing a strong ministry presence among these newcomers. The growth of German Baptist life in western Canada was in great part due to the work of Friedrich August Petereit (1850–1922) and was closely associated with the First Baptist Church of Winnipeg, organized 31 December 1889. Other noteworthy pioneers of Canadian German Baptist life were F. A. Müller and Abraham Hager.[38] In the middle of the twentieth century, from after the Second World War through the early 1950s, Canada received another large influx of German speakers that the United States did not experience. Many of these were Baptists already, and their arrival added 12 new churches and roughly 1,250 new members to the Canadian rolls. Since this time, the North American Baptist Conference membership has been roughly 40 percent Canadian, with a particularly strong presence in the province of Alberta.

Throughout the nineteenth century and into the twentieth, the German churches in North America were closely related to their English-speaking sister churches. Many were dually aligned either with what we now call American Baptists or the Baptist Union of Canada, the smaller German churches receiving home mission funds for their support. A number of churches were also members of English-speaking Baptist associations.[39] Over time, tension developed both within German Baptist life and between German-speaking and English-speaking Baptists, largely over the use of the German language and questions of assimilation in general.

This led to varying results. By 1920, it was more proper to speak of Baptists of German descent in eastern Canada rather than "German Baptists," and these churches became fully part of the Ontario-Quebec Baptist Convention of Canada. The western churches, whose members were more recent immigrants, politely and graciously declined an invitation at this time to become likewise part of the Baptist Union of Western Canada and aligned themselves fully with the German Baptist

---

[38] Ibid., 91; and Kerstan, *Historical Factors*, 152–61.

[39] Woyke, *Heritage and Ministry*, 88; and Kerstan, *Historical Factors*, 161–62.

Conference.[40] That same year, the German Baptist General Mission Society relinquished monetary support from other conventions. Steps toward independence had begun.

The 1920s and 1930s brought a move toward still greater independence by the German Baptist Conference. A unified budget was adopted for the 1925–1928 triennium, and in 1934 a General Council was formed to provide central coordination of the work of the various concerns supported by the conference.[41] In 1940, the German Baptists were invited to become fully part of the Northern Baptist Convention. Again, they graciously refused, noting during the age of comity agreements that one in five of their churches were in the territory of the Canadian and Southern Baptists, and they did not wish to jeopardize their good relations with either.

In 1942, the German Baptist Conference voted to adopt the name North American Baptist General Conference. This became the official name in 1946 with the adoption of a new constitution. The conference's move toward independence was complete.[42] Incorporated in Illinois, the denominational headquarters were first located in Forest Park, with a later relocation to larger facilities in Oakbrook Terrace in 1976. The conference has long been a member of the Baptist World Alliance and joined the North American Baptist Fellowship in 1967. Since 1954, the conference has been a member of the Baptist Joint Committee on Public Affairs.[43] In the early 1970s, the conference underwent a restructuring, with the associations becoming the more basic regional administrative units rather than the regional conferences.[44]

---

[40] Link, "North American (German) Baptists," 96; Kerstan, *Historical Factors*, 161–62; and Woyke, *Heritage and Ministry*, 294.

[41] Woyke, *Heritage and Ministry*, 294.

[42] Ibid., 294–362. "General" was dropped from the name of the conference in 1975.

[43] Woyke, *Heritage and Ministry*, 389–90.

[44] Ibid., 379–81.

Work

Without question, missions deserves first place in discussion of the work undertaken by North American Baptists. Indeed, the German Baptist work in North America was itself a missionary endeavor. Early German Baptist workers received substantial support from the ABHMS in order to evangelize the rapidly growing German immigrant population in the nineteenth century and also to assimilate them into American life and culture. Unified missions work was not discussed at the first general conference. In a way, this shows the depth of commitment to missions in the German Baptist community. It was simply understood that responsibility for missions rested with each local community and believer. Questions of origin and influence aside, the North American Baptists have resonated with the declaration of Oncken, "*Jeder Baptist ein Missionar*!" ("Every Baptist a missionary!").[45]

The general conference of 1883, meeting in Cleveland, proposed the establishment of a General Missionary Society (GMS). Some had been hesitant, wanting neither to diminish the emphasis upon each regional conference as a missionary organization nor to encroach upon the autonomy of the local congregations. Still, another influx of German-speaking immigrants in the last two decades of the century made the need for coordinated work more pressing. The GMS worked in tandem with the ABHMS. The German Baptists supplied the workers and raised funds for their support and for the support of small German Baptist congregations not able to function in financial independence. The appointment of the missionaries, and additional funds for the support of them and of the churches, rested with the English-speaking society.[46]

While home missions was the first concern, the call to overseas missions did not go unheeded. Interest arose early in the Western

---

[45] Cf. H. Leon McBeth, *The Baptist Heritage: Four Centuries of Baptist Witness* (Nashville: Broadman, 1987) 472.

[46] Ibid., 304.

Conference. Indeed, there were regular reports in *Die Biene* on foreign missions work by various denominations. In this case as well, German Baptists worked through various other missions societies in North America and Europe. In the early days of this work, they sent missionaries to India, China, and the Philippines. One of the first young people appointed to foreign service from the German churches was Emma Rauschenbusch, daughter of August, who was sent to India and served with distinction along with the daughter of Konrad Fleischmann.[47]

Signal leadership in North American Baptist missions was provided by Dr. William Kuhn, General Missionary Committee secretary from 1916–1946. For a long time, he held steadfast to a goal of "a mission field of our own" for North American German Baptists. While he likely had in mind a European field, the fulfillment of his hope took another shape.[48] Ramaker's 1924 history lamented that with the transfer of German colonies to England and France following the First World War, "one of the most flourishing and promising mission fields of modern times has been cut off with no immediate prospect of restoration."[49] His reference was to Cameroon, a nation in western Africa. His tone reflects the fact that Cameroon had over the previous three decades assumed first place in the hearts of German Baptists in America. The work had been under the direction of a mission society in Berlin, and most German missionaries were interned when governance was transferred. Two years after Ramaker wrote, however, German missionaries were once again admitted to British Cameroon, and in 1928 the North American Baptist General Mission Committee assumed shared administration of the field with the Germans. The first missionary appointed by the General Missionary Committee was Paul Gebauer in 1931, who served for another thirty years. The work of the North Americans became completely separated from German influence in

---

[47] Ramaker, *German Baptists in North America*, 90–96; and Woyke, *Heritage and Ministry*, 128–31.

[48] Lang, "Glimpses of Selected North American Baptist Leaders," 19–20.

[49] Ramaker, *German Baptists in North America*, 96.

1935. This greatly reduced the disruption of the work at the beginning of World War Two, when the British exempted the North Americans from the internment of German missionaries.[50] In 1944, North American Baptists assumed full administration of the Cameroonian mission field.

The centerpiece of North American Baptist foreign missions work remains Cameroon. This story deserves a more detailed accounting than is provided here.[51] The history of North American Baptist foreign missions includes a record of insight and progressive thinking about the work of missions. In the 1920s, missionary C. J. Bender wrote, "It is also wrong to impose our forms of worship on the mission field and use them as a standard by which to judge the spiritual life and the religious quality of our Cameroonian Christians."[52] There are approximately sixty foreign missionaries currently serving under North American Baptist appointment. Other mission fields include Japan, Brazil, Mexico, Nigeria, the Philippines, Russia, and Romania.

Also significant in the work of the North American Baptist Conference has been its ministries of care, publication, and education. Ramaker observed with admiration the remarkable array of ministries funded by the contributions of German Baptists, who tended to be farmers in the Plains region and wage workers in the cities.[53] Over the years, they have supported an active press that produces literature to inform (periodicals), instruct (Sunday school curriculum), and edify (hymnals) its constituents. North American Baptists have established during the course of their existence an orphanage, nine nursing homes, eleven summer camps for children and families, and homes for single working women in Chicago and New York City.[54] The nursing homes and camps are still in existence.

---

[50] Woyke, *Heritage and Ministry*, 304–15.

[51] John Siewert and Daphne Dunger are currently writing one. A publisher had not been selected at the time of this writing.

[52] Woyke, *Heritage and Ministry*, 314.

[53] Ramaker, *German Baptists in North America*, 42–43.

[54] Woyke, *Heritage and Ministry*, 249–58, 355, 422–27.

There have been two North American Baptist schools. The oldest, as noted above, began as the German Department of the University of Rochester Divinity School and operated in a relationship similar to that of the missionaries and the ABHMS. The 1930s and 1940s were a significant period in the life of the school. The parent school became Colgate-Rochester Divinity School in 1929, and its relationship with the German Department underwent changes through the 1930s that entailed dwindling support for the latter that became nominal by the end of the decade. In response, the German Department moved toward a greater independence, symbolized by the mid-decade adoption of the name German Baptist Seminary. This name proved problematic as World War Two commenced, so the name was changed once again to the Rochester Baptist Seminary, though this name proved not to be popular with Colgate-Rochester Divinity School because of possible confusion of the two. In 1940, the seminary became independent and soon began to explore the option of relocation. In 1944, there was yet another name change to reflect the new identity of the conference, North American Baptist Seminary. In 1949, the school relocated to its present site in Sioux Falls, South Dakota. The school received full accreditation by the Association of Theological Schools in 1968.[55]

In 1939–1940, E. P. Wahl established a school for laity, the Christian Training Institute, in Edmonton, Alberta, to serve the growing German Baptist community there and in other western provinces. The school quickly grew and prospered. In 1967, a long-range plan was announced to upgrade the institute to an undergraduate theological school, adopting the new name North American Baptist College (NABC). A new campus was built in 1968, and the following year the school received accreditation as a Bible college. In 1988 the school established an affiliation with the University of Alberta, enabling students at NABC to work toward a liberal arts degree. Divinity coursework was added in 1980, and one decade later, Edmonton Baptist Seminary was formally established. Growth and development has

[55] Ibid., 331–49, 411–15.

continued to the present, including the designation of "university college" for the undergraduate school. In 2002 the school adopted its current name, Taylor University College and Seminary.[56]

Challenges

North American Baptists have had disagreements and discussions, yet have been blessedly spared controversy that led to strife and division. Because some of their early leaders were Separatists who embraced a range of variation in ecclesial practices, open Communion was a question before the first conference in 1851.[57] Their blending of theological conservatism and pietistic temperament kept them to a middle course during the fundamentalist-modernist controversy of the early twentieth century and encouraged them to take a moderate stance on the question of the ordination of women later in the century.[58] They have been led from their beginnings to declare what they believe to be the mind of Christ on social issues. The first resolution adopted by the first general conference gave thanks for the Union victory in the Civil War and declared, "We greet with great joy, as the glorious fruit of the

---

[56] Ibid. 419–21.

[57] Woyke, *Heritage and Ministry*, 3–5. August Rauschenbusch successfully guided the German Baptists to a closed Communion position, but not on the same logic as would characterize Landmarkism. Woyke notes (*Heritage and Ministry*, 27) that closed Communion was a principal obstacle to K. A. Fleischmann's becoming Baptist.

[58] A 1985 task force commissioned by the conference reached the conclusion that it is biblically permissible to ordain women to a wide range of ministries including associate pastor, yet women are biblically prohibited from the office of senior pastor. These findings were reaffirmed in 1992 and ratified by the triennial meeting in Dallas. Worth noting is that this task force discovered an ordained woman, Rev. Grace Domes, who had served the church in Folsomdale, New York, from 1938–1942. Her ordination by another Baptist body fully was recognized, and she was listed as pastor in the conference directory without protest ("Ordination Guidelines and Study Document," 32).

struggle, the equal rights of the Negroes with those of the white citizens of the land."[59]

North American Baptists have at times encountered tension over the question of the precise focus of their orthopraxis. Is life faithful to Christ a matter more of interiority or activity? Alexander von Puttkamer, for example, served as commander of the Union's Fort Ellsworth in Alexandria, Virginia. In this service he made Bible reading and church attendance requirements for the men under his command. After the war, he served in English-speaking Baptist churches, possibly because of German Baptist criticism of the decision by a minister of the gospel to take the earthly sword.[60]

Beginning in September 1890, discussion of the sort of life required of Christians and the end result of that decision occupied the pages of *Der Sendbote*. Ironically, while it had little effect on the life and thought of German Baptists in America, it was perhaps the most ecumenically significant episode in the history of this community. The theme was the "Social Question," and the interlocutors were Walter Rauschenbusch, son of August and pastor of Second German Baptist Church of New York City, and Ernst Anschütz, pastor of the church in West Hoboken, New Jersey. Anschütz argued that if all could be brought to embrace and follow the teaching of the Lord, "love thy neighbor as thyself," the social problems and inequities of Gilded Age America could be remedied within the existing order. Rauschenbusch countered that Christianity proclaims a new kingdom and is therefore inescapably revolutionary. "I am a member," he wrote, "of the most revolutionary society that has ever existed on earth—the disciples of Jesus."[61] It was the earliest articulation of what would become in the following decades the theology of the Social Gospel.

Retention of the German language was the most enduring question and challenge to the German Baptist community. As noted above, the

---

[59] Woyke, *Heritage and Ministry*, 104.

[60] Ibid., 37–38.

[61] Ibid., 273–81. Woyke provides helpful, lengthy quotations from this exchange.

German Baptist work in America was largely a mission by English-speaking Baptists in its early period. From the beginning, speakers of German and English alike had the expectation that the German language ministry would be temporary and for the sake of assimilation into American culture almost as much as for evangelization. As some German communities became more Americanized, they had to begin using English to retain the younger generations.[62] All the while, new waves of immigrants continued to arrive and constitute new fields for German work. These subsequent arrivals tended to be more socially conservative and were more intent on clinging to the language of the homeland.

Broader social issues affected the retention of the German language as well. From the beginning, German Baptists in Canada were caught up in the anti-German sentiments of World War One. In 1917 the city of Berlin, Ontario, changed its name to Kitchener. This may well have been a factor in the eastern Canadian churches by and large leaving the German Baptist Conference and joining the Ontario-Quebec Baptist Convention of Canada.[63] Some states, such as Iowa, banned all use of German during this time.[64] Again during World War Two, churches in western Canada felt pressure because of their German identity. Throughout these times, the German Baptists helped allay fears in the English-speaking community through demonstration of their loyalty to the United States and Canada.[65]

The period during which the conference moved to autonomy, 1920–1946, brought a gradual, though not total, shift from German to

---

[62] Ramaker, "The Seventy-Fifth Anniversary of the German Department," 39, who notes that there was already in the 1890s a demand on the seminary from older congregations for ministers who could provide services in English; Woyke, *Heritage and Ministry*, 282; and Link, "North American (German) Baptists," 96.

[63] Link, "North American (German) Baptists," 96, notes that the younger churches in western Canada were more determined to retain German identity and language.

[64] Woyke, *Heritage and Ministry*, 282.

[65] Link, "North American (German) Baptists," 98, notes that the Northern Conference canceled its 1941 meeting because of suspicions about attending large meetings of German speakers.

English. The loss of members and churches to English-speaking congregations and conventions led to a 1928 emphasis on bilingual ministry. Even then, the move toward English continued to gain strength. A significant event was the Burlington, Iowa, general conference of 1940. This was the first meeting of the Triennial, the sessions of which were almost entirely in English, as was the printed conference program.[66] During the time that followed, the English language *Baptist Herald*, which was started as a youth paper, became the principal periodical of the conference. Even so, *Der Sendbote* continued to be printed on a regular basis until 1971. At this time, it became an eight-page supplement to the *Herald*, but only for those who subscribed to receive it. It ceased to be published altogether in 1986. While the conference has not been a "German denomination" since the mid-1940s if not earlier, even today Triennial meetings are seasoned with the sound of conversations in *Die Mütersprache*.

Today[67] there are 64,565 North American Baptists in 394 churches.[68] As a small denomination now shorn of its ethnic identity, it faces distinct challenges. As does North American evangelicalism generally, the NAB Conference faces the effect of a post-traditional environment in which denominational identity counts for less and less among many Protestants. Part of this is due to an inward turning of local churches and with it a weakening of congregational relation to denominational structures and to sister churches. Current executive director Ron Berg has identified a key challenge as that of enabling the churches to maintain a sense of community that has long characterized North American Baptists. To this end, he has set forth a vision for "church

[66] Woyke, *Heritage and Ministry*, 359–60.

[67] I am grateful to Rev. Ron Berg and Dr. John Binder, current and former executive directors of the NAB Conference, for their insight that assisted me in writing this section of the essay.

[68] Rokki Espie, ed., *2004 NAB Directory* (Oak Brook Terrace IL: Development Department, North American Baptist Conference, 2004) 5. These figures reflect 2002 statistics.

clusters" to form closer bonds among churches in close proximity, forming smaller units within the associations. It is a time of transition in the North American Baptist churches. The greatest numerical growth is now along the Pacific coast and in western Canada in suburban and urban areas. Some of the churches in the east are now African American and Latino inner city congregations, continuing in another key the historic vision of North American Baptists, seeking to embody the love of Christ by bringing persons into Christ's community.

Along the way, surprises of grace abound. In 1999, former Executive Director John Binder went to Boca Raton, Florida, as interim pastor of Evangel Baptist Church, one of a dwindling number of NAB churches in that state and Georgia that arose largely met Chris Cowen, pastor of SonCoast Christian Ministries, a growing independent evangelical congregation that lacked adequate facilities. Following a period of discernment, the congregations merged in March 2000, retaining the name SonCoast, occupying the former Evangel property, and affiliating with the NAB Conference. Cowen had been involved with a fellowship of pastors from a diverse group of independent churches that had come together for support and accountability. He shared the story of SonCoast's merger with Evangel and the reasons for NAB affiliation. A number of these other pastors were drawn to his vision, and "before we knew it the Florida association was formed with 11 churches at that time..."[69] The Association is comprised of Brazilian, Hatian, African-American, and Euro-America congregations. The establishment of this Association also brought a vibrant mission to Haiti into the fold of NAB work. What lies ahead for the North American Baptist Conference is not clear. It is clear, however, that the Holy Spirit's *Gemeinde*-creating grace remains present among them.

---

[69] Personal Correspondence with Rev. Chris Cowen, 31 August 2006. Chris Cowen and John Binder, phone conversation of 30 August 2006.

Chapter 9

BAPTISTS IN CANADA

William H. Brackney

Baptists in Canada reflect a multiplicity of origins and continuing types over a span of about two and a quarter centuries. Canadian Baptists are in many ways an amalgam of British, American, and indigenous Canadian influences. The term "Canadian Baptists" usually refers to those churches in the three traditional regions—Maritimes, Central Canada, and the West—who belong to one of the four historic conventions: the Convention of Atlantic Baptist Churches, the Baptist Convention of Ontario and Quebec, L'Union d'Eglises Baptistes Francaises au Canada, and the Baptist Union of Western Canada. They are also distinguished as "Convention Baptists," and nationally they comprise what is called "Canadian Baptist Ministries." Beyond the "Convention Baptist" family are several robust groups of Baptists found across the country.

The idea of "planting" was an early Maritime motif, as the English settlers to the region following the expulsion of the Acadians in the 1750s were known by the term "planters."[1] The first Baptists arrived from the United States in the wake of the French and Indian War. The fires of the Great Awakening were burning brightly, and this fervor reached Canadian territory. A bold start was made in 1763 at the head of

---

[1] William H. Brackney, *Polyglot Past: Making Sense of Canadian Baptist Identity, The John Gilmour Lectures for 1996* (Peterborough ONT: Murray Street Baptist Church, 1997). The heritage of the Planters in Nova Scotia has become a significant historical pursuit among regional colonial historians.

the Bay of Fundy at what was later Sackville, New Brunswick. Nathan Mason of Rehoboth, Massachusetts, planted a congregation in Sackville that dissolved in 1771.[2] Ebenezer Moulton (1709–1783) is usually credited with starting the first surviving congregation also in 1763 at Horton (later Wolfville), Nova Scotia. Originally a pastor at South Brimfield in western Massachusetts, Moulton had been quite active in the 1750s in Massachusetts campaigns to unite Baptists against oppressive taxation.[3] He fled his creditors in Massachusetts and settled in Nova Scotia, earning a living as a surveyor and preacher in the Yarmouth area. Moulton itinerated extensively along the Fundy Shore, and the Horton congregation was one of the results of his labors.[4] The floundering congregation was revived and strengthened in part through the preaching of Henry Alline (1748–1784), and it reconstituted itself in 1778. Located at the head of the Annapolis Valley, what became the Wolfville Church was influential for the entire region.

Next in the "planting" sequence were black Baptists who in 1782 arrived in the Maritimes under the leadership of David George. George (1743–1810), a freed slave from Virginia, and later Georgia, commenced preaching at various places in Nova Scotia and New Brunswick and started a permanent church at Birchtown near Shelburne on the South Shore.[5] Discrimination against the African Canadian community was strong, and after a decade, George led many of the black planters to establish a colony in Sierra Leone, West Africa. Later, black Baptist

---

[2] Robert Gardner, *Baptists of Early America: A Statistical History 1639–1790* (Atlanta: Georgia Baptist Historical Society, 1983) 130.

[3] William G. McLoughlin, *New England Dissent, 1630–1833: The Baptists and the Separation of Church and State*, vol. 1 (Cambridge: Fellows of Harvard College, 1971) 481–82.

[4] Compare Maurice K. Armstrong, *The Great Awakening in Nova Scotia* (Hartford, 1950) and William Brackney, "Ebenezer Moulton," in *Dictionary of American National Biography*, ed. John A. Garraty and Mark C. Carnes (New York: Oxford University Press, 1999) 16:26–27.

[5] Grant Gordon, *From Slavery to Freedom: The Life of David George, Pioneer Black Baptist Minister* (Hantsport NS: Lancelot Press, 1992) 43–71.

settlements were formed as termini to the Underground Railway in the far western area of Upper Canada at Amherstburg.[6]

A separate set of circumstances surrounding the plantation of Baptist communities ensued in Upper Canada (later Ontario). Missionaries from the United States played an important role in this region, planting congregations from Hallowell and Beamsville (1796) to Charlotteville (1803) and Queenston (1808) around the edges of Lake Ontario.[7] Sponsoring the U.S. missionaries were the Shaftsbury Association in Vermont, the Black River Association in northern New York, the Lake Baptist Missionary Society in central New York, Maine Baptist Missionary Society, New York (City) Baptist Missionary Society, and the Massachusetts Baptist Missionary Society.[8] Scottish Baptists under the sponsorship of the Haldanite movement came to Upper Canada as early as 1816, settling in the Ottawa Valley and eventually in Lower Canada (Quebec). John Edwards at Clarence, John Gilmour at Montreal, and William Fraser at Breadalbane were among the pioneer English/Scottish Baptists. In contrast to the closed Communionism of the American Baptists in Canada, the Scottish Baptists were of an open Communion persuasion. John Gilmour became a long-term link with English Baptists through the establishment of the Baptist Colonial Missionary Society and Baptist Canada Missionary Society, also of the open Communion kind. Montreal became the English center, with both missionaries and funds mostly directed at Canada Baptist College, a school to train pastors that commenced in 1838.[9]

---

[6] Dorothy S. Shreve, *The Afri-Canadian Church: A Stabilizer* (Jordan Station ONT: Paideia Press, 1983) 46–60.

[7] Stuart Ivison and Fred Rosser, *The Baptists in Upper and Lower Canada Before 1820* (Toronto: University of Toronto Press, 1956) 82–97.

[8] The work of the Massachusetts society is summarized in Elmer G. Anderson, "The Work of American Baptist Missionaries in Upper Canada to 1820" (B.D. thesis, McMaster University, 1952), and William H. Brackney, "Yankee Benevolence in Yorker Lands: Origins of the Baptist Home Missions Movement," *Foundations* 24/4 (October 1981): 293–309.

[9] Ivison and Rosser, *Baptists in Upper and Lower Canada*, 95.

Other Caucasian Baptist groups immigrated to Canada and established a presence as well. As German settlers came into the United States, many continued on into what is now the province of Ontario. Three areas were of special significance to Baptists: Berlin (later Kitchener), London and southwestern Ontario, and Hamilton.[10] From 1889 to the 1920s, German immigrants found their ways to Winnipeg, thence to Saskatchewan and Alberta, creating in Edmonton a center of their work. Eventually the population of Baptist congregations in the Prairies reached nearly 7,000 in more than 50 congregations. So strong was the church community that other German Baptist institutions grew up locally, and eventually the Canadian congregations won a separate corporate existence from the parent North American Baptist Conference in the United States.[11]

Likewise, Swedish Baptists, who were originally from Sweden but came through the United States, started churches as early as the 1850s in Quebec. Other congregations were commenced at Winnipeg, Manitoba, and at Battle River and Camrose, Alberta, among the Swedish settlements. From the Winnipeg church, several others were started in Manitoba and northwestern Ontario that formed the Central Canada Conference. Originally the churches were listed as part of the Baptist General Conference, and leaders were trained at the University of Chicago or Bethel Seminary in Sweden. With new growth indicated after World War II, and growing Canadian nationalism among the congregations, in 1981 the Baptist General Conference of Canada was formed. Related to the Swedish congregations were a few Danish and Norwegian Baptist churches, mostly isolated and under the care of those respective conferences in the United States. In the Niagara Peninsula of

---

[10] Frank Woyke, *Heritage and Ministry of the North American Baptist Conference* (Oakbrook Terrace IL: NABC Press, 1979) 184–86.

[11] David T. Priestly, "The Effect of 'Home Mission' Among Alberta's German Immigrants," in *Memory and Hope: Strands of Canadian Baptist History*, ed. David Priestley (Wilfred Laurier University Press, 1996) 55–68, and Ernest K. Pasiciel "The Socio-Cultural Transformation of the North American Baptist Conference" in ibid., 69–80.

Ontario and stretching from Manitoba to Alberta there were also pockets of Russians, often referred to in the Canadian West as Galicians and Ruthenians, as well as Ukrainians, Czechoslovakians, Polish, and Hungarians.[12] Last of the "ethnic" types are the Southern Baptists in western Canada who planted congregations first in British Columbia (BC) then in the Alberta oilfields where small numbers of emigrants from Texas and Louisiana had settled.[13]

Baptists and Institutional Development in Canada

In the Baptist way, organizational and institutional establishments ensued after sufficient congregations were planted. Baptist institutional life included regional associational and convention development, education, care and benevolence, and publishing concerns. The first association of churches established was convened in 1800 in Nova Scotia and New Brunswick, to be followed by three congregations in the Bay of Quinte region who established the Thurlow Association of Upper Canada in 1802. The associational principle fostered church planting, ministerial recognition, missionary cooperation, and fellowship among the churches across Canada. Several attempts at a larger, inter-provincial union were made, including the Canada Baptist Missionary Society (1837), the Canada Baptist Union (1843), the Baptist Convention of Nova Scotia, New Brunswick, and Prince Edward Island (1846), Regular Baptist Missionary Union of Canada (1848), Regular Baptist Missionary Union of Canada West (1858), the Canada Baptist Missionary Convention East (1858), the Baptist Convention of Ontario and Quebec (1888), the Baptist Convention of Manitoba and the Northwest (1884),

---

[12] C. C. McLaurin, *Pioneering in Western Canada: A Story of the Baptists* (Calgary: self-published, 1939) 357–74, 381–98.

[13] Southern Baptists first tried to affiliate with the fundamentalist Regular Baptists in B.C., then found opportunities to conduct both "home" and "foreign" missions in Canada from their base in Oregon and Washington. A Canadian Southern Baptist Conference was first organized in 1963. See G. Richard Blackaby, "The Establishment of the Canadian Convention of Southern Baptists" in *Memory and Hope*, 99–110.

the British Columbia Baptist Convention (1897), the United Baptist Convention of the Maritime Provinces (1905), Baptist Convention of Western Canada (1907), the Baptist Union of Western Canada (1909), the Canadian Baptist Foreign Mission Board (1911), the Baptist Federation of Canada (1944), and, lastly, Canadian Baptist Ministries (1995–). In the half-century course of its history, several distinguished pastoral leaders guided the Baptist Federation of Canada, including Abner Langley, Thomas McDormand, Fred Bullen, and Richard Coffin.[14] In a step ostensibly driven by economy and efficiency, in 1995 the federation was merged with the Canadian Baptist International Mission Board (CBIM) to form Canadian Baptist Ministries, now the sole pan-Canadian Baptist organization.

The establishment of educational institutions in the Canadian context was of more than passing importance to various parts of the Baptist family. First, education was a mark of the sophistication and maturation of denominational interests for all the "dissenter" groups. The "established" groups like the Anglicans and Presbyterians had long cherished an educated ministry and won the respect of colonial society. Second, the institutions themselves were often a microcosm of denominational character, exhibiting theological and organizational peculiarities.

Somewhat of a historical rivalry has existed over the years about the "first" educational institution's founding among Baptists. Acadia University traces its beginnings to the establishment of Horton Academy in Wolfville in 1828. When Nova Scotia Baptists were denied faculty positions in the chartered schools, Kings College and Dalhousie University, a plan was laid to upgrade the small academy at Horton. This reached fruition in 1838 with the chartering of Acadia University.[15] Its

---

[14] The best coverage of this organizational history is in Harry A. Renfree, *Heritage and Horizon: The Baptist Story in Canada* (Mississauga ONT: Canadian Baptist Federation, 1988) 86–89; 103; 166–67; 185–86.

[15] Baptists had originally petitioned to have the school named "Queens University," but Queen Victoria declined permission, doubtless because the school was associated with dissenters.

theological faculty was much influenced by Newton Theological Institution in New England; Acadia served the needs of the Maritime congregations throughout the nineteenth century. Chief among its faculty were Edmund Crawley (1799–1888), a protégé of Alexis Caswell at Brown University, and John Mockett Cramp (1796–1881), a Stepney College alumnus who once edited the *Baptist Magazine* in England. The theological department closed in 1883 in favor of sending ministerial students to McMaster in Toronto.[16]

Ultimately, however, Maritime sympathies favoring their own theological program led to a reinstatement of ministerial training at Acadia in 1889. During the early decades of the twentieth century, the university sought theological faculty who earned doctorates in a variety of fields. Gradual modernization took place until many felt Acadia had moved beyond its essentially rural, small-church constituency. A celebrated judicial proceeding in 1935 involving church property, the "Kingston Parsonage Case," focused the liberal leanings of a prominent faculty member, and more conservative churches moved to support other institutions for training pastors.[17] Noteworthy among these were New Brunswick Bible Institute and Gordon College and Gordon Conwell Theological Seminary in Massachusetts. Enrollment in the theological department dwindled in the 1950s and 1960s, and concerns were raised in the Maritime Convention that brought changes in the administration. When Acadia became a provincially supported university in the 1960s, the theological program evolved into Acadia Divinity College, related to Acadia University. New faculty were recruited, several with degrees from Scottish universities, and the college consciously pursued a definitively evangelical direction, notably under principals Andrew A. MacRae and Lee M. MacDonald. Practical studies became predominate over the classical disciplines, with emphases upon Maritime Baptist heritage and Anabaptist studies under MacRae and

---

[16] Ronald Stewart Longley, *Acadia University 1838–1938* (Wolfville NS: Acadia University, 1938) 63–65.

[17] George Rawlyk, "Fundamentalism, Modernism and the Maritime Baptists in the 1920s and 1930s," *Acadiensis* 17/1 (Autumn 1987): 24–27.

smore attention to biblical studies under MacDonald. At present, the school is under the auspices of the Convention of Atlantic Baptist Churches, and there continues to be a Baptist representation on the Acadia University Board of Governors.

McMaster University's roots are found in Montreal in the Canada Baptist College, mentioned earlier. From its beginning in 1838, its objectives and courses were more advanced than those of Acadia, but much of the dream fell short of realization in the early years. The college at Montreal was administered by missionary scholars whose expectations of ministerial students reflected more of a British orientation than the frontier of Canada warranted. Benjamin Davies,[18] an early principal, was frustrated and returned to Stepney College near London after only a few years. John M. Cramp, another English Baptist educational missionary to Canada, helped to close the school in 1849, and he moved to Acadia where he continued his career as an educator, historian, and administrator.

A second chapter in McMaster's story opened in the agricultural heartland of southwestern Ontario in 1861. At Woodstock, Robert A. Fyfe, one of the faculty from Montreal, started the Canadian Literary Institute, based on the model of literary and theological institutions in the United States. The program at Woodstock (later called Woodstock College) was designed to prepare students for university studies elsewhere. In 1887, Senator William McMaster of Toronto gave generous funds to the Baptist educational project on the proviso that the Woodstock school would be focused as a preparatory school and the theological program moved to Toronto. This occurred, and the new institution became Toronto Baptist College.[19] In many minds, the institution was intended to be a "national" Baptist school, serving all the regions of the country from its most prosperous city.

---

[18] Benjamin Davies (1814–1876) earned the first doctorate in any theological institution in Canada. He later returned to Canada to head the Classics Department at McGill University from 1847–1857.

[19] Charles M. Johnson, *McMaster University: The Toronto Years*, vol. 1 (Toronto: University of Toronto Press, 1976) 18–44.

Toronto Baptist College received university status in 1887 from the Province of Ontario and the next year benefited from the estate of Senator McMaster, prompting the trustees to rename the school McMaster University. It remained in Toronto under the shadow of the University of Toronto until 1928 when it relocated to Hamilton, Ontario. During this period, McMaster was arguably the most thoroughly Baptist institution in North America, controlled by a Baptist board, administered by Baptist clergy, with its property owned by the convention.[20] Following World War II, McMaster was unable to meet the rising demands of its region as a church-related institution, so in 1957 it became provincially related with a separate theological school, McMaster Divinity College, which continued under the Baptist Convention of Ontario and Quebec.

McMaster University was much affected by the fundamentalist movement between 1915 and the 1960s. Repeated investigations of its faculty and curricula by both fundamentalists and moderates led to a widening gap between the churches and the school. Eventually McMaster's acceptance among Baptist churches dwindled to a reduced number of congregations in the immediate area of Hamilton-Burlington. In the 1980s, a resurgence of evangelicalism that began with Clark H. Pinnock[21] and continued under principal William H. Brackney in the nineties led to a renewal of McMaster as an open evangelical Baptist school with ecumenical ties to the Toronto School of Theology. Emphasis was placed upon Baptist studies, New Testament research and publications, and evangelical thought.[22] In recent years, however, under

---

[20] See the discussion in William H. Brackney, "Secularization of the Academy: A Baptist Typology," *Westminster Studies in Education* 24/2 (2001): 119–21.

[21] Pinnock's interpretation of the fundamentalist struggle at McMaster, which is sympathetic to a need to reinterpret the era in evangelical terms, is found in his essay, "The Modernist Impulse at McMaster University, 1887–1927," in *Baptists in Canada: Search for Identity Amidst Diversity*, ed. J. K. Zeman (Burlington ONT: G. R. Welch, 1980) 193–207.

[22] Brackney's last faculty appointment was to fill the newly created Bentall Chair in Evangelical Thought with a world-class evangelical theologian from Oxford. Following his departure, the college withdrew the offer.

new leadership, the school has turned toward extreme conservatism, and the Baptist Convention of Ontario and Quebec (BCOQ) has lessened its financial support for McMaster. From the 1960s, significant numbers of Baptist ministerial candidates have bypassed McMaster to study at Ontario Bible College and Seminary, later Tyndale University College in Toronto.

As McMaster's fortunes fluctuated after the 1960s, Ontario Baptists gave increasing support to a leadership training center on the model of the Baptist Leadership Training School in Alberta. First known as "Baptist Training Institute" in Toronto in 1955, it moved to Brantford in 1959 and to Whitby, Ontario, in 1984, where it became the Baptist Leadership Education Center (BLEC).[23] The later program was funded in part by Leonard Cullen, a local horticulturalist, and by diminishing convention funds. Never entirely successful as a residential program, BLEC closed in 2002.

Francophone Baptists in Quebec constitute a fourth part of mainstream Baptist educational work in Canada. Several evangelical mission groups in Britain and Europe developed an interest in witnessing to the French Canadians of Lower Canada (Quebec). The most effective of these was that of Swiss evangelicals Louis Roussey (1812–1880) and Henriette Feller (1800–1868) in 1835. This led to the Grand Ligne Mission south of Montreal, an academy for men, and to a school for young ladies at Longueuil. From these roots was to come an association of francophone churches, le Union des Eglises Baptiste Francaises.[24] Over the years of the nineteenth century and well into the twentieth, persecution of Protestants and meager results were the story of that noble effort. However, with increased plurality and secularization in Quebec, as well as Francophones marrying into English families, indigenization of the Baptist mission seemed more promising from the 1960s onward. In 1982, behind the mission efforts of John Gilmour and

---

[23] Renfree, *Heritage and Horizon*, 333.

[24] The older work is Walter N. Wyeth, *Henrietta Feller and the Grande Ligne Mission: A Memorial* (Philadelphia: Wyeth, 1898), to be supplemented with W. Nelson Thompson, "Witness in French Canada" in *Baptists in Canada*, 45–65.

W. Nelson Thompson, a Bible college was established in Montreal, the Facultie de Theologie Evangelique. It is related academically to Acadia Divinity College.

In the Prairie provinces, education for ministry was limited to those who traveled east to either McMaster or Acadia universities, went south to the United States, or after 1930 received minor training at one of several Bible colleges in the Prairie provinces. From the 1890s through the 1930s, McMaster students took summer assignments in June, July, and August in small outposts in Manitoba and Saskatchewan under the support of the Home Mission Board of Ontario and Quebec. Leaders of the West realized the great limitations of this system and began to lay plans for various Western institutions. In 1879, John Crawford and G. B. Davis attempted a school at Rapid City, Manitoba, a short-lived scheme called Prairie College.[25] The most successful of them was Brandon College in Brandon, Manitoba, founded in 1890, an amalgam of earlier institutions in Rapid City and Winnipeg. The struggling college was under the auspices of McMaster for many generations and then chartered in Manitoba. It continued to be Baptist-related until 1939 when it became a provincial institution. Among those who taught at Brandon were D. C. Mackintosh, D. R. Sharpe, J. B. McLaurin, and Howard P. Whidden. The venerable Tommy Douglas, author of the Canadian national health plan, was a Baptist student at Brandon.[26]

In the far West, early attempts at starting a denominational school met with stiff challenges. In 1879, the churches of British Columbia formed an independent convention and made plans for a university. It took more than two decades for Ockanagan College to open at Summerfield, B.C., in 1907, and it ran into insurmountable obstacles after only seven years. Almost at once, yet another college was proposed at Edmonton, Alberta. Named for a prominent Baptist citizen of that city, McArthur College was launched under the principalship of Dores R. Sharpe, but failed at its outset to raise sufficient funds. Meanwhile, beginning in the 1920s, several Bible colleges emerged in Saskatchewan

---

[25] McLaurin, *Pioneering in Western Canada*, 286–95, 314–24.

[26] Ibid., 296–314.

and Alberta to fill the need for Christian workers. While the colleges were not under Baptist auspices, many Baptist students attended them. In 1949, a one-year residential school, the Baptist Union of Western Canada, began the Baptist Leadership Training School (BLTS) at Calgary, Alberta, a Baptist version of a Bible college that sought to orient students toward Christian service and study in a denominational setting. The BLTS program ranged from a residential pre-university experience to a training effort for youth workers. Its residential program ceased in 1995.

At length, a bold step was taken in 1959 to commence Carey Hall under union auspices. A charter was granted by the British Columbia legislature, and the school began near the campus of the University of British Columbia with forty-two students. After a decade on its own, the Baptist Union of Western Canada studied possible relationships for Carey Hall with Regent College and with North American Baptist College and Edmonton Seminary (both related to the German Baptists in Canada). In 1980, a long-term agreement was signed with Regent College, a trans-denominational evangelical school, also adjacent to UBC. Carey Hall continued as a residence with a small faculty that contributed to a Master of Divinity program. The combined Carey/Regents faculty included nationally known theologians and biblical scholars like J. I. Packer, Bruce Waltke, W. Ward Gasgue, and Clark Pinnock, and this in turn attracted the majority of ministerial candidates for the West to the school. In 1991, Carey Hall further evolved into Carey Theological College and now offers a full range of degree programs, still in conjunction with Regent College. The faculty at Carey, inclusive of a chair in honor of the western Canadian church planter Pioneer MacDonald, has been limited in number, yet inclusive of Canadian evangelical scholars like Samuel Mikolaski, Roy Bell, and the late Stanley Grenz. In 2004, the school commenced a North American Chinese Studies Program under the direction of Chung Yan Joyce Chan. While library privileges are shared with the university, there is no formal academic relationship between Carey and UBC or the Vancouver School of Theology.

The smaller Baptist bodies in Canada have built important educational institutions in addition to those of the Convention Baptists. Some developed along sharp theological confessions. Fellowship Baptists[27] struggled for many years to develop adequate educational institutions for their needs. T. T. Shields created Toronto Baptist Seminary in Jarvis Street Church in 1927, but it was wracked by division among its leadership. Two Toronto Fellowship pastors, W. Gordon Brown (1904–1979), pastor at Runnymede Baptist Church, and Jack Scott, pastor at Forward Baptist Church, split with Shields and Toronto Baptist Seminary in 1948–1949 and started Central Baptist Seminary in Toronto.[28] Another Fellowship institution emerged in 1976 in southwestern Ontario, London Baptist Bible College; in its early years it also added a seminary division. The two schools, Central and London, merged in 1993, first located at London (1993–1995) and later on a new campus in Cambridge, Ontario, called Heritage Baptist College and Theological Seminary. In Quebec, the Fellowship administers Seminaire Baptiste Evangelique du Quebec (SEMBEC) for its francophone ministry candidates.

Some of the "smaller" ethnic bodies also started schools. Early in the Baptist settlement of the Prairies, the need for ethnic ministerial education was recognized. In 1915 and 1918, respectively, Brandon opened Scandinavian and Slavic departments, built on models at Rochester and Colgate seminaries. Likewise, German Baptists moved to build a separate Canadian identity and recognized a need to train Christian leaders for their congregations in the West. At Edmonton, Alberta, in 1940, they commenced the Christian Training Institute on a modified Bible college plan. The institution prospered, and in 1967 the

---

[27] The Fellowship of Evangelical Baptist Churches in Canada arose in the 1920s during the Fundamentalist/Modernist Controversy in the United States. See "Fellowship of Evangelical Baptist Churches in Canada" in William H. Brackney, *Historical Dictionary of the Baptists*, Lanham, MD: Scarecrow Press, 1999): p. 157-58.

[28] Leslie K. Tarr, *This Dominion, His Dominion, The Story of the Evangelical Baptist Endeavour in Canada* (Willowdale ONT: Fellowship of Evangelical Baptist Churches, 1968) 98.

North American Baptist Conference approved the name change to "North American Baptist College." NABC received full accreditation as a Bible college in 1964 and proceeded in the 1970s to develop an advanced theological studies program. This was first called North American Baptist Seminary, then Edmonton Baptist Seminary.[29] Recognizing a desire to grow beyond its natural constituency, Edmonton Baptist Seminary (and North American Baptist College) became Taylor University College and Seminary in 2002, named for the famous missionary J. Hudson Taylor. Similarly, the Swedish Baptists who pioneered churches in the Prairie provinces started their own program related to Bethel Theological Seminary in St. Paul, Minnesota. It began in Wetaskiwin, Alberta, a center of Swedish settlement. Originally a Bible institute, it discontinued work after only a few years. At length, Trinity Western University (related to the Evangelical Free Church), founded in 1962, invited the Baptist General Conference to join a consortium to be called Associated Canadian Theological Schools (ACTS) in Langley, B.C., in 1985. The consortium now includes Canadian Theological Seminary (Christian and Missionary Alliance), Mennonite Brethren Biblical Seminary (Mennonite Brethren), and Canadian Pentecostal College (Pentecostal Assemblies of Canada). Finally, Southern Baptists from an intensive "home" missions program that commenced as early as 1951 determined to have a Canadian institution and in 1987 built Canadian Southern Baptist Seminary in Cochrane, Alberta, in the heart of their Canadian Southern Baptist constituency. In 1997, an undergraduate division, Canadian Baptist College, was added to the seminary program.

Baptists also have other benevolent institutions across Canada. To serve the retirement needs of seniors, Ontario Baptists founded Lynde Creek in Whitby, Maritimers opened four retirement homes across their region, and those in the West sponsor a residence at White Rock, B.C. German Baptists have built four homes for the aged in Canada at Winnipeg, Manitoba; Medicine Hat and Leduc, Alberta; and White

[29] The earlier history is recounted in Woyke, *Heritage and Ministry*, 419–22.

Rock, B.C. Fellowship Baptists have an extensive Christian camp program, with sites in Ontario, Quebec, British Columbia, and Yukon. They also have senior citizens' homes managed through foundations.

Theological Issues Unique to Baptists in Canada

Among the earliest theological issues was that of New Light preaching. As an extension of the Great Awakening, numbers of New Light preachers came to Nova Scotia and New Brunswick from the 1760s to 1790s. This gave a distinctively revivalist flavor to the first wave of pastoral leaders. Revivals could be synonymous with evangelistic services or times of refreshing and renewal. Their sermons stressed personal religious experience and narrative rather than rigid confessionalism. Full-time revivalists traversed the Maritimes, holding protracted meetings throughout the nineteenth century and well into the last century. Camp meetings or "ashrams" institutionalized some of this religious fervor. Reinforcement of the New Light tradition was seen in the Freewill Baptist development in the Maritimes and Lower Canada. Freewillism began in upper New England in the wake of Benjamin Randall, a self-taught Baptist preacher who stressed "free grace, free will, free communion, and free pews." Randal and his "Connexion" reacted strongly to Calvinist theology and elite congregationalism. Beginning in the 1790s his preachers entered New Brunswick and fanned out into Nova Scotia and Lower Canada, adopting the name "Free Baptists." Another group in the early nineteenth century that entered Upper Canada from New York State of the same ilk was the "Free Communion" Baptists. They placed more stress on free access to the Lord's Supper and emphasized the perseverance of the saints more than the Freewill Baptists.[30] In 1837, there was a split among Maritime "Free" Baptists that led to the establishment of the Free Christian Baptists. The two groups reunited in 1867 as the Free Baptist Conference of Nova Scotia. However, another rift developed in the 1880s over the doctrine

[30] Renfree, *Heritage and Horizon*, 122–31.

of entire sanctification, and this led to two come-outer groups, the "Primitive" Baptists who disliked educated and salaried pastors, and the "Reformed Baptists" who favored perfectionism but were also immersionists and local congregational in their definition of the church. The Reformed Baptists were concentrated in eastern New Brunswick and operated "Beulah Camp-meeting" and eventually a school at Sussex, the Bethany Bible College. The Reformed Baptists published a newspaper, *The King's Highway*, until they merged in 1968 with the Wesleyan Methodist Church and the Pilgrim Holiness Church to form the Wesleyan Church of America.[31] Most of the remaining Free Baptists, belonging to the New Brunswick Conference, voted overwhelmingly to join the regular Baptists, and in 1905 the merged body, the "United" Baptist Convention of the Maritimes, was born, thus closing a longstanding theological rift.

In contrast to the revival tradition was the establishment of First Baptist, Halifax, actually an outgrowth of St. Paul's Anglican Church in Halifax. That congregation has exhibited a more liturgical worship and progressive theological tradition than most congregations in the Annapolis Valley or eastern Nova Scotia. It had strong ties to regular Baptists in New England and fostered an educated ideal for ministry. A similar worship tradition can be seen in Toronto at Yorkminster Park Church; in Hamilton at James Street Church; in Montreal at First Baptist and Westmount Baptist churches; in Manitoba at Broadway First, in Winnipeg and First Baptist Church, Brandon; in Saskatchewan at First Baptist Saskatoon; and in Alberta at First Baptist Edmonton. Most of these congregations have been influenced over the years by McMaster University graduates. Less revivalist and conversionist in style, these Baptists favored Christian nurture and cooperation with other denominations.

In the Ontario community, open versus closed Communion provided divergent opinions in the Baptist communities. American

---

[31] My thanks for this detail to Professor Emeritus of Philosophy and Religion Lawrence Mullen of Houghton College in New York, a relative of the editor of the paper and himself a former instructor at Bethany Bible College.

Baptists in the Northeast were uniformly of the closed Communion position. This meant that their doctrine of the church mandated a believer's church of individuals who were baptized by immersion upon profession of their faith. Participation in the Lord's Supper was limited to such people in full membership. On the other hand, a significant number of Baptist ministers and laity immigrated to Canada from England, and they were open or mixed Communionists. An open Communion advocated admission to the Lord's Table on the basis of one's Christian profession, regardless of baptismal status or mode. Open Communionists were inspired by Robert Hall, Jr., and others who placed emphasis in the ordinance upon fellowship and the interdenominational table over strict rules not found in Scripture. Strict or closed Communion was associated with a continuing eighteenth-century Calvinistic perspective, while open Communion tended to be associated with progressive, urban, evangelical, and revivalist thinkers of the nineteenth-century British context. The Communion question laid appropriate focus upon the Baptist doctrine of the church as well as the cultural division between American and British Baptist influences in the Canadian provinces.[32]

A third issue that dominated discussion among Baptists and with the other major denominations was that of religious voluntarism. Baptists, of course, more or less favored religious liberty and disestablishment. In the 1840s, a major attempt was made to use proceeds from the sale of the Clergy Reserves lands for the support of King's College (Anglican) in Upper Canada. Baptists led the campaign against this legislation, supported by the Methodists and lukewarmly by Presbyterians. Robert A. Fyfe (1816–1878), the leading Baptist of the era, wrote numerous editorials and petitions in favor of a completely voluntary system, by which he meant that all theological schools should be supported by the denominational interests that sponsored them. Fyfe, much influenced by New York State Baptists, held tenaciously to religious liberty and the

---

[32] For a discussion of this issue and the relevant documents, see William H. Brackney, *Baptist Life and Thought: A Sourcebook*, rev. ed. (Valley Forge: Judson Press, 1998) 489–91.

doctrine of a voluntary church and opposed any system whereby the King's College or any other denominational institution would receive funds favoring its religious affiliation. In 1842, the newly organized Canada Baptist Union resolved "each member of the civil community, of whatever faith, is entitled to an equal share in the benefits conferred by government upon the people....the exhibition of favoritism to any one encourages religious dissention...and is a direct violation of the rights of conscience."[33]

Already the die was cast in the Maritimes, however, where Baptists shared bounteously with Anglicans and Presbyterians in Wolfville and Fredericton. What emerged was a uniquely Canadian understanding of religious freedom and voluntarism, namely that denominations could share proportionately in the distribution of public funds for education, as long as their membership deserved such recognition.[34] More a model of religious equalitarianism than separation of church and state, it has remained in place to the present time in several Canadian provinces.

A serious rift opened in the early twentieth century among Baptists in central Canada that eventually led to two separate denominational entities. In 1908 and 1909, investigations of liberal teaching targeting Old Testament professor Isaac G. Mathews occurred at McMaster. A prominent Toronto pastor and contributing editor to the *Scofield Reference Bible*, Elmore G. Harris, led the effort. Although Mathews was "cleared," he departed Canada for Crozer Theological Seminary, one of the bastions of anti-fundamentalist thought in the Northern Baptist Convention in the U.S. Harris went on to help found Toronto Bible Training Institute, a major new evangelical center in Ontario that he hoped would counter the liberal tendencies of McMaster University.[35]

---

[33] Quoted in J. E. Wells, *Life and Labors of Robert Alexander Fyfe D.D.* (Toronto: W. J. Gage and Co., 1885) 148–49.

[34] See the discussion of voluntarism in Theo T. Gibson, *Robert Alexander Fyfe: His Contemporaries and His Influence* (Burlington ONT: G. R. Welch, 1988) 147–65. The author of this book, a retired Baptist minister and regional minister, is a stalwart defender in the Canadian context of separation of church and state.

[35] Johnson, *McMaster University*, 91–93; Renfree, *Heritage and Horizon*, 206.

Renewed impetus was given to critics of the convention and the university in the following decade by American fundamentalists.

The new leader of the "charge" and the charges in the 1920s was Thomas Todhunter Shields (1873–1955), pastor of Jarvis Street Baptist Church in Toronto.[36] He found unacceptable traces of evolutionary, ecumenical thinking at McMaster and called upon the Baptist Convention of Toronto and Ontario to adopt a creedal statement. Shields was especially troubled by McMaster's awarding an honorary doctorate in 1923 to Brown University president W. H. P. Faunce, an avowed critic of creedalism, plus the appointment in 1925 of L. H. Marshall, pastor of the Baptist church in Coventry, to the chair in practical theology.[37] Marshall, a protégé of the distinguished British Baptist scholar H. Wheeler Robinson, became the center of a rancorous debate at the convention assembly in 1925, and after a few teaching terms, he left Canada to return to Rawdon College in England. Sensing continued infidelity at McMaster, however, Shields started a rival school in Toronto and used the pages of his paper *The Gospel Witness* to criticize the convention and rally his support. At length, in 1926, the convention censured Shields and, with a change in their charter in 1927, the BCOQ voted to expel Jarvis Street Church as Shields openly organized a new body, the Union of Regular Baptist Churches of Ontario and Quebec.[38] A small group of Ontario congregations remained independent and in 1931 began to call themselves the Fellowship of Independent Baptist Churches, in part signaling some disaffection with Shields's autocratic leadership. Devotees of Shields appeared in British Columbia in the later 1920s and formed the Convention of Regular Baptist Churches of British Columbia in 1928. Until the late 1940s, T. T. Shields remained a dominant factor in the anti-convention forces in central and western Canada. His paper *The Gospel Witness* and Toronto Baptist Seminary were constant sources of vituperative attacks on both the convention and

---

[36] The best study of Shields is Mark C. Parent, "The Christology of T. T. Shields: The Irony of Fundamentalism" (Ph.D. thesis, McGill University, 1981).

[37] Johnson, *McMaster University*, 174–75; 182–83.

[38] First called the Regular Baptist Missionary and Educational Society.

rivals in his own group. At length, new leaders came forth in the West, like Morley R. Hall in Calgary and W. H. McBain and Gordon Brown among the central Canadian factions, with a vision to unite the theologically conservative evangelical Baptists. The result was the formation of the Fellowship of Evangelical Baptist Churches of Canada in 1953, bringing together churches in the central and western regions.[39]

For the last several decades, the Fellowship Baptist churches have held forth a platform of inerrancy, biblical separationism, opposition to charismatic renewal and women in ministry, and dispensationalist interpretation of Bible prophecy that has characterized their denominational life. Their main numerical strength and flagship congregations are found in Ontario.[40]

Recently, the impact of charismatic renewal in various forms has had a pronounced effect upon mainstream Baptists across Canada. John Wimber, formerly of Fuller Theological Seminary, has made forays into Baptist territory, and the Toronto Airport Blessing, started by a former Fellowship Baptist pastor, John Arndt, has drawn support across the BCOQ. At McMaster Divinity College in the 1990s, Clark Pinnock, a former inerrantist with Southern Baptist connections, adopted a charismatic agenda and was openly supportive of the "Airport Ministries."[41]

Canadian Baptists Today

Baptists represent a form of evangelical tradition among major religious groups in Canada. There are conservative evangelical examples, such as the Fellowship Baptists, the Baptist General Conference and the North American Baptist Conference, and there are moderate to liberal factions,

[39] For the story of Fellowship Baptists, consult Leslie K. Tarr, *This Dominion, His Dominion*, 127–36.

[40] Tarr, *This Dominion, His Dominion*, 102–103.

[41] On Pinnock, see William H. Brackney, *A Genetic History of Baptist Thought* (Macon GA: Mercer University Press, 2004) 504–509, and Doug Koop, "Closing the Door on Open Theists," *Christianity Today* 47/1 (January 2003): 24–25.

especially in the Baptist Convention of Ontario and Quebec. Most Maritime Baptists would consider themselves evangelicals on the conservative side, and those belonging to the western Union are certainly mostly in that tradition. Of primary importance are American institutional influences, including Gordon College and Gordon Conwell Theological Seminary, Fuller Theological Seminary, Trinity Evangelical Divinity School, Wheaton College, InterVarsity Canada, and World Vision Canada. Most Baptist groups have a limited ecumenical perspective, leaning toward membership in the Evangelical Fellowship of Canada. The Baptist Convention of Ontario and Quebec is the sole Baptist presence in the Canadian Council of Churches, and those conventions and unions comprising the organization Canadian Baptist Ministries, plus the Seventh Day Baptists, relate to the Baptist World Alliance.

Numerically, among Convention Baptists there are 62,000 Baptists in 540 congregations in Atlantic Canada; 32,344 members in 387 congregations in Central Canada; and 20,000 members in 175 congregations in Western Canada. The North American Baptist Conference includes 17,527 members in 140 congregations from Ontario westward, and the Baptist General Conference of Canada has 101 churches with 7,000, mostly in the West. The Fellowship of Evangelical Baptist Churches in Canada, highly concentrated in Ontario and British Columbia, number 56,215 members in 493 congregations, and there are 3 congregations of Seventh Day Baptists with about 140 members, all in Ontario. Southern Baptists in Canada claim a membership of 10,622 in 209 congregations, located in the Western provinces and Ontario. Afri-Canadian Baptists number 20 congregations and 3,500 members located in Nova Scotia and Ontario. Statistically, as of 2005, the smaller and newer Baptist groups are close approaching the aggregate numbers of convention Baptists across the country.[42]

---

[42] An update of the statistics compiled by J. K. Zeman for *The Canadian Encyclopedia*, vol. 1 (Edmonton AB: Hurtig Publishers, 1988).

Chapter 10

SEVENTH DAY BAPTISTS

Don A. Sanford

Seventh Day Baptists have been a part of the Baptist family for three and a half centuries. They hold to such basic Baptist concepts as (1) salvation by grace through faith in Jesus Christ; (2) the Bible as the inspired message of God and the final authority for both faith and conduct; (3) baptism of believers by immersion witnessing to one's acceptance of Christ as Savior and Lord; (4) freedom of thought under the guidance of the Holy Spirit; (5) the congregational form of church government granting all members the right to participate in the decision-making process of the church.

The distinctive that sets Seventh Day Baptists apart from other Baptists is their observance of the biblical seventh day Sabbath, the day established and blessed by God at creation and held sacred by Jesus and the New Testament church. Historically the observance of Sunday stemmed from the anti-Jewish attitude of Rome and the accommodation to pagan worship of the sun. It was not until the Protestant Reformation of the sixteenth century and the availability of the Bible to the people that the question of the day for Christian worship was seriously challenged.[1]

---

[1] See Don A. Sanford, *A Choosing People: The History of the Seventh Day Baptists* (Nashville: Broadman Press, 1992) for a comprehensive discussion of Seventh Day Baptist history both in England and North America.

Seventh Day Baptist Beginnings in England

In 1595, Nicolas Bownde wrote a book titled *The Doctrine of the Sabbath* that attempted to secure a biblical basis for a strict, disciplined observance of the Puritan Sunday. Bownde argued that "the Sabbath must needs be still upon the seventh day as it always hath beene."[2] His book supported the stern Calvinistic discipline of the time that promised punishment for all lawbreakers and demonstrated who might be considered the elect.

Bownde's book had considerable impact upon the churches of the seventeenth century. To the Church of England it confirmed the idea that the church had the power and the precedent for establishing doctrine and practice. On the other hand, it was so restrictive in what could be done that King James had published in 1618 *The Book of Sports*, which prescribed in detail what activities might be undertaken after attendance at worship in the morning. To those who used the Bible as the source of teaching and doctrine, Bownde's book posed a serious dilemma. His early argument for the Sabbath they could accept, but there were some who saw an inconsistency in the General Baptists' Orthodox Creed of 1678. Article XL, on religious worship and the Sabbath day, calls for all to worship

> according to God's own institution and appointment. And hath limited us by his own revealed will, that he may not be worshipped according to the imaginations and devices of men, or the suggestions of Satan, under any visible representations whatsoever, or any other way not prescribed in the holy scriptures.... Yet the assembly of the church ought not to be neglected by any. And in order to his being worshipped and served, God hath instituted one day in seven for his sabbath to be kept holy unto him, which from the resurrection of Christ is the first day of the week which is called the Lord's day, and

[2] Nicolas Bownde, *The Doctrine of the Sabbath: Plainely layde forth, and soundly proved by testimonies both of holy Scripture, and also of olde and ecclesiasticall writers* (London, 1595) 35.

is to be observed to the end of the world as a Christian sabbath, the last day of the week being abolished.[3]

The first known writing in support of the seventh day Sabbath by a Baptist was from James Ockford, who in 1650 published *The Doctrine of the Fourth Commandment, Deformed by Popery, Reformed & Restored to its Primitive Purity*. Ockford's book was met with great opposition and controversy, ultimately causing Parliament to ban the book and order all copies burned. Only one copy is known to exist.

It is difficult to determine an exact date for the beginning of the Seventh Day Baptists in England as a distinctive denomination for several reasons. First, to avoid persecution, some who held Sabbatarian views wrote anonymously, or as in the case of the Tewksbury Baptist Church, the membership list was written in code and contained members who kept the seventh day as well as the first day. Such was also the case of Stephen and Anna Mumford, who eventually came to America and were among the first members of the Seventh Day Baptist Church in Newport, Rhode Island, when it was formed in 1671.

Second, beliefs changed as people began to experience freedom. B. R. White observed that many people changed their convictions impulsively, and therefore it is unwise to assume that a person remained in a particular group "at the moment when some fragment of evidence brings him to the historian's note."[4]

Third, although individuals may have had distinct beliefs concerning the Sabbath, or believers' baptism, they shared many tenets of faith with other churches. Therefore, a number of those that history would claim as Seventh Day Baptists were participating members of churches who worshipped on Sunday. Some even served as pastors of other churches while maintaining private or small group worship on the Sabbath. Henry Jessey, the famous dissenting pastor of the separatist church known as the Jacob, Lathrop, and Jessey Church, was a case in

---

[3] "An Orthodox Creed or Protestant Confession of Faith," in William L. Lumpkin, *Baptist Confessions of Faith* (Valley Forge: Judson Press, 1989) 327–28.

[4] B. R. White. *The English Baptists in the Seventeenth Century*, 3 vols. (London Baptist Historical Society: 1983) 1:30.

point. According to his biographer, for two years he "kept his opinion much to himself and observed the day in his own chamber with four or five others, but on the first day he preached as before."[5]

For more than a century the Stennett family was associated with the cause of both Baptists and Seventh Day Baptists. Through writings, hymns, and other representations of the free church tradition, their influence has extended to modern times. Edward Stennett was a strong contender for the Sabbath and suffered persecution because of his belief. His son, Joseph, was pastor of the Pinner's Hall Seventh Day Baptist Church in London, but preached at other churches on Sunday. Joseph Stennett II was primarily the pastor of the Little Wild Street Baptist Church (non-Seventh Day Baptist), but maintained a close relationship with his father's church and often filled the pulpit there. It was said of him that "as to his personal religion, he was a Seventh Day Baptist but vocationally, he always served the first-day Baptist churches. Historians of both denominations claim him as an important person."[6]

In England during the seventeenth century, hymn singing was frowned upon or even forbidden among many Baptists. Seventh Day Baptists were among those who took Paul's instructions to worship with psalms, hymns, and spiritual songs (Col 3:16). Some of the early hymn writers tried to show that the words of their hymns were all scriptural by placing in the margin biblical references to words used in the text, even though not necessarily in the context of the hymn. In 1732, Joseph Stennett published fifty hymns to be used in Communion services, twenty-five for baptism and three that proclaim the Sabbath. Samuel Stennett wrote two well-known hymns that are still included in some of the older hymnbooks: "Majestic Sweetness Sits Enthroned" and "On Jordan's Stormy Banks I Stand."

---

[5] Edward Whiston, *The Life and Death of Mr. Henry Jessey* (n.p., 1671).

[6] Oscar Burdick, "The Stennett Family," (Ph. D. diss., Alfred University School of Theology, 1953) 167.

Seventh Day Baptists in America

Although there were some early connections with English Seventh Day Baptists, American Seventh Day Baptists had roots more closely tied to Baptist traditions within the American colonies, with three independent beginnings in Rhode Island, Pennsylvania, and New Jersey.[7] The first Seventh Day Baptist Church in America began in 1671 as the result of a schism in John Clarke's Baptist Church of Newport in Newport, Rhode Island. Five members of the congregation—Roger Baster, William Hiscox, and Samuel and Tacy Hubbard along with their daughter—joined with Stephen and Anna Mumford, who had migrated from England in 1665, to form a congregation committed to Sabbath observance. Unity in the Newport Baptist Church existed between Sabbatarians and non-Sabbatarians until two of the members who had previously accepted the Sabbath reversed their views. The seventh day observers felt betrayed and had difficulty maintaining fellowship with those who had once accepted the Sabbath but recanted. The resulting schism led to the formation of the first Seventh Day Baptist Church in Rhode Island.[8]

Because the Mumfords had been Sabbatarians in England before migrating to America, it has often been assumed that they were the founders of the Seventh Day Baptist Church in Newport. However, the evidence points to Samuel and Tacy Hubbard as the more likely founders. In 1647, they subscribed to the doctrine of believers' baptism. Samuel credited his wife with taking the lead in this enlightenment. He wrote, "God having enlightened both, but mostly my wife, into his holy ordinance of baptizing only visible believers, and being very zealous for it, she mostly was struck at and answered two times publicly; where I was said to be as bad as she, and are threatened with imprisonment to

[7] See Sanford, *A Choosing People*, 94–113 for a detailed description of the origin of the first Seventh Day Baptist Churches in America.

[8] *Abington Baptist Association Records*, cited by Oscar Burdick, *The Great Decade, 1650–1660*, June 1984 draft ms., Seventh Day Baptist Historical Society (SDBHS) Library, Janesville WI, 25.

Hartford jail, if not to renounce it or to remove."[9] In 1648, they moved to Newport, were baptized by John Clarke, and became active members in Clarke's church. Samuel Hubbard assumed considerable leadership in the church as a sign of his Baptist commitment and suffered persecution on several occasions from the Massachusetts Bay Puritan establishment. In 1665, the Hubbards accepted the seventh day Sabbath. Their daughters, Ruth, Rachel, and Bethiah, along with their son-in-law Joseph Clarke, the nephew of John Clarke, followed. Considerable correspondence exists between the Hubbards and Sabbatarian Baptists in England.

In spite of the separation, there remained a considerable spirit of cooperation and ecumenicity within the Baptist community in Newport. In 1694, when the First Baptist Church was without a pastor, its members voted to place themselves under the ministry of Rev. William Hiscox of the Seventh Day Church. The sharing of pulpits continued for years, and several Baptist churches in the Newport area jointly owned and maintained a chapel at Green End, where baptisms were held until its maintenance became a problem after the American Revolution.

Several members of the Newport Seventh Day Baptist Church migrated to the Westerly or Hopkinton region of Rhode Island, where in 1708 they formed a branch church. Among its most prominent members was the Ward family. Richard Ward was governor of Rhode Island from 1740 to 1742, and his son, Thomas, was secretary of state. Richard Ward's most noted son, however, was Samuel, who in 1762 became governor. He was the only colonial governor who refused to sign the Stamp Act, and he later served in the First and Second Continental Congresses. He would have signed the Declaration of Independence had he not died of smallpox less than four months prior to its enactment.

A continuing role of the Seventh Day Baptists of Rhode Island in both cooperation and education is demonstrated in the establishment of Rhode Island College, later known as Brown University. When the

---

[9] Register of Mr. Samuel Hubbard, transcript MS 196x.6, SDBHS Library, Janesville WI, 97.

Philadelphia Association decided to establish a Baptist college, they chose Rhode Island because it was the only colony that had a Baptist governor, and a majority of its legislature were Baptists. The original charter specified that of the thirty-six trustees, twenty-two shall forever be elected of the denomination called Baptists. Seventh Day Baptists were listed among the Baptist trustees as well as the Board of Fellows that was charged with the academic affairs of the college. The first four-year graduate of the university was Ebenezer David, a Seventh Day Baptist who served at Valley Forge as a chaplain in the American Revolution.[10]

About thirty years after the organization of the Newport church, a second group of Baptists committed to the seventh day Sabbath organized near Philadelphia. Like Rhode Island, the Pennsylvania colony was founded on principles of religious freedom. Unlike Rhode Island, which was a haven for colonists from England, Pennsylvania acted like a magnet attracting settlers from among the persecuted from the continent of Europe. Many of them came from countries with strong state churches, deeply rooted in traditions and customs that made it difficult for a minority group to attain the strength needed to survive beyond the colonial period.

The Seventh Day Baptists' beginnings in Pennsylvania stemmed from the Quaker settlement of the late seventeenth century. There is some evidence that the Quaker use of numerical designation of the days of the week rather than the pagan origin of the names in common usage showed an inconsistence of worshipping on Sunday rather than on the seventh day, Saturday. Four churches were established in the Philadelphia area around 1700 that lasted through the period of the American Revolution.

It is ironic that those who had suffered persecution in Europe were often intolerant of those who disagreed with them. William Penn's *Frame of Government* (1682) contained provisions for freedom of religion, but it was not an unrestricted freedom. One prevision was

---

[10] See Walter Bronson, *The History of Brown University* (Providence RI: Brown University, 1914).

particularly restrictive for those who chose to worship on the seventh day Sabbath, for it required abstaining from common daily labor "every First Day of the week called the Lord's Day."[11] Such so-called "blue laws" were created to work a hardship on those who did not work on the Sabbath for religious convictions or on Sunday for legal requirements.

The third Seventh Day Baptist beginning in America came as a result of Baptist migrations from Massachusetts to the Piscataqua River that separated Maine from New Hampshire. Puritan persecution followed them there, but the restoration of the Stuart monarchy in England strengthened their claim on New Jersey, where religious freedom was granted. A strong Baptist contingent founded a church at Piscataway in 1686. In 1705, when Edmund Dunham was on his way to church, he chastised a neighbor who was doing servile work on Sunday. Hezekiah Bonham challenged him to find one passage in the Bible stating it was wrong to work on Sunday. Dunham enlisted his Sunday school class in his search for a proof text, but found none. As a result, seventeen members of the Baptist church separated and established their own church. Dunham was sent to Rhode Island, where the Hopkinton branch of the Newport church ordained him. The ordaining minister was William Gibson, who had been recruited from England by the Newport Church, thus solidifying a tie that eventually led to the organization of the Seventh Day Baptist General Conference a century later.[12]

Expansion into New Territories

The American Revolution had a direct effect upon Seventh Day Baptists. Their sense of covenant placed them in the mainstream of those who yearned for the political freedom for which they had labored in their

---

[11] William Penn, article 36, *The Frame of the Government of the Province of Pennsylvania in America* (London 1682), reprinted in Donald S. Lutz and Jack D. Warren, *A Covenanted People: The Religious Tradition and Origins of American Constitutionalism* (Providence: John Carter Brown Library, 1987) 32.

[12] Sanford, *A Choosing People*, 111–12.

practice of religion for more than a century. Not only did they loyally contribute to the struggle for independence, but they were also vitally affected by it. The expansion of territory resulting from the Treaty of Paris in 1783 opened new regions into which they could settle. Many chose to settle where they could establish their own community of faith. At the same time, this expansion challenged them to develop ways in which a close covenant relationship of clustered churches could be maintained.

With the exception of a few industries, such as shipbuilding and textile-related work, a large number of Seventh Day Baptists made their living from the land. Farming was one occupation in which a person could set his or her own workdays and thus observe the seventh day Sabbath. From the Rhode Island area, the pattern of migration westward generally followed the Housetonic River in western Connecticut to Rensselaer County in New York, where a church was established. From there the migration moved across central and western New York, with the group establishing churches as they moved. From this migration, a second stage moved into Wisconsin territory in the later 1830s.

The Philadelphia and New Jersey churches tended to follow military roads and trails across the Appalachian region into western Pennsylvania and then up the Monongahela River into West Virginia. The West Virginia migration spawned a move into the more fertile regions of Ohio and the Great Plains area, establishing churches as they moved. This westward migration tended to be by families within the faith who gathered for worship, and fellowship had lasting effects on the character of the denomination.

Churches tended to be family oriented through intermarriage with common ancestry. It was not unusual for two or three brothers to marry a like number of sisters in a neighboring family. It was highly probable that their parents might have been related. Thus, when a new person moved into the community or attended a worship service, an often-asked question was "Who are you related to?"

Additionally, isolation from others with a differing theological practice created a longing for a sense of community. This eventually led to the organization of the general conference in 1802, which is typical of many Baptist churches and done for several reasons.[13] (1) It gave the people an identity; (2) it helped define doctrine; (3) it stimulated education, both for laity and ministers; (4) it helped develop programs; (5) it was a vehicle of communication; (6) it was a stimulus for evangelism and missions; (7) and it was a vehicle for ecumenical cooperation with other Christians.[14]

The first article of the early constitution adopted in 1805 used the title "Sabbatarian General Conference," but in 1817 a more definitive name was adopted: Seventh Day Baptist General Conferene. Since many other churches referred to Sunday as the Sabbath, the term Seventh Day clearly indicated which day was observed. Using "Baptist" in the name revealed both the historic roots and the major distinctive of believers' baptism upon profession of faith in Christ. The recognition of Seventh Day Baptists as a distinct denomination has been important in ecumenical relations as well as clearly defined in state, national, and international affairs.

Closely related to the sense of identity, the corporate body of the general conference set guidelines for membership, examined and ordained ministers, and developed statements that have reflected the basic beliefs supported by both Scripture and history. Expressing an aversion to creedal statements, Seventh Day Baptists adopted *A Statement of Belief* in 1937 that declares, "Seventh Day Baptists cherish liberty of thought as an essential condition for the guidance of the Holy Spirit. Therefore they have no binding creed to which members must subscribe. They hold, however, that certain beliefs and practices, having the support of Scripture and adhered to by followers of Christ through the centuries are binding upon all Christians."[15]

---

[13] See Sanford, *A Choosing People*, 145–58 for a good discussion of the formation of the Seventh Day Baptist General Conference.

[14] Sanford, *A Choosing People*, 148–49.

[15] *A Statement of Belief of Seventh Day Baptists*, located at http://www.seventh-day-baptist.org.au/library/books/sdbbook.htm (accessed 24 May 2005).

In both England and America, Seventh Day Baptists have relied upon an educated populous for both belief and practice. While many attribute the Sunday school movement to Robert Raikes of England, who in 1780 established a reading and catechism school, it is a fact that forty years prior to Raikes, Ludwig Hocker of the German Seventh Day Baptists at Ephrata, Pennsylvania, established a Sabbath school for religious education of the children. The colonial migration of families into the frontier Sabbath schools often became the first step in the organization of a church. The churches in turn often took the lead in the establishment of schools and academies that served the whole community. In places such as Alfred, New York; Milton, Wisconsin; and Salem, West Virginia, the academies became colleges. In Alfred, Seventh Day Baptists established a seminary for ministerial training in 1871.

Because the normal school week was Monday through Friday, a higher than average number of Seventh Day Baptist students entered the teaching profession, where a five-day workweek allowed freedom for Sabbath observance. Where coeducation was encouraged, this was true for both men and women. Women doctors and teachers were among the early missionaries to China beginning in 1847. The first woman graduate from the seminary at Alfred was Experience Fitz Randolph, who was ordained in 1885. She later married Rev. Leon D. Burdick. The two of them served both separate and joint pastorates and even conducted a number of evangelistic crusades together.

The constitution adopted in 1805 by the Seventh Day Baptist General Conference limited general conference transaction to that of "advice, counsel and recommendation."[16] Yet in practice, there were times when conference provided the facility for bringing together special interests such as the selection of a hymnbook suitable for use in the

---

[16] Article 3, General Conference Constitution (1805), reprinted in Henry Clarke, *A History of the Sabbatarians or Seventh Day Baptists, in America Containing Their Rise and Progress to the Year 1811, with Their Leaders' Names, and Their Distinguishing Tenets, etc.* (Utica NY:Printed by Seward and Williams for the author, 1811) 70.

churches. The first such hymnbook was published in 1826, with others following in 1832 and beyond.

Through its power of recommendation, the general conference has initiated a number of programs. It was instrumental in the organization and support of the Missionary Society, the Tract Society, and the Education Society during the first half of the nineteenth century. As other needs were perceived, it responded to requests for a Sabbath School Board, a Women's Board, a Young People's Board, and a Historical Board. In celebration of the 200th anniversary of the 1671 founding of the Newport church, a Memorial Board was established to manage some of the investments and distribution of both designated and undesignated funds. The conference was responsible for setting up area associations and suggesting ways to make them more effective in the total work of the denomination.

The general conference has served as communicating agent both within and outside denominational bounds. Basically, there were four targets for denominational growth: (1) overseeing biological growth in order to retain those who had been brought up or married into the covenant relationship; (2) convincing Christians of other denominations of the validity of the Sabbath and other Seventh Day Baptist distinctives; (3) going to non-Christian Sabbath keepers; and (4) reaching those who had neither Christ nor the Sabbath and evangelizing them.[17]

The earliest efforts of the general conference in communicating the gospel were to frontier settlements of the westward migrations. Annual homecomings and circular letters helped some maintain connections with the home churches, but they lacked the personal preaching and teachings furnished by a pastor. The conference sponsored a number of circuit riders to bring a sense of belonging. The riders' reports to the general conference show that their visitation and preaching was not limited to Seventh Day Baptists, but the gospel was shared throughout the scattered settlements of the frontier, often in school houses, in other

---

[17] See Sanford, *A Choosing People*, 176–84.

churches, or even outdoors. Some reports give accounts of the cutting of ice in frozen ponds or streams in order to baptize new converts.

The first periodical published by Seventh Day Baptists was the *Seventh Day Baptist Missionary Magazine* (1821–1825). Its objectives were both denominational and ecumenical in scope. It aimed "to acquaint the public with sentiments and religious observances which distinguish this people from other Christian denominations, and to circulate religious and missionary information among the societies of our denomination."[18] It also attempted to "cultivate harmony among all evangelical Christians, and to unite with others in the laudable work of holding up the doctrine of the cross."[19] This endeavor was followed in succession by the *Seventh Day Baptist Register* (1840–1844) and the *Sabbath Recorder*, which began in 1844 and continues to the present time.

In 1843, those in the general conference decided to make a direct appeal by letter to the various other Christians to consider the validity of the Sabbath. The letter was directed specifically to other Baptists and acknowledged a commonality of many basic beliefs and polity. It stated, "your baptism is our baptism; your church government is our government; your doctrinal principles are ours; and there is nothing which constitutes any real ground or separation except the great and important subject we now urge upon your attention."[20]

Several tract and evangelizing societies were established during the first half of the nineteenth century that eventually led to the formation of the American Sabbath Tract Society in 1840. Several attempts were made to evangelize Jews who were already observers of the Sabbath. The first target was centered on the large population of Jews in New York City, but the cultural differences and prejudices were too great for those

---

[18] "Editor's Address to the Patrons and Friends of This Magazine," foreword, *Seventh Day Baptist Missionary Magazine* 1 (August 1821).

[19] Ibid.

[20] Thomas B. Brown, ed., *An Appeal for the Restoration of the Bible Sabbath: in an Address to the Baptists, from Seventh-day Baptist General Conference* (New York: American Sabbath Track Society, 1852) 22. See Sanford, *A Choosing People*, 152–53 for a discussion of the letter and its results.

who had little in common beyond Sabbath observance. An unsuccessful later venture sent two missionary couples to Palestine.[21]

With the establishment of the Missionary Society in 1847, Seventh Day Baptists developed a vision for foreign missions. After briefly considering Ethiopia as a field of foreign mission, China was decided as a better mission opportunity. The mission to China lasted for a century until the Communist takeover in 1950. It encompassed not only preaching and evangelization but also a strong medical and educational mission. At one time the Shanghai church had the largest membership in the denomination, and the medical mission included a hospital staffed largely by certified women doctors and nurses. A number of graduates from the mission school enrolled in church-related colleges in the United States.[22]

Most of the twentieth-century missionary efforts of Seventh Day Baptists were centered on what has been termed the "five P's of mission activity": (1) Purpose: why become involved? (2) Priority: should home missions or foreign missions be stressed? (3) Place: where should effort be expended? (4) Personnel: who would go and what training is needed? (5) Process: what is the relationship between planting a mission and cultivation of seed already planted?[23]

One opportunity for foreign missions came from the Gold Coast (Ghana) of Africa in a village called Ayan Maim. A man from that village named Joseph Ammokoo learned by reading *Watson's Theological Dictionary* about the Seventh Day Baptists. Through his own study of the Bible, he became convinced that he should keep the Sabbath, so naturally he became interested in the Seventh Day Baptists. He contacted a church in Richburg, New York, and requested that the church assist him in bringing two young men to America to be educated in English and in the beliefs of the Seventh Day Baptists. This contact

---

[21] See Sanford, *A Choosing People*, 177–79.

[22] Ibid., 179–84.

[23] Ibid., 287 ff.

led to a fruitful mission endeavor that lasted for more than half of the twentieth century.[24]

Another successful mission effort in the twentieth century was in Jamaica. The close proximity of Jamaica led to close personal relationships, and in time some who migrated to the United States became leaders in both the United States and Canada among Seventh Day Baptist churches. In addition, since Jamaica was part of the British Empire, the relationship allowed many Jamaicans to migrate to England where they became the dominant leaders and members of the 300-year-old mother church of Seventh Day Baptists at Mill Yard in London.

Similar responses for help and fellowship have led to mission efforts in other areas. In 1965, a World Federation of Seventh Day Baptist Conferences was organized and has embraced seventeen conferences from six continents. The World Federation meets periodically about every five years, but through its executive committee it functions to provide increased communication, stimulate fellowship, promote evangelism, evaluate needs, and act as a liaison between individuals in different conferences.

The ecumenicity demonstrated in English and Colonial beginnings has been continued on local and denominational levels in the twentieth and twenty-first centuries. Winthrop Hudson called Seventh Day Baptists "Separate, but not sectarian, being separate in organization and practice but ecumenical in spirit."[25] When the Ecumenical Conference on Foreign Missions was held in 1900, Seventh Day Baptists were represented. They were charter members of the Federal Council of Churches, which first met in 1908. Issues such as temperance, immigration, international arbitration, child labor, and religious training of the young were leading topics of the first meetings. Over the next sixty-five years, the denomination participated in the Federal Council and its successor, the National Council of Churches.

---

[24] Ibid., 293–96.

[25] Winthrop S. Hudson, "Separate But Not Sectarian," Willis Russell Lecture, Alfred University, 14 February 1977; reprinted in *Sabbath Recorder* 199 (April 1977): 28.

Seventh Day Baptists were among the supporters of the World Faith and Order Conference that met in Lausanne, Switzerland, in 1927, with A. J. C. Bond as the official denominational representative. From this conference came the proposal to form a World Council of Churches. A conference of delegates from around the world was held at Utrecht, Holland, in 1938. Of the eighty delegates, ten were from the United States with the addition of ten alternates. Two Baptists were chosen—Kenneth Scott Latourette of Yale Divinity School and W. O. Carver of the Southern Baptist Theological Seminary. Carver was unable to attend, and A. J. C. Bond of the Alfred School of Theology took his place. As it turned out, Latourette and Bond were the only two Baptists at the constituting conference, and because of their presence they were able to make a significant contribution to the constitution.[26] In 1976, the Seventh Day Baptist General Conference voted to withdraw membership from the World Council of Churches. What began as an evangelistic goal of reaching the world for Christ was largely eclipsed by social and political activism that led Seventh Day Baptists to depart. However, Seventh Day Baptists have been active in partnership with other Baptist groups through the Baptist World Alliance, the North American Baptist Fellowship, and the Baptist Joint Committee on Public Affairs.

---

[26] A. J. C. Bond, "The Utrecht Conference," *Sabbath Recorder* 124 (27 June 1938): 414–15.

Chapter 11

THE COOPERATIVE BAPTIST FELLOWSHIP

Walter B. Shurden

The Cooperative Baptist Fellowship, often referred to by insiders simply as CBF or "the Fellowship," describes itself as "a fellowship of Baptist Christians and churches who share a passion for the Great Commission of Jesus Christ and a commitment to Baptist principles of faith and practice."[1] That sentence, while true, probably could be written of most Baptist groups. It may be more descriptive and specific to say that CBF is a denomination of non-fundamentalist Baptist Christians who separated from the Southern Baptist Convention in 1990. In this manner, one at least describes the historical and theological origins of CBF. CBF began in August 1990 as a vigorous reaction to the fundamentalist takeover of the Southern Baptist Convention (SBC). The fundamentalist takeover of the SBC, usually known in SBC and CBF circles simply as "the Controversy," began in 1979, reached its apex in 1990, and continues in some forms to the present day in 2005.[2]

---

[1] See http://www.thefellowship.info/Inside%20CBF/Who%20we%20are.icm (accessed 28 February 2005).

[2] Many accounts of the controversy have been written, both from the fundamentalist and moderate points of view. For a brief account from the moderate perspective, see chapter 7, "The Fundamentalist-Moderate Controversy," of the revised edition of my book *Not a Silent People* (Macon GA: Smyth and Helwys Publishing, 1995). For book-length versions of the controversy from different points of view, you may consult the following sources. For the fundamentalist interpretation see Jerry Sutton, *The Baptist Reformation* (Nashville: Broadman & Holman Publishers, 2000); for the moderate interpretation see David T. Morgan,

How else should we describe CBF? Ethnically, CBF is completely open to all races, while predominantly white in its ethnic composition. However, it works closely with Hispanics in America, and CBF's moderator (president or elected leader) for 2005–2006 is an Asian American woman. The moderator-elect for 2006–2007 is an African American male. CBF has made it a point to be racially inclusive. Moreover, CBF is open to the leadership of women in its organizational life. Of the fifteen moderators, individuals who preside over a meeting of CBF in its general assembly, six have been women.

In terms of membership, CBF consists of both Baptist individuals and churches. While it is difficult to gain an accurate count of the number of individuals who support it, CBF has approximately 1,800 Baptist churches supporting its ministries. CBF has an estimated total membership of 400,000 people. Geographically, CBF's numerical strength centers in the South, Southeast, and Southwestern United States. Comprised primarily of traditional ex-Southern Baptist individuals and ex-Southern Baptist churches, CBF, in terms of its mission and ministry, passionately advocates Christian missions, historic Baptist distinctives, non-fundamentalist theological education, women in ministry, the prominence of the laity, and a decentralized approach to denominational life. Presently, CBF has 146 appointed missionaries, and it "partners" with 13 theological schools in North America. These 13 schools recently enrolled 1,800 seminary students. CBF also has endorsed more than 450 chaplains who work in diverse settings such as hospitals, the military, and pastoral counseling centers.[3]

The New Crusades, The New Holy Land: Conflict in the Southern Baptist Convention, 1969–91 (Tuscaloosa: University of Alabama Press, 1996). For more personal memoirs of the conflict, you may consult the following: for the moderate position see Grady C. Cothen, *What Happened to the Southern Baptist Convention: A Memoir of the Controversy* (Macon GA: Smyth and Helwys Publishing, 1993); for the fundamentalist perspective see Paul Pressler, *A Hill on Which to Die: One Southern Baptist's Journey* (Nashville: Broadman & Holman Publishers, 1999).

[3] See http://www.thefellowship.info/News/050222chaplains459.icm (accessed 28 February 2005).

Because they are non-fundamentalists in theological and ethical outlook, CBFers are often dubbed "moderate" Baptists, a name many CBF people disdain because it fails to communicate their sense of passion about Christ and the gospel. The name "moderate," however, accurately suggests a centrist position in matters biblical, theological, and ethical. And while that description certainly fits most CBFers, one finds Baptists of all theological and ethical persuasions within the CBF network. The theological spectrum within CBF runs from the Right to the Left, from liberal to conservative, but most CBFers are theological centrists with a tolerance that willingly embraces considerable diversity within their ranks.

An ecumenical Baptist group, CBF enthusiastically embraces other Christian denominations as well as other Baptist bodies. Working closely with eighteen state and regional CBF organizations, CBF is also a member of the Baptist World Alliance, the international organization of Baptists. CBF has worked especially close in some ventures with the American Baptist Churches, USA. CBF also cooperates with the "Christian Churches Together in the U.S.,"[4] a new emerging ecumenical body in the United States. Moreover, while believing firmly in the unique revelation of God in Christ, CBFers tend to be tolerant of other great world religions.

During its brief history (1990–present), the most public and prominent names associated with the Cooperative Baptist Fellowship are the former president of the United States and his wife, Jimmy and Rosalynn Carter. President Jimmy Carter gave the keynote address at the general assembly of CBF in 1993. Among other things, he said, "In the Cooperative Baptist Fellowship, my wife and I have found a home."[5] On 17 February 2005, the coordinating council of CBF (CBF's executive committee) voted unanimously to name the offering taken at the CBF general assembly the "Jimmy and Rosalynn Carter Offering for

---

[4] For more information on this movement, see http://www.ncccusa.org/about/cctusa.html (accessed 28 February 2005).

[5] See "Jimmy, Rosalynn Carter Embrace Fellowship; Fellowship Blesses 25 New Missionaries," *Baptists Today*, 27 May 1993, 1.

Religious Liberty and Human Rights." In addition to the Carters, most of the major denominational leaders of the Southern Baptist Convention prior to 1979, names preeminent among Southern Baptists for years, eventually embraced CBF as their denominational home.[6]

Beginnings and Background

Historical beginnings of Baptist denominational bodies are often important in understanding the specific characteristics of the various groups. This is especially true with the Cooperative Baptist Fellowship. It is impossible to understand CBF apart from the twelve-year struggle (1979–1990) that raged within the Southern Baptist Convention between SBC fundamentalists and SBC moderates. The SBC moderates evolved into the CBF. The fundamentalists retained the denominational apparatus of the SBC.

Like the Protestants who rebelled against the Catholics in the sixteenth century Reformation, much of what characterized CBF, especially in its earliest years, emerged from their protests of developments within the SBC. These "protests," while still present today as shaping factors in CBF life, are not currently the exclusive concerns of CBF. One can understand these protests by placing alongside each other the contrasting features of SBC fundamentalism with those of the CBF moderates.

---

[6] This list of SBC leaders was long. Illustrative of these SBC leaders who embraced the CBF were the following: Duke K. McCall, former president of the Southern Baptist Theological Seminary and president of the Baptist World Alliance; Grady C. Cothen, president of the Sunday School Board; Randall Lolley, president of Southeastern Baptist Theological Seminary; Roy L. Honeycutt, Jr., president of the Southern Baptist Theological Seminary; Foy Valentine, president of the Christian Life Commission of the SBC; Darold H. Morgan, president of the SBC Annuity Board; Carolyn Weatherford Crumpler, president of the Woman's Missionary Society; Russell Dilday, president of Southwestern Baptist Theological Seminary; James M. Dunn, executive director of the Baptist Joint Committee on Public Affairs; and Keith Parks, president of the Foreign Mission Board.

SBC Fundamentalists	CBF Moderates
Denominational centralization	Denominational decentralization
Biblical inerrancy	Biblical authority under the Lordship of Christ
Male clergy	Women and men in ministry
Pastoral authority	Congregational authority
Prominence of clergy	Prominence of laity
Sectarian	Ecumenical
Creedal	Anti-creedal
Missions as evangelism	Missions as evangelism and justice issues
Religious control	Religious freedom

During the hot days of 23–25 August 1990, 3,000 moderate Southern Baptists gathered in a historic meeting in Atlanta known as the Consultation of Concerned Southern Baptists. Called by Daniel Vestal, who had been defeated only two months previously as the moderate candidate for the presidency of the SBC, this "consultation" launched the Cooperative Baptist Fellowship. Though the formal organization of CBF came the next year in 1991, the consultation in 1990 clearly marked the beginning of what came to be the Cooperative Baptist Fellowship.

Vestal's defeat marked the twelfth consecutive time that the SBC fundamentalists had defeated the SBC moderates for the presidency of the Convention. The SBC presidency, because of its appointive powers, symbolized the power struggle between the two groups. While defeated a dozen times in their efforts to retain the traditional character of the SBC, the moderates had enormous strength in the SBC. The strength of the moderates in that struggle often goes untold.[7] Unable to win,

[7] When non-incumbents competed for the SBC presidency during the decade-long conflict, fundamentalists certainly won. However, they won only by the following margins: 1979, 51.36%; 1980, 51.67%; 1982, 56.97%; 1984, 52.18%; 1986, 54.22%; 1988, 50.33%; 1990, 57.68%. Fundamentalists had their largest margin of victory in 1990, only after moderates had begun to separate from the SBC.

however, and unwilling to continue the constant and debilitating furor within the denomination, moderates pulled out and followed Daniel Vestal to Atlanta. The participants in the consultation, in addition to providing momentum to the moderate cause, took three important actions in 1990. They (1) elected an Interim Steering Committee,[8] charging it to bring a constitution to a general assembly the next year in Atlanta, (2) named Daniel Vestal chair of the Interim Steering Committee, and (3) created a financial mechanism that allowed local churches to contribute to the infant organization.[9] Though Daniel Vestal had called the meeting and was clearly the dominant personality present, Jimmy Allen, a former president of the SBC, presided at the Consultation of Concerned Southern Baptists. At the closing session of the consultation, Allen wept as he said, "This will be a day we will look back to and long remember."[10] Another Baptist movement/denomination was being born! But its future denominational shape was unclear at the beginning.

During the years 1990–1991, both SBC moderates and fundamentalists intensified the process of alienating themselves from each other. The consultation in Atlanta and the creation by moderates of a financial conduit through which churches bypassed the old SBC financial program was Exhibit A of that increasing separation from the moderate side. However, other acts during these years underscored this process of alienation. In 1990, for example, Baylor University of Texas and Furman University of South Carolina amended their charters so as to make them independent of their respective Baptist state conventions. Fearful that the fundamentalist takeover at the national SBC would trickle down to the state Baptist conventions, an increasing number of

---

[8] For a list of the members of the Interim Steering Committee, see Walter B. Shurden and Randy Shepley, eds., *Going for the Jugular: A Documentary History of the SBC Holy War* (Macon GA: Mercer University Press, 1996) 262–63.

[9] See Duke K. McCall, "The History of the Baptist Cooperative Missions Program," in Walter B. Shurden, ed., *The Struggle for the Soul of the SBC* (Macon GA: Mercer University Press, 1993) 241–51.

[10] See "Moderates Create New Funding Mechanism for SBC Fellowship; Set Spring Convocation," *SBC Today*, September 1990, 1.

Baptist schools took this preventive action. Significantly, in 1990 moderate Baptists launched a new Baptist publishing company, Smyth & Helwys. This new venture provided a publishing outlet for moderate Baptists, since Broadman Press, the SBC publishing arm, was no longer hospitable to them.

In 1991, the distancing between moderates and fundamentalists increased. In that year, for example, the SBC fundamentalists forced Lloyd Elder, moderate president of the Baptist Sunday School Board, to retire. Moreover, the SBC financially began squeezing moderates out of the SBC system, dropping all monetary support for the Baptist Joint Committee on Public Affairs and defunding the Baptist Theological Seminary in Rüschlikon, Switzerland.

Moderates responded by dropping the "SBC" name from aspects of their movement. In March 1991, the "Southern Baptist Alliance," the most progressive wing of the moderate movement, became merely the "Baptist Alliance." Likewise, in May of that year, *SBC Today*, the moderate newspaper, changed its name to *Baptists Today*. Theological education also got in the picture as moderates opened their first seminary, the Baptist Theological Seminary in Richmond. Every aspect of SBC denominational life fragmented during these first years of the 1990s. All of these events gave momentum to what became the Cooperative Baptist Fellowship, the most dominant expression of the moderate movement among Baptists of the South.

Beliefs and Convictions

While the particular denominational structure of the organization took more than a decade to tumble into anything like its final shape, the major convictions of the emerging Baptist body stood starkly clear from the earliest years. At the general assembly in Atlanta on 9 May 1991, delegates formally constituted the Cooperative Baptist Fellowship. Fiercely opposed to any kind of mandatory creed, CBFers nonetheless loudly applauded at that meeting for the public declaration of some of their most cherished Baptist ideals.

The Interim Steering Committee presented to the 1991 general assembly a document known as "An Address to the Public." The historic character of the document could not have been lost on anyone who knew the history of the formation of the Southern Baptist Convention in 1845. In that year, Southern Baptists issued their own "Address to the Public," stating their reasons for taking the historic step of separating from Northern Baptists and creating the SBC. Likewise, CBF's 1991 address distinguished moderate Southern Baptists from fundamentalist Southern Baptists. It also provided insight into what CBFers believed to be consistent with the Baptist tradition of freedom and responsibility, and it gave reasons for the creation of the new Baptist body.[11]

Often called CBF's "Declaration of Independence," the address began with these words: "Forming something as fragile as the Cooperative Baptist Fellowship is not a move we make lightly. We are obligated to give some explanation for why we are doing what we are doing. Our children will know what we have done; they may not know why we have done what we have done. We have reasons for our actions."

Stating first that the reasons for forming CBF were "larger than losing," the document asserted that moderate Southern Baptists had been excluded from any significant participation in SBC denominational life. While moderates had not been excluded from giving their money to the SBC, sending messengers to the national convention, or voting their convictions at those national meetings, they had been excluded from meaningful governance on the SBC boards and agencies. The situation was comparable to a nominating committee in a local church excluding minority and dissenting voices from any church committees. The controversy in the SBC had culminated in a "winner-take-all" policy by

[11] You may see copies of this document in the following books that I have either edited, co-edited, or written: *The Struggle for the Soul of the SBC: Moderate Responses to the Fundamentalist Movement*, 309–14; *Going for the Jugular: A Documentary History of the SBC Holy War*, 266–70; and *The Baptist Identity: Four Fragile Freedoms* (Macon GA: Smyth & Helwys Publishing, Inc., 1993) 97–102. For a brief history of the document, see "A Brief History of 'An Address to the Public,'" in Walter B. Shurden, *Not an Easy Journey: Some Transitions in Baptist Life* (Macon GA: Mercer University Press, 2005) 261–65.

fundamentalists. "We have no voice," stated "An Address to the Public." CBFers affirmed that their voicelessness within the SBC constituted a major reason for creating CBF. It was not the only reason, however.

The heart of the address listed six critical differences of beliefs between fundamentalist and moderate Southern Baptists. Since the nature and interpretation of the Bible, especially the fundamentalist claim of the "inerrancy" of the Bible, had been the centerpiece of much of the controversy, the document began with a statement on the Bible: "Many of our differences come from a different understanding and interpretation of Holy Scripture. But the difference is not at the point of the inspiration or authority of the Bible." Acknowledging that moderates "interpret the Bible differently" from fundamentalists and illustrating that point with differences over the role of women and the authority of the pastor, the document also said, "We also, however, have a different understanding of the nature of the Bible." The address went on to affirm, "We want to be biblical—especially in our view of the Bible. That means that we dare not claim less for the Bible than the Bible claims for itself. The Bible neither claims nor reveals inerrancy as a Christian teaching. Bible claims must be based on the Bible, not on human interpretations of the Bible." Fundamentalists characterized moderates as not "believing the Bible." "An Address to the Public" made it clear that the Bible was central for CBFers.

The address listed the differences in attitude toward "education" as the second critical difference between the two groups. Alleging that fundamentalists viewed education as indoctrination and possessed a monopolistic view of truth, the CBF document staked out a more humble approach to truth and education: "Moderates, too, are concerned with truth, but we do not claim a monopoly."

According to the address, a third contention between the two groups was "what a missionary ought to be and do." "We think the mission task is to reach people for faith in Jesus Christ by preaching, teaching, healing and other ministries of mercy and justice. We believe this to be the model of Jesus in Galilee." Fundamentalists, on the other hand, "allow their emphasis on direct evangelism to undercut other biblical ministries of mercy and justice."

The role and task of the pastor comprised the fourth difference. Moderates claimed that the pastor of a Baptist church is to be a "servant/shepherd," while fundamentalists argued that the pastor is the "ruler" of the church. This contrast between the two groups was highlighted at the 1988 meeting of the SBC when the fundamentalist majority adopted a resolution minimizing what they called the "Priesthood of the Believer" and maximizing the authority of the pastor.[12]

The fifth difference between the two groups proved to be one of the major and clearest distinctions between them, and that was the role of women in the church. Moderates affirmed that women could be called to serve both as ministers and as deacons. Fundamentalists denied those roles to women. CBF began and has continued as a passionate advocate of women in ministry. The SBC attitude, on the other hand, intensified over the years and codified itself into a rigid and exclusive posture toward women in ministry and as deacons.[13]

"An Address to the Public" listed different understandings of the "church" as the final and sixth difference between moderates and fundamentalists. The document said that for CBF, "an ecumenical and inclusive attitude is basic to our fellowship." It went on: "So, we are eager to have fellowship with our brothers and sisters in the faith and to recognize their work for our Saviour. We do not try to make them

---

[12] See the resolution and my article on this topic, "The Priesthood of all Believers and Pastoral Authority in Baptist Thought," *Faith and Mission* 7/1 (Fall 1989): 24–45. See Shurden, *Not an Easy Journey*, 64–87.

[13] See articles 6 and 18 of the 2000 edition of "The Baptist Faith and Message," in which women are excluded from being pastors and are to be submissive to their husbands. See also http://www.abpnews.com/news/news_detail.cfm?NEWS_ID=282 (accessed 1 March 2005), which notes that the North American Mission Board of the SBC approved guidelines saying all new Southern Baptist congregations should have male-only deacons. The SBC also decided no longer to endorse women as military chaplains; see "Southern Baptists Stop Endorsing Women as Military Chaplains," *Baptists Today*, March 2004, 14.

conform to us." The CBF document contrasted the sectarianism of SBC fundamentalism with the more ecumenical and open attitude of the CBF. These contrasting attitudes became more sharply profiled in 2003/2004 when the SBC withdrew from the Baptist World Alliance, while the CBF joined and supported the alliance.

While CBF identified some of its cardinal convictions as early as 1991 in its address, the Baptist group also clarified its convictions more recently with a statement of seven of its "Core Values." Two of those seven core values speak directly to issues of CBF's Baptist convictions and Christian beliefs. These are listed on the CBF Web site. Regarding Baptist principles, CBF affirms the following:

> Soul Freedom—We believe in the priesthood of all believers. We affirm the freedom and responsibility of every person to relate directly to God without the imposition of creed or the control of clergy or government.
>
> Bible Freedom—We believe in the authority of Scripture. We believe the Bible, under the Lordship of Christ, is central to the life of the individual and the church. We affirm the freedom and right of every Christian to interpret and apply scripture under the leadership of the Holy Spirit.
>
> Church Freedom—We believe in the autonomy of every local church. We believe Baptist churches are free, under the Lordship of Christ, to determine their membership and leadership, to order their worship and work, to ordain whomever they perceive as gifted for ministry, and to participate as they deem appropriate in the larger Body of Christ.
>
> Religious Freedom—We believe in freedom of religion, freedom for religion, and freedom from religion. We support the separation of church and state.[14]

---

[14] See http://www.thefellowship.info/Inside%20CBF/Core%20Values.icm (accessed 2 March 2005).

When CBF describes what the Bible teaches about "biblically-based Global Missions," it affirms the following traditional Christian doctrines:

> God is the one triune God, Creator of all people in God's own image
>
> All people are separated from God by sin.
>
> Christ is the Savior and Redeemer for all peoples.
>
> The Holy Spirit convicts and converts all who believe in Christ, teaches the church in the voice of the Living Christ, and empowers the church and all believers for the mission of Christ in the world.
>
> Christ calls us to minister redemptively to the spiritual, physical, and social needs of individuals and communities.
>
> Every believer and every church is responsible for sharing the Gospel with all people. We want to enable believers and churches to work cooperatively with other Great Commission Christians to activate this global missions calling in their communities and throughout the world.[15]

Even though CBF described its core beliefs through the above documents, the organization is thoroughly anti-creedal. CBF has adopted no doctrinal statement that individuals or churches are coerced to sign to be part of the organization. While a few voices within CBF have called for a doctrinal statement or creed of some nature, it is highly unlikely that such will occur in the near future. On the other hand, the SBC in 2000 revised and tightened its doctrinal statement, the *Baptist Faith and Message*, so as to make it a controlling document in SBC life. CBF sympathizers reacted quickly, negatively, and almost unanimously to this development, noting the dangers of creeds in Baptist life. For example, Daniel Vestal, the coordinator of CBF, addressed the creedal issue at the general assembly in Orlando, Florida, in 2000. "We believe the Bible is inspired by God and is true for faith and life," said Vestal.

---

[15] Ibid.

He continued, "But we resist man-made documents that require everyone to interpret the Bible the same way."[16] Because the SBC, in its 2000 revision of the *Baptist Faith and Message*, deleted the phrase saying that Jesus is the criterion by which the Bible is to be interpreted, Vestal responded that CBF is a Jesus People who did not put the Scripture above Christ.[17] His major objection was to the revisionist and creedal nature of the new edition of the *Baptist Faith and Message*.

Mission and Purpose

From its earliest beginnings, CBF, through its spokespeople, policy statements, and budgets, unambiguously stated that Christian missions, both global and domestic, stood at the center of its existence. Cecil Sherman, CBF's first executive officer, often, and to the dismay of CBFers who wanted a comprehensive mission statement, referred to the movement as "a missions delivery system."[18] In 1995 at the CBF general assembly in Ft. Worth, Texas, CBF took a historic step as it adopted a formal mission statement with a dual passion for Christian missions and historic Baptist convictions. The statement opened with the following words: "We are a fellowship of Baptist Christians and churches who share a passion for the Great Commission of Jesus Christ and a commitment to Baptist principles of faith and practice. Our mission is to network, empower, and mobilize Baptist Christians and churches for effective missions and ministry in the name of Christ."[19]

As late as 2005, the dual passions of Christian missions and historic Baptist principles remained central in CBF. Significantly, however, when

---

[16] See "Leader Defines CBF Identity; New Strategic Plan Approved," *Baptists Today*, August 2000, 3.

[17] Ibid.

[18] See "CBF Rejects Motion to Stop Seminary Funding for Southern Baptists; Names 10 Missionaries," *Baptists Today*, 26 May 1994, 1.

[19] *Cooperative Baptist Fellowship: 1995 General Assembly Resource Book*, 20–22 July, Tarrant County Convention Center, Fort Worth TX, p. D2. See also "Cooperative Baptist Fellowship Appoints 16 New Missionaries, Considers Becoming Convention, Adopts Formal Mission Statement," *Baptists Today*, August 1995, 1.

CBF listed its "primary emphases" on its 2005 Web site, the first of those emphases was "Global Missions." The first of CBF's "primary emphases" reads as follows: "Global missions and ministries that focus primarily on partnerships with local congregations and other mission groups, planting the gospel among the world's unevangelized peoples (ethno-linguistic people groups, comprising nearly one-fourth of the world's population, who have little or no exposure to the Christian message), and ministries among the urban poor and other marginalized peoples in America's inner cities."[20]

If one wants to know the heartbeat of a church or religious movement, one must look to budgets and to ministry priorities in those budgets. Over the years, the dominant part of the CBF annual budget has been targeted for global missions. This continues to be the case, though as CBF assumes new ministries, the percentage of the budget supporting global missions naturally declines somewhat. Nonetheless, CBF's 2004–2005 budget is $16,008,123, and of that amount $9,044,566 is earmarked for global missions.

R. Keith Parks, more than any other single person, stamped the cause of global missions on the life of the CBF. The longtime and admired president of the Southern Baptist Convention Foreign Mission Board (FMB), Parks announced his retirement from the FMB in March 1992 because of differences with fundamentalist trustees of the FMB. At the general assembly of CBF in May 1992, the moderator introduced Parks to the audience. He received a sustained, standing ovation from CBFers. Later that same year, in November, he stated that he would become the missions head for CBF. In January 1993, the coordinating council elected Parks CBF missions coordinator, and he immediately challenged CBF to center its mission strategy on the unreached people of the world.

In terms of its mission and purpose, CBF experienced another significant turning point in the year 2000. Meeting in Orlando, Florida, the general assembly approved the first phase of a new strategic plan that

---

[20] See http://www.thefellowship.info/Inside%20CBF/At%20a%20glance.icm (accessed 3 March 2005).

rearticulated the mission and purpose of CBF in a comprehensive and challenging fashion. CBF succinctly restated its mission as "Serving Christians and churches as they discover and fulfill their God-given mission."[21]

In spelling out that new mission, CBF adopted four strategic initiatives. These four mission initiatives continue to define the life and ministry of CBF. First, CBF affirms "Faith Formation." Faith formation means two important things for CBF. It means the act of encouraging Christians in their journeys toward Christ-likeness through wholesome and effective evangelism. Also, it means motivating Christians in their spiritual growth through corporate worship, spiritual disciplines, Bible study, and the life of love. CBF embraces "Building Community" as their second strategic initiative. This initiative contains several dimensions: developing and sustaining healthy congregations, affirming traditional Baptist values, bringing wholeness to relationships through acts of reconciliation and justice, nurturing healthy family life, and supporting specialized ministries such as chaplains and pastoral counselors. CBF's third strategic initiative focuses on "Leadership Development." This initiative includes developing effective leaders, both lay and clergy, within congregations, supporting quality theological education for future church leaders, and facilitating an effective collegiate ministry. The fourth and final strategic initiative reaffirms the centrality of "Global Missions and Ministries" for CBF. Each of these initiatives places the local congregation of believers at the heart of CBF life.[22] "Serving Christians and churches as they discover and fulfill their

---

[21] See http://www.thefellowship.info/Inside%20CBF/Mission.icm (accessed 3 March 2005).

[22] See more about these four strategic initiatives at http://www.thefellowship.info/Inside%20CBF/Strategic.icm (accessed 4 March 2005). I have tried to address the issue of the mission and purpose of CBF from its own history. One can do this in more dramatic and contemporary ways, however. Daniel Vestal, coordinator of CBF, wrote a helpful article on 1 May 2004 titled "Cooperative Baptist Fellowship...A Status Report," in which he not only answered the question "What is CBF?" but also pinpointed the mission of CBF. He finished the sentence "CBF is..." with four descriptive sentences. First, he said, "CBF is a movement of spiritual and

God-given mission" is, once again, the reason for CBF's continuing existence.

Denomination, Convention, Fellowship?

One of the most vexing issues for CBF since its beginning in 1990 has been the nature of the religious movement itself. Is CBF a denomination? Is it a denomination separate from the SBC? If so, is it a "convention" like the SBC? If not a convention, is it a mission society, concerned primarily with missions? What is a "fellowship"? Precisely what is CBF? Answers to these questions have ranged all over the board, both inside and outside of CBF.

A major reason for the ambiguity concerning the nature of CBF is its origin. When it began in 1990, CBF consisted almost entirely of individuals and churches that considered themselves Southern Baptists or ex-Southern Baptists. Some of these individuals and churches continued to think of themselves as "Southern Baptists" who simply had created a new mechanism for supporting selected SBC agencies and institutions. This may have been a majority attitude in the early years of CBF. When Daniel Vestal, for example, delivered the keynote address at the 1990 Atlanta Consultation of Concerned Southern Baptists, he said, "We're not here to form a new denomination. We're not here to plan political strategy. We're not here to wish anyone ill will or harm. But we are here to explore how we can cooperate with each other for the cause of Christ in ways which do not violate our conscience, or the principles which inform our conscience." What Vestal and others at that initial meeting of CBF may not have clearly seen or intended, at least one outsider lucidly discerned. Peter Steinfels, a writer for the *New York*

---

congregational renewal in Baptist life." Second, "CBF is a network for nurturing and developing congregational leaders." Third, "CBF is a congregational partner for global missions." Finally, Vestal said, "CBF is a denomination-like fellowship for an increasing number of Baptist Christians and congregations." See http://www.thefellowship.info/News/040501%20Status.icm (accessed 2 March 2005).

Times, reported with less nuances and more candor that a new Baptist denomination was being birthed. "Leaders of the new Fellowship," Steinfels wrote, "deny that its establishment means taking final leave from the 14 million member SBC, but after failing for 12 years to stem the growing control of the Convention by staunch conservatives, the Fellowship's founders clearly intend to redirect most of their loyalties, energies and funds toward the new group."[23] Whether or not Steinfels correctly assessed the intentions of CBF's leaders, he accurately predicted the destination of the Cooperative Baptist Fellowship.

The separation between the SBC and CBF, however, has been gradual and, for some people, yet unfinished. Four years after the launching of CBF, delegates to the 1994 general assembly refused to defund SBC seminaries. Some moderates were still teaching in the SBC seminaries, and friends in CBF did not want to "hurt" friends by withdrawing financial support. One month later, however, the SBC accelerated the separation between the two groups. In June 1994, messengers to the annual meeting of the SBC approved a motion "to decline to receive funds channeled through the Cooperative Baptist Fellowship."[24] This constituted a pivotal moment in CBF life. Had this SBC action "made" CBF a distinct denomination? No! The tension continued within CBF life, though Cecil Sherman wrote on the tenth anniversary of CBF, "The bridges are out and the road is closed. There is no way back into the SBC for an honest Baptist."[25]

The debate continues, but it is safe to say that CBF now has all the marks of a denomination, completely separate and with an identity distinct from the SBC. By 1997, the CBF general assembly approved a recommendation that said CBF is "a religious endorsing body." Relating especially to endorsing military chaplains and pastoral counselors, this action constituted another gradual step toward denominational status.

---

[23] As cited in "The Cooperative Fellowship; What About It?" *SBC Today*, 11 July 1991, 6.

[24] *Annual of the Southern Baptist Convention*, 1994, pp. 99–100.

[25] See his article "Taking Stock After Ten Years," in *Baptists Today*, February 2000, 24.

When CBF first applied for membership in the Baptist World Alliance, it was declined membership in the world body because the membership committee "felt the CBF did not meet certain criteria and especially in the area of their identity."[26] Translated, that meant the BWA was not convinced that CBF had a separate identity from the SBC. Only after CBF convinced the BWA that the Fellowship was distinct from SBC would BWA admit CBF into their membership.[27]

But if CBF is a separate entity from the SBC, which it surely is, what kind of "denomination" is it? It is a new entity in Baptist life. It does not represent the old "convention" model of Baptist life where the Convention owns and controls institutions and agencies. Neither is CBF a missionary society with a single purpose, that of missions alone, though CBF does appoint its own missionaries. CBF clearly has multiple ministries, as shown above. Daniel Vestal, CBF coordinator, probably described it best when he said CBF is "a partner," "a network," "a denomination-like fellowship." Apart from its missionaries and the staff at the National Resource Center in Atlanta, CBF has no personnel nor does it own institutions. CBF describes a partner "as an organization that receives support through funds, volunteers or joint projects from the Fellowship."[28] CBF partners with individuals, churches, seminaries,[29]

---

[26] See "CBF Membership Not Approved at BWA Meeting," *Baptists Today*, September 2001, 10.

[27] See "Baptist World Alliance Accepts Cooperative Baptist Fellowship," *Baptists Today*, August 2003, 13.

[28] See http://www.thefellowship.info/Inside%20CBF/Partners/ (accessed 2 March 2005).

[29] CBF partners with thirteen schools of theological education. These schools may be divided into four distinct categories. First, some of these are freestanding "Baptist" schools, unaffiliated with a college or university. Among these seminaries are Baptist Seminary of Kentucky, Baptist Theological Seminary at Richmond, Central Baptist Theological Seminary of Kansas City, and International Baptist Theological Seminary in Prague (Czech Republic). A second group of theological schools with which CBF partners are five seminaries affiliated with Baptist colleges and universities. These include Campbell University School of Divinity, Gardner-Webb University School of Divinity, Logsdon School of Theology at Hardin-Simmons University, McAfee School of Theology of Mercer University, and Truett

publishing agencies, religious liberty agencies, ethics organizations, regional CBF organizations, news services, a youth camping ministry, the Baptist World Alliance, and many other such bodies. One can count at least twenty-six "partners" alongside whom CBF ministers. In most instances, CBF offers financial support to its "partners." However, it does not control those partners. One may say that CBF is a Baptist denomination, but one must immediately say that it is an exceedingly decentralized Baptist denomination. The nature and shape of CBF, it is safe to say, is still unfolding.

At least four terms are important if one is to understand the structure and organizational leadership of the CBF. These four terms are coordinator, moderator, coordinating council, and general assembly. The coordinator of CBF is the chief executive officer, the person who spearheads the daily operations of the Fellowship. Up to this point in CBF history, only two people have served in this role, and they are Cecil E. Sherman and Daniel Vestal.

Sherman, the first coordinator of CBF, served moderate Baptists during most of the SBC controversy as their major spokesperson and leader. Acting upon the recommendation of a search committee,[30] the CBF coordinating council elected Cecil Sherman as their first coordinator in January 1992. He began his work at CBF in April 1992, and he served in that capacity until June 1996. Tommy Boland, a businessman from Atlanta, served as interim coordinator. In September

---

School of Theology of Baylor University. Standing in a third and unique category is Wake Forest Divinity School. An ecumenical school of theology belonging to former Baptist Wake Forest University, the Wake Forest Divinity School has functioned as a vital partner with CBF. The fourth category of CBF's partners in theological education are non-Baptist schools with a Baptist House of Studies. These include Brite Divinity School of Texas Christian University, Candler School of Theology of Emory University, and Duke University Divinity School.

[30] That committee consisted of James Slatton, Richmond VA, chair; R. Kirby Godsey, Macon GA; Carolyn Cole Bucy, Waco TX; Lavonn Brown, Norman OK; Daniel Vestal, Atlanta GA; Dorothy Sample, Flint MI; Walter B. Shurden, Macon GA; Martha Smith, Gastonia NC; and John H. Hewett, Asheville NC. See *SBC Today*, 6 September 1991, 1.

1996, the coordinating council elected Daniel Vestal as national coordinator, and he has effectively served in that capacity since.

The moderator of CBF is the president and presiding officer of CBF. Limited to a one-year term of service, the moderator conducts the business of CBF at the general assembly and at all coordinating council meetings. Depending on how one counts, there have been either fourteen or fifteen CBF moderators. Technically, CBF did not exist until it adopted a constitution in 1991. Historically, however, Daniel Vestal already had served as chair of the Interim Steering Committee in 1990–1991, and he was the first person to "preside" at a meeting of what became CBF. For the sake of historical accuracy, historians should mark the beginning of CBF at the Consultation of Concerned Southern Baptists of 1990, and Daniel Vestal should be noted as the first moderator of CBF. Nine men and six women have served as CBF moderators. The moderators, the date of their year of service, and the place of meeting when they presided are listed in the endnotes.[31]

The coordinating council, elected by the general assembly of CBF, meets three times a year and conducts the business of the CBF when the fellowship is not in general assembly. Among other activities, the

---

[31]

Moderator	Year	Place of General Assembly
1. Daniel Vestal*	1990/91	Atlanta
2. John Hewlett	1991/92	Ft.Worth
3. Patsy Ayres	1992/93	Birmingham
4. Hardy Clemons	1993/94	Greeensboro
5. Carolyn Crumpler	1994/95	Ft. Worth
6. Patrick Anderson	1995/96	Richmond
7. Lavonn Brown	1996/97	Louisville
8. Martha Smith	1997/98	Houston
9. John Tyler	1998/99	Birmingham
10.Sarah Frances Anders	1999/00	Orlando
11.Donna Forrester	2000/01	Atlanta
12.Jim Baucom	2001/02	Ft. Worth
13. Phil Martin	2002/03	Charlotte
14. Cynthia Holmes	2003/04	Birmingham
15. Robert B. Setzer, Jr.	2004/05	Grapevine TX

*Vestal served as chair of the Interim Steering Committee

coordinating council employs and terminates the coordinator, establishes financial policy, determines procedures for the operation of the staff and ministries of the fellowship, and plans and coordinates the general assembly. Each person elected to the coordinating council serves a three-year term.

The general assembly is the annual meeting of CBF for the purposes of worship, fellowship, and business. While serious business is conducted at the general assembly, the assembly gives much of its attention to missions, inspiration, and Christian education, the latter through what are known as "Breakout Sessions." During the fifteen-year history of CBF, the general assembly has met in ten different cities.

CBF Today and Tomorrow

In this closing section, I want to echo some themes in CBF history, both old and new, and then point to some challenges that are either already present or on the horizon. Both past themes and future challenges will work to sharpen the identity and mission of this young Baptist movement.

Four themes that echo throughout the CBF house deserve to be mentioned. First, the theme of Baptist "freedom" has birthed, nourished, and sustained CBF during its brief history. A synonym for CBF is "Free and Faithful Baptists." John Hewett, at the time a young North Carolina pastor, coined the phrase at the 1990 Consultation of Concerned Southern Baptists. "An Address to the Public," CBF's declaration of independence from the SBC, spoke of freedom in many ways: freedom from fundamentalist tyranny, freedom to interpret Scripture according to conscience, freedom for free inquiry in education, freedom to include justice issues in the missions movement, freedom of the local congregation from pastoral authoritarianism, freedom for gender equality, and freedom to be ecumenical in attitude and action. The issue of "control vs. freedom" hung as a generic canopy over the SBC controversy. Fundamentalists argued for and achieved stricter control;

moderates, on the other hand, lobbied for Baptist freedom, and they embodied that idea in CBF.

When Cecil Sherman became the first coordinator of CBF, he said he was going to Atlanta to run up a flag for Baptist freedom. His successor, Daniel Vestal, has struck the same note repeatedly. During his address to the 1998 CBF general assembly, Vestal said, "We were born in a struggle for freedom and in our brief history we have been champions for freedom."[32] In an article dated 1 January 2004, Vestal described CBF in freedom terms. He said,

> Cooperative Baptist Fellowship was born out of a struggle for freedom: soul freedom, Bible freedom, church freedom, religious freedom. The birth of this renewal movement came from the pain of freedom fighters. These noble men and women resisted fundamentalism, authoritarianism and just plain meanness. We will not be cut off from those roots that birthed us; nor will we be separated from the principles of freedom that continue to form us; nor will we shrink from the struggle against any form of tyranny that enslaves the soul or imprisons the mind. We will continue to be a freedom movement.[33]

Freedom never meant a license for irresponsibility at CBF. Freedom was a call to stewardship. CBF Baptists were called to be both free *and faithful*. A second theme in CBF history, therefore, has been global missions and the call to help heal a hurting world. "Global Missions" is the first link on the home page of CBF's Web site. In a brief period of time, CBF has placed approximately 150 missionaries around the world. What Keith Parks began, Barbara and Gary Baldridge, his successors, have continued: keeping before CBF the world for whom Christ lived and died.

Global missions takes on many forms and shapes at CBF. One example of this multifaceted ministry is Partners in Hope. Partners in

---

[32] See "CBF General Assembly Focuses on Spirituality," *Baptists Today*, 23 July 1998, 1.

[33] See "In Praise of Freedom" at "Vestal Online," http://www.thefellowship.info/News/010104%20Freedom.icm (accessed 3 March 2005).

Hope is the Rural Poverty Initiative of CBF that focuses on a twenty-year commitment to twenty of the poorest counties in the United States. Led by Tom Prevost, this is an effort to respond to the biblical mandate of caring for the poor. The hope is not only to meet the needs of the poor but to make the non-poor more aware and attentive to the needs of the poor in our own communities.[34] Partners in Hope fits well with CBF's mission strategy of focusing on marginalized people.

A third theme in CBF life has been the centrality of the local congregation. CBF works hard to reverse the idea that local congregations exist to feed and serve the denomination. To the contrary, the CBF exists to serve and "resource" the churches. Call the CBF offices in Atlanta, and they answer the phone with "Good morning, CBF Resource Center." The nomenclature is not accidental but intentional. In an address to the 2003 general assembly, Daniel Vestal asked, "What does 'today' mean for CBF?" He emphatically answered, "It means several things, but first it means helping churches discover and fulfill their God-given mission."[35]

A fourth and emerging theme to watch in CBF is ecumenism. That theme, while present in "An Address to the Public," has received little publicity in CBF's history. However, with the close working relationship that CBF has forged with the American Baptist Churches, USA, their new membership in the Baptist World Alliance, and their commitment to Christian Churches Together in the USA, CBF is emerging as an ecumenical partner with both Baptists and non-Baptists. This, doubtless, will increase in the future.

The fellowship faces numerous and huge challenges in the future. Some of these are unique to CBF, but some are common to other Christian denominations as well. One challenge, maybe peculiar to the

---

[34] See "Cooperative Baptists Make Long-Term Commitment to Nation's Poorest Counties," *Baptists Today*, October 2003, 2–3, 17. See also http://www.thefellowship.info/Global%20Missions/PIH/ (accessed 2 March 2005).

[35] See "CBF Being the Presence of Christ" at "Vestal Online," http://www.thefellowship.info/News/070103%20CBF%20Being%20the%20Presence%20of%20Christ.icm (accessed 3 March 2005).

CBF, is its ongoing effort to relate to its organizational "partners," entities such as seminaries, news services, and various other types of partners. This is a polity or governance issue. Remember that the CBF does not own any of these "partners." Moreover, CBF, up to this point, has not established significant guidelines for any kind of mutual accountability between the partners and CBF. Determining who is a partner, devising how much financial support a partner should receive, and establishing criteria for evaluating "partnerships" constitute nagging, complex, and important questions for the CBF future. The fact that CBF must now struggle with these issues reflects its growing denominational character. At the 2003 meeting of the general assembly, a CBF Task Force on Budget Priorities recommended the establishment of a Partnership Study Committee. That committee has been appointed and, at this writing in 2005, is hard at work. Doubtless, the report of the committee will be another hinge moment or turning point in CBF life.[36]

A second challenge that CBF confronts is the diversity within its own ranks. As indicated earlier, the Fellowship includes varying theological, ethical, political, and ideological positions. "Moderates" have never been of one stripe. Although CBF has not experienced serious divisions in its short life, disagreements abound. The "culture wars" that divided the SBC and many other Christian denominations, as well as America itself, are not completely alien to CBF life.

One of the most controversial issues to come before CBF has been homosexuality. CBF coordinators, Cecil Sherman and Daniel Vestal, have spoken as with one voice in solid opposition to homosexuality. Indeed, no one could speak more plainly than they have. Sherman, in his typically candid and blunt way, wrote, "The Bible teaches homosexuality is a sin.... God made woman for man. God made man for woman. The

---

[36] For a CBF news release on this committee and its work, see "Fellowship Coordinating Council Receive Report from Partner Study Committee," at http://www.thefellowship.info/News/050218partner.icm (accessed 3 March 2005). To see the interim report of "The Partnership Study Committee," go to http://www.thefellowship.info/documents/PartnershipStudyReport.pdf (accessed 3 March 2005).

Bible does not give mixed signals on the subject."[37] Likewise, Daniel Vestal said, "I believe the practice of homosexuality violates the teaching of scripture." Responding to stories published by Baptist Press, the SBC press agency, that CBF funded pro-homosexual organizations, Vestal wrote, "The Cooperative Baptist Fellowship has never issued any statement, taken any action, or spent a single dollar that was intended in any way to condone, endorse or promote the gay-lesbian lifestyle."[38]

Sherman and Vestal know well that they do not speak for everyone in CBF. They also know that even the actions of CBF in opposition to homosexuality do not signal unanimity on this highly incendiary issue. In 1995, the CBF coordinating council defunded the Baptist Peace Fellowship in North America because the organization urged local churches to welcome gays and lesbians.[39] Additionally, delegates to the 2001 general assembly voted 701–502 to uphold a ban on hiring gays or funding organizations that "condone, advocate, or affirm homosexual practice." Some opponents to the ban voted as they did because they believed that the coordinating council had violated its bounds, since the general assembly had never voted on the issue. Some, however, obviously voted against the ban because of principle. Regardless of why they voted against the ban, those 502 votes suggest that "moderate Baptists" are not of one mind on this inflammatory issue. CBF, like other Baptist bodies, must learn in the future to negotiate the turbulent waters of diversity.

A third, and maybe the most serious issue facing CBF, is attracting the younger generation to its ranks. Again, like many denominations, CBF is a graying group. It will not be enough to depend upon CBF churches to replenish the aging and vanishing leaders who have shaped the movement. CBF will have to learn creative ways to make its peculiar

---

[37] See "About Homosexuality," in *Baptists Today*, 1 April 1993, 23.

[38] See "CBF and the Issue of Homosexuality: A Response to Recent Reports from Baptist Press," in *Baptists Today*, September 2000, 8.

[39] See "Cooperative Baptist Fellowship Appoints 16 New Missionaries; Considers Becoming Convention, Adopts Formal Mission Statement," *Baptists Today*, August 1995, 1.

past, with its stress on freedom, Baptist convictions, Christian missions, and issues of justice, attractive to the coming generations. Fortunately, it has a good story to tell!

Baptists Today asked CBF coordinator Daniel Vestal in an interview in June 2000, "What do you envision when you dream and pray about the future of CBF?" Vestal answered:

> I dream of a Fellowship that is much more multicultural and multiethnic and that will attract multitudes of churches that never heard of the SBC controversy. I dream of CBF networks in all 50 states, on college and university campuses and in cities across the country. I dream of missionaries appointed and churches mobilized to reach hundreds of unreached people groups. I dream of thousands of women and men being trained for effective leadership in Baptist life in our consortium schools. I dream of partnering with state conventions, associations and other Baptist bodies (especially the American Baptists), and even SBC institutions. I dream of a new Baptist ethos that while prophetic is not embarrassing, and while pastoral, does not accommodate the popular culture.[40]

In an article in the April 2004 issue of *Baptists Today*, Bob Setzer, Jr., moderator-elect of CBF, asked the question, "How is CBF doing?" He answered, "About as well as any 13 year old I know." Setzer continued, "I am amazed by the vitality of this young movement. Our far-flung missionaries, combined with a partnership network of state and regional groups, ethnic networks, partnering schools and institutions, make for a powerful force for healing in a broken world. And all is done with a Christlike spirit of cooperation and a healthy dose of Baptist freedom."[41] CBFers hope Setzer spoke the truth about the future. Time will tell.

---

[40] See "A Conversation With Daniel Vestal," *Baptists Today*, June 2000, 9.

[41] See Bob Setzer, Jr., "How is CBF Doing?" in *Baptists Today*, April 2004, 9

Chapter 12

BAPTIST AMERICANUS

Lydia Huffman Hoyle

According to the *World Christian Encyclopedia*, there are 322 Baptist denominations worldwide.[1] In the United States alone, more than 60 Baptist groups associate with each other on a national level (although some of these reject the "denomination" descriptor.)[2] That number does not include all of the independent Baptist churches that dot the American landscape—some of which boast thousands of members—or the numerous local associations of churches that reject broader organization as being contrary to the Bible. Preceding chapters have discussed the history and distinctives of ten of the more widely known Baptist denominations. Although these groups account for more than 90 percent of all Baptists in the United States, several million Baptists are scattered across the remaining denominations. They represent some of

---

[1] David Barrett et al., eds., *World Christian Encyclopedia*, 2nd ed. (New York: Oxford, 2001) s.v. "World Summary."

[2] The exact number of Baptist denominations is difficult to state with confidence. Sources written across the last twenty-five years are inconsistent—listing anywhere from twenty-seven to fifty-seven Baptist groups. The fact index located online at http://www.fact-index.com/l/li/list_of_baptist_sub_denominations.html#North%20America [no longer accessible] (accessed 28 February 2005) lists a total of fifty-seven Baptist denominations. This total, however, includes several denominations under a single heading in at least two cases. Thus, it appears that there are more than sixty Baptist denominations in the United States. It does seem, however, than a number of small Baptist denominations listed are in the process of disassociating as their numbers dwindle. Thus, the number of Baptist denominations is in flux.

the more colorful and less well-known denominations in the Baptist family. This chapter will provide a sense of the wide variety of small denominations that share the Baptist name. Although Baptists may all look the same to those outside the tradition, lines of separation tend to run deep. Here, we will trace some of those lines, providing added detail and subtlety to the amorphous "Baptist" designation.[3]

Many people perhaps wonder why there are so many different kinds of Baptists. Although Baptists are certainly not unique in their tendency to divide rather than tolerate diversity, they have developed church division into an art form. According to Baptist historians O. K. and Marjorie Armstrong, Baptists have the dubious honor of "establishing more independent bodies than has any other religious group in the United States—or the world."[4] Although the Baptists have been superseded by the Pentecostals in this claim to fame, it is certainly true that the nature of the Baptist tradition is one that provides fertile soil for the seed of division. As folks who generally eschew creeds, Baptists are left with the Bible alone to sort out matters that the Bible does not always address clearly. In addition, as Christians who emphasize the freedom of the local congregation, Baptists tend to be uncomfortable establishing broad authoritative bodies that might usurp the Holy Spirit and make decisions under which all must unite. Thus, while universally affirming the authority of the Bible, most Baptists have felt free to ignore biblical admonishments to seek unity in Christ—at least when it comes to extra-church structures.[5] As noted in the introduction, Baptists can be defined, in part, by their penchant for division.

Although there is no obvious taxonomy of Baptists, it is evident that Baptists have followed patterns of division found elsewhere in American

---

[3] Please note that the groups discussed here will be representative. For a more exhaustive listing, consult Bill J. Leonard, *Dictionary of Baptists in America* (Downers Grove IL: Intervarsity Press, 1994).

[4] O. K. Armstrong and Marjorie Armstrong, *The Baptists in America* (New York: Doubleday, 1979) 253.

[5] Bill Leonard outlines eight dialectics that create inevitable tension in Baptist lives and churches. See *Baptist Ways: A History* (Valley Forge: Judson Press, 2003) 6–10.

Protestantism. In his book *Dissent in American Religion*, Edwin Gaustad outlines seven elements common in the American context that have contributed to Protestant schism: piety, liberty, frontier, evangelicalism, ethnicity, race, and ecumenism.[6] For the most part, Baptist divisions can likewise be organized around these areas of description and dispute. In an effort to bring some order to what otherwise seems to be a mind-boggling array of Baptists, this chapter will adopt and adapt Gaustad's categories.[7] It will focus on the seeds of discontent and conflict that impelled Baptists to divide again and again.

Understanding the context for schism also helps explain why multiple Baptist groups might share similar theologies and practices but nonetheless remain separate. History and the shared culture and heroes that grow from that history help maintain distinctions that to the outsider may seem insignificant. And so we look back at denominational beginnings in hopes of better understanding the "Baptist Americanus" genus.

Evangelicalism (or Evangelism)

Baptists, from the beginning, have been divided regarding the centrality or importance of evangelism in the mission of the church. Although the great majority of Baptists have shared a concern regarding the ultimate salvation of human souls, they have been less ready to agree on the role of human participation in the salvation process and the proper understanding of the atonement. The earliest Baptists taught that Christ died for all people. These English men and women came to be known as General Baptists because of their adherence to this belief in a general atonement. Particular Baptists, who began forming churches some thirty years later, were convinced that Christ died only for the elect. Thus, the Calvinist/Arminian division among seventeenth-century Protestants in

---

[6] Edwin Scott Gaustad, *Dissent in American Religion* (Chicago: University of Chicago, 1973) 10–40.

[7] Please note that in many cases, Baptist schism may be a result of disagreements that fit into several of these categories.

general was reflected among the earliest proponents of the "Baptized Way."[8]

Both Particular and General Baptists were among those that settled the American colonies. Once here, the theological distinctions that had kept them separated in England seemed to lessen in importance. Perhaps because Baptists were few in number,[9] scattered, and frequent recipients of ridicule by those from established churches, Baptist congregations in the New World sometimes included members who did not share the same views on the atonement. As churches grew and Baptists multiplied, however, this theological disagreement, present from the outset, eventually led to schism. Across four centuries, churches, associations, and ultimately denominations formed that trace their roots back to either the General or Particular Baptists.

Although the Calvinist theology of the Particular Baptists was shared by most colonial Baptists, the move away from Reformed theology after the first Great Awakening (in the late eighteenth century) and the establishment of missionary societies (in the early nineteenth century) resulted in the reactionary formation of a number of Baptist denominations committed to reaffirming Calvinist doctrine. The Primitive Baptists were one such group. (See chapter 7.) Another was the Two-Seed-in-the-Spirit Predestinarian Baptists. The Two Seeds drew their name and theology from the teaching of Daniel Parker. Although he apparently looked like a wild man, with long hair and a tobacco-juice stained beard,[10] Parker was able to draw followers with his unique version of Calvinism. He taught that every person was born with one of two seeds. Those born with the good seed would be drawn to repent. Those born with the bad seed would not. Because these two seeds were planted before birth in the human soul, nothing could alter their

---

[8] Early Baptists often referred to themselves in this way. The "Baptist" designation was not one they chose.

[9] In 1700, there were only a total of fourteen Baptist churches in the American colonies. See O. K. Armstrong and Marjorie Armstrong, *Baptists in America*, 83.

[10] Leon McBeth, *The Baptist Heritage: Four Centuries of Baptist Witness* (Nashville: Broadman, 1987) 373.

presence.[11] Parker, nonetheless, thought it worthwhile to preach and start churches. Those with the "good seed" would respond. Although committed to this personal mission activity, Parker was quite troubled that some Baptists were forming missionary societies to evangelize non-Christians. He could find no reference to supra-church organizations in the Bible. Building on his Two-Seed doctrine and his anti-mission society stance, Parker preached across Texas, Illinois, Oklahoma, and elsewhere, starting small churches where he could. His seeds took root in several areas, and a number of congregations were born. By 2003, only four congregations remained with a total of eighty members.[12]

Since the nineteenth century, a minority of Baptists have held the view that Jesus died only for those God elected to save. The Primitives and Two-Seeds, nonetheless, have been joined by other denominations whose belief in limited atonement is central to their self-definition. These include a number of associations formed in the nineteenth century like the (Regular) United Baptists. In addition, several like-minded groups have formed in the last twenty-five years. These include Continental Baptist Churches (formed in 1983), the Sovereign Grace Baptist Association of Churches (1984), and the Association of Reformed Baptist Churches of America (1997). In general, these organizations have formed in part to proclaim their commitment to some type of Reformed Theology. They have separated themselves from denominations less certain about such matters.

Other Baptist groups have carefully defined themselves by using the name of their denomination to announce their more Arminian view of the atonement or their desire to take the message of Christ to the world. The Free Will Baptists (discussed in chapter 6) are the most obvious of these. They are joined by others like the General Association of General

---

[11] Bill J. Leonard, *Dictionary of Baptists in America*, s.v. "Two-Seed-in-the-Spirit Predestinarian Baptists."

[12] See http://fact-index.com/t/tw/two_seed_in_the_spirit_predestinarian_baptists.html (accessed 28 February 2005). Statistics compiled by the American Religion Data Archive list only sixty-five Two-Seed adherents as of 2000.

Baptists (1870),[13] who revived the General Baptist name and heritage, and the recently organized General Six-Principle Baptists (2003), who emphasize not only the general nature of the atonement but the rite of laying on of hands on new believers. (This practice common among early English General Baptists involved church members laying their hands on the head of a new convert and praying for that person. Baptists in America did not practice this rite widely.)

Perhaps the Baptist organization with the most obvious evangelistic commitment (and name!) has been the National Baptist Evangelical Life and Soul Saving Assembly of the United States of America (NBELSA). This predominantly African American group was first formed in 1920 as an auxiliary to the National Baptist Convention of America. Following the model of the Salvation Army, the NBELSA developed a military-type structure and sought to provide social and evangelistic outreach in North American cities. The group began work in Kansas City, Missouri, but soon expanded to other cities. By 1937, they had broken away from the National Baptist Convention. Building on their urban ministry as well as on the production of Bible correspondence courses, the organization grew quickly. In 1951, the group reported 264 congregations with a total of 50,000 members.[14]

Piety

A second area of dispute and division for Baptists has been in the area of piety—particularly as piety is expressed in personal religious experience. The question of the proper role of religious experience in the life of faith came to be prominent in America during the First Great Awakening.

[13] In 2001, the General Association of General Baptists reported 1,415 churches with 129,407 members. See Eileen W. Lindner, ed., *Yearbook of American and Canadian Churches 2004* (New York: Abington Press, 2004) 371.

[14] Larry G. Murphy et al., eds., *Encyclopedia of African American Religions* (New York: Garland, 1993) s.v. "National Baptist Evangelical Life and Soul Saving Assembly of the United States of America." None of the common sources of contemporary religious data include more recent statistics for the group.

Those who were enthusiastic supporters of the more emotional and evangelistic style of worship common in the revival services began to organize churches separated from their traditionalist brethren. These "Separates" or "New Lights," with their major emphasis on the sole authority of the Bible, frequently found themselves in harmony with the Baptists.[15] Soon, this division among Congregationalists and others came to be reflected in the Baptist family. The Separate Baptists separated from their "Regular" sisters and brothers. Although most Separates reunited with the Regular Baptists in the decades following the division, some maintained their distinctive identity. Today, the Separate Baptists in Christ are the largest of these groups with 7,500 members (1999). The Separates, unlike most Baptists, maintain the ordinance of foot washing in addition to baptism and the Lord's Supper and do not hold to the eternal security of the believer.[16]

In the late twentieth century, differing beliefs regarding religious experience again brought division to Baptists. The Full Gospel Baptist Church Fellowship, which traces its foundations to English Baptists, Methodists, and the Pentecostal Movement, began in 1994. According to the denominational Web site, it encourages "the free expression of the gifts of the Spirit" while utilizing a hierarchical structure within the church.[17] Although the organization maintains a commitment to local church autonomy and the ultimate authority of Scripture (beliefs common to most Baptists), classic Pentecostal emphases on the "Holy Ghost" and "spiritual gifts" also play a central role. The Baptist designation of the denomination points to its institutional roots. Churches that have joined the Full Gospel Baptist Church Fellowship generally have ties to the National Baptist Convention, U.S.A. Many of the Full Gospel churches are jointly affiliated. From its inception, the group seemed to strike a chord with many National Baptists. By 1995, it

---

[15] Leonard, *Baptist Ways*, 120.

[16] http://www.fact-index.com/sl.se/separate-baptists-in-christ.html (accessed 28 February 2005; no longer accessible).

[17] The history of the denomination is described at its web site.

included approximately 5,000 churches with a total membership of 500,000.[18]

Liberty

Building on their strong commitment to "soul competency" and local church autonomy, some Baptists have bristled under the felt dominance of others and have started new denominations where they can have freedom from outside control. The Original Free Will Baptists are one such liberty-loving denomination. This group of Baptists, primarily located in North Carolina, broke away from the National Association of Free Will Baptists in 1962. Though doctrinally similar to their sisters and brothers in the national association, the North Carolina Free Will Baptists wanted to own and operate their own press and develop their own Sunday school materials.[19] This, in combination with some polity disputes[20] and a disagreement over the establishment of a liberal arts college, led to the formation of the new convention. Today, there are more than 46,000 Original Free Will Baptists. Almost all of them live in eastern North Carolina.[21]

North Carolina was also the home of another liberty-seeking denomination. This group, known as the Christian Unity Baptist Association, organized in 1935. These mountain Baptists from the

---

[18] David Barrett et al., eds., *World Christian Encyclopedia*, s.v. "United States of America." The Full Gospel Baptist Church Fellowship is not the only Baptist denomination with Pentecostal and Wesleyan traits. The General Conference of the Evangelical Baptist Church, organized in 1935, also shares these ties.

[19] See www.fact-index.com/o/or/original_free_will_baptist.convention.html (accessed 7 October 2004).

[20] William F. Davidson, *The Free Will Baptists in History* (Nashville: Randall House, 2001) 330.

[21] These statistics are compiled by the American Religion Data Archive and can be accessed through their Web site at www.arda.com. See http://216.122.145.46.cgi-bin/Mapcompare.exe (accessed 28 February 2005). Paradoxically, the Original Free Willers, though desirous of freedom from the National Association, are more ready than their mother denomination to cede authority to the associations or districts of which they are a part.

northwest corner of the state shared much of their theology with the Missionary and Primitive Baptists from whom they came. The Christian Unity folks, however, did not like the fact that women in their denominations were not allowed to preach. At the group's organizational gathering, two women preached.[22] Among the articles of faith crafted at this first meeting stood these simple statements: "We believe in the unity, liberty, and equality of God's children," and "We believe in a God-called ministry."[23] For the Christian Unity folks, this, among other things, meant that women should not be prevented from responding to God's call. In the midst of Depression-era mountain life, the formation of a new association was perhaps the only way those with convictions regarding gender equality could embody their beliefs.[24]

The early twentieth century also saw the formation of new denominations by those who felt compelled to announce their freedom from the modernism that shook the theological world in the late nineteenth and early twentieth centuries. The American Baptist Churches, U.S.A. (then known as the Northern Baptist Convention), included a number of modernist scholars and denominational leaders. Conservatives who became a part of the new fundamentalist movement tried to root out what they believed to be liberal "heresy" from their schools, missionaries, and denominational literature. When these efforts saw only minimal success, two groups withdrew to pursue the faith free from the "errors" of the modernists. The first group to withdraw was the General Association of Regular Baptist Churches (1933). A second group, which held on longer in hopes of convincing the mother

---

[22] "Christian Unity Baptist Association," in Wikipedia. See http://www.fact-index.com/c/ch/christian_unity_baptist_association.html (accessed 16 September 2004).

[23] "Articles of Faith," in Statistical Table of the Christian Unity Baptist Association, n.d. See www.Is.net/~newriver/nrv/cuba.htm (accessed 16 September 2004).

[24] In 1969, most of the association chose to affiliate with the General Association of Separate Baptists. Howard Dorgan, however, found that in 1990, six Christian Unity congregations continued an association. See Howard Dorgan, *In the Hands of a Happy God* (Knoxville: University of Tennessee Press, 1997) 13.

denomination to adopt their understanding of the truth, eventually pulled out, forming the Conservative Baptists of America (1947).[25] Additional Baptist fundamentalist organizations developed across the country in the twentieth century. Due to their tendency to emphasize church autonomy, these groups were frequently loosely organized and emphasized the independence of the churches. Several of these are discussed in chapter 5.

Frontier

According to Gaustad, the frontier spirit was one that not only sought liberty from external authorities but also sought simplicity and valued common sense. In the church setting, this frontier spirit meant that ministers did not need education so much as morality, piety, and the ability to preach.[26] The Old Regular Baptists are one of a number of frontier-spirit denominations that take the primitivism common to most Baptists to a deeper level. Believing that their doctrines closely mirror those of the New Testament church, the Old Regulars call adherents to maintain ways of worship and life consistent with Appalachian mountain traditions. Many of these traditions revolve around the organization of the family. The Old Regulars maintain a patriarchal family structure. Men rule their families and the church. Women are called to be silent in the church and are admonished to avoid wearing men's clothing (i.e., slacks) and cutting their hair. Pastors preach extemporaneously and baptize outdoors.[27] Baptisms are routinely delayed until the person is thirty-five or forty.[28] This "Christ against culture" mentality of the Old Regulars has never enjoyed a wide appeal. As a result, this denomination that developed across the nineteenth century has remained small and confined to the Appalachian region. Nonetheless, in 1990, there were

---

[25] McBeth, *Baptist Heritage*, 571–78.

[26] Gaustad, *Dissent in American Religion*, 18–19.

[27] Howard Dorgan, *The Old Regular Baptists of Central Appalachia: Brothers and Sisters in Hope* (Knoxville: University of Tennessee Press, 1989) 5–8.

[28] Ibid., 24.

326 Old Regular Baptist Churches with a total of more than 15,000 members.[29]

The Old Regulars are joined by a number of other frontier-spirited Baptist denominations—especially in the central Appalachian area. These include several types of Primitive Baptists (see chapter 7), Regular Baptists, and others. All of these groups are remarkable in their persistence in maintaining traditions in the face of modern and post-modern culture. Among the Baptists generally categorized as "Primitives," there is one small group known as the Primitive Baptist Universalists. These folks stretch the definition of Baptists held by most. Although some Baptists may maintain a lived theology that gives little thought to the existence of hell, the Universalists argue that hell exists only in the temporal world. Hell is what you experience here on earth when you pull away from God. It is not an option in the afterlife. If Christ died for all, then everyone will be blessed in the afterlife. For the "no-hellers," this is the simple truth of Christ's atonement.[30] The Universalists, who developed separate organizations in the 1920s, have remained a small group. In 1995, Howard Dorgan, who spent three years studying the group, counted a total of only 571 members.[31] In the era of the mega-church, the Primitive Universalists and their "frontier" brethren have nonetheless been successful in maintaining their own distinct stream flowing into the Baptist river.[32]

Ethnicity

Some Baptists have joined the Old Regulars in their efforts to maintain their own culture but have approached the task with a somewhat

---

[29] Martin B. Bradley et al., eds., *Churches and Church Membership in the United States* (Atlanta: Glenmary Research Center, 1990) 3.

[30] Dorgan, *In the Hands*, 40. The Universalists come together in several associations. There is no over-arching denomination.

[31] Ibid., 181.

[32] Howard Dorgan describes several of these churches in *Giving Glory to God in Appalachia: Worship Practices of Six Baptist Subdenominations* (Knoxville: University of Tennessee Press, 1987).

different motivation. Thousands of Baptists have come to America from well-established European traditions and have resisted assimilation into the melting pot. German and Swedish Baptists, in particular, have developed their own independent Baptist organizations utilizing the languages of their heritage.

One German group, the German Baptist Brethren, have a particularly interesting history. According to an account published by the contemporary Brethren Church, approximately 140 Brethren families immigrated to America in the early 1700s. Some left the Brethren to join the Ephrata Cloister, a celibate communal organization. (This is probably the closest Baptists have ever come to being either celibate or communal in character.) Others remained, founding congregations in the mid-Atlantic states as well as in Virginia and in the Carolinas.[33] Though practically all Baptists by this time practiced baptism by immersion, the German Baptist Brethren held the distinction of baptizing each believer three times. The minister would press the candidate facedown into the water from a kneeling position once for each member of the Trinity.[34] In addition, the Brethren included foot washing and a love feast in their celebration of Communion.[35]

The German Baptist Brethren were able to maintain their distinctives, in part, by continuing to worship using the German language. Their move toward becoming an English-speaking denomination in the 1830s and 1840s raised many issues in the churches regarding the extent of American enculturation that should be allowed or encouraged. Out of this ongoing debate, the church, in the 1880s, divided into four parts. Only two of the groups, the Old Order German Baptist Brethren, who fought modern innovations like Sunday school and higher education, and the Old German Baptist Brethren maintained the Baptist name.[36]

---

[33] See www.brethrenchurch.org/bhamer.html (accessed 7 February 2005).

[34] H. C. Vedder, *A Short History of the Baptists* (Philadelphia: The American Baptist Publication Society, 1907) 390.

[35] See www.brethrenchurch.org/bhamer.html (Last accessed 7 February 2005).

[36] Ibid.

While Swedish Baptists joined the Germans in establishing denominations that reflected the language and ethnicity of their heritage, some ethnic Baptists have been more likely to form their own associations within denominations that are primarily Anglo. This has been true among Hispanic Baptists. As the Hispanic population in America expanded in the nineteenth century, both Northern and Southern Baptists actively sought to plant churches among the new immigrants. These efforts were largely successful. Today, most Hispanic Baptists continue to associate with either Southern Baptist state conventions or the American Baptist Churches, U.S.A. There are, however, separate Hispanic associations as well as institutions for theological education that operate within these denominations. This has apparently been a formula that works. The Hispanic Baptists have experienced notable growth as the number of Hispanics in the United States has likewise multiplied.

Today, while German, Swedish, Hispanic, and other ethnic Baptists continue to maintain some distinct organizations, most have tried to extend their arms to embrace folks who do not share their ethnic roots. In an increasingly diverse population, this is perhaps necessary for survival.

Race

It is certainly no secret that race has been a central factor in the division of American Protestantism. Churches have divided over race and by race. The Baptist denomination best known for its racist foundations is the Southern Baptist Convention. (See chapter 3.) Such roots are an embarrassment to those who must acknowledge the heritage today. Though no twentieth-century Baptists have claimed racial prejudices as a reason for establishing a new denomination, Baptists, like most American Protestants, continue to be divided by race. Few Baptist denominations can boast significant racial diversity.

Division by race began in the late eighteenth century but accelerated during the Civil War Reconstruction period. Baptist denominations prominent in the 1860s soon found their African American members withdrawing to establish first congregations and ultimately denominations in which they could have a stronger voice. African American Primitive Baptists formed the Colored Primitive Baptists of America in the 1860s. African American Free Will Baptists formed the General Conference of United Free Will Baptists (1901). Other societies also formed. Notably, the African American churches did not find the need to establish a separate black denomination for each white Baptist group. Instead, the great majority of African American Baptist churches and associations began coming together in 1886, ultimately forming the National Baptist Convention in 1895.[37] (See chapter 4.) Most predominantly, African American denominations in existence today are a result of disputes within the National Baptist Convention. These include the Lott Carey Baptist Foreign Mission Convention (1897), the National Baptist Convention U.S.A. (1915), the Progressive National Baptist Convention (1961), and the National Missionary Baptist Convention of America (1988).

Ecumenism

According to Gaustad, "bringing churches together also drives them apart." Thus, in the somewhat rare cases when Baptists of different stripes have laid aside their differences to unite in one denomination, this very act has propelled some to start something new. One example is the formation of the Old Time Missionary Baptists. The Old Timers apparently began in the early nineteenth century. At that time, many Regular Baptists and Separate Baptists came together to become United Baptists. Although the two groups did not share the same theology regarding the atonement, they were able to lay aside their differences to work together.[38] The Old Timers did not like the degree to which the United Baptists united. They supported missionary outreach but rejected

---

[37] Hans J. Hillerbrand et al., eds., *Encyclopedia of Protestantism* (Routledge: New York, 2004) s.v. "Baptist Family of Churches."

[38] Howard Dorgan, "United Baptists," in Leonard, *Dictionary of Baptists*, 274.

missionary boards and conventions. They were also concerned that converts experience conviction of sin and a period of mourning prior to repentance and faith in Christ. They did not believe a person could simply make a decision to follow Christ. For these reasons, the Old Timers, from the beginning, have maintained only weak associations with each other and have refused to unite with brethren too enamored with the role of human decision-making in the conversion process. Today, the Old Timers number around 60,000 and primarily live in Kentucky, Tennessee, Missouri, and Georgia.[39]

Anti-ecumenism has also caused division among Baptists in another way. One group of Baptists, broadly known as the Landmark Baptists, arose in the mid-nineteenth century. These folks, who originally represented a strong minority voice in the Southern Baptist Convention, believed that Baptist churches were the only true churches. They worked to trace the continuous presence of the Baptist church across history to Jesus. In their view, because Baptists had the only true churches, only Baptist baptism and Baptist Communion were valid. Although many Landmarkers stayed within the Southern Baptist Convention and worked to instill their version of history and theology in others, some left to form separate churches and organizations. The American Baptist Association (1924), the Baptist Missionary Association of America (1950), and the Interstate and Foreign Missionary Baptist Association of America (1950) all have their roots in this nineteenth-century controversy. In 2000, these three associations included more than 450,000 members in more than 3,300 churches.[40]

Conclusion

The "Baptist Americanus" genus is certainly one that includes a wide variety of species. Few descriptors can be used to speak accurately of all

---

[39] "Old Time Missionary Baptist," http://encyclopedia.thefreedictionary.com (accessed 7 October 2004).

[40] Martin B. Bradley et al., eds., *Churches and Church Membership in the United States* (Atlanta: Glenmary Research Center, 1990) 1.

Baptists. Even believer's baptism, a hallmark of all Baptists, is practiced in a number of different ways. Most simply immerse the believer once, but some dip the convert facedown into the water three times. Some add the requirement of laying on of hands following the baptism. Some refuse the rite to anyone who has not reached adulthood. Baptists, it seems, disagree even in areas of common belief. Hopefully, however, in these brief glimpses into some of the smaller Baptist denominations, it is possible to see not only those things that have divided Baptists but also the independence of spirit and desire to "get it right" that binds all Baptists together.

CONTRIBUTORS

William H. Brackney is currently the Millard R. Cherry Distinguished Professor of Christian Thought and Ethics at Acadia Divinity College, Acadia University, in Wolfville, Nova Scotia. Previously, he was Professor of Religion and Chair of the Department at Baylor University where he instituted the Program in Baptist Studies where he also taught Baptist Studies and Church History at George W. Truett Theological Seminary. Previously he was dean of Theology at McMaster University and principal of McMaster Divinity School (1989–2000). He has also been professor of the history of Christianity at Eastern Baptist Theological Seminary (1985–1989). Dr. Brackney was educated at the University of Maryland (BA), Eastern Baptist Theological Seminary (MA), and Temple University (MA, Ph.D.), where he received his Ph.D. with distinction. He is the author or editor of twenty-five books including the recent *A Genetic History of Baptist Thought* (Mercer), *Human Rights and the Christian* (Praeger), and *Baptists in North America: An Analyical Survey* (Blackwell's).

John G. Crowley is associate professor of History at Valdosta State University. He was educated at Valdosta State University (BA, MA) and Florida State University (Ph.D.). He has served on the History faculty at Valdosta State since 1994. He is the author of *The Primitive Baptists of the Wiregrass South* (1998). A lifelong Primitive Baptist, he was ordained a Primitive Baptist minister in 1977.

William F. Davidson taught at Columbia Biblical Seminary and School of Missions (a division of Columbia International University) for twenty-nine years before retiring in 2002. He was educated at Peabody College for Teachers (BA), Northern Baptist Theological Seminary (BD), and New Orleans Baptist Theological Seminary (Th.D.). He is the author of *The Free Will Baptists in History*. Since retiring in 2002, he has continued to teach brief intensive courses at Columbia Biblical Seminary, Free Will Baptist Bible College, and at in the graduate school at Hillsdale Free Will Baptist Bible College in Moore, Oklahoma. An active interim pastorate ministry still keeps him involved in the local church during retirement.

Jerry L. Faught is the Dickinson Assistant Professor of Religion at Oklahoma Baptist University. He was educated at Oklahoma Baptist University (BA), Southwestern Baptist Theological Seminary (M.Div.), and Baylor University (Ph.D.). He has published numerous articles in the field of Baptist Studies. His article "The Ralph Elliott Controversy: Competing Philosophies of Southern Baptist Seminary Education" won the Norman W. Cox Award from the Baptist History and Heritage Society in 1999 for the best article published in *Baptist History and Heritage.*

Lydia Huffman Hoyle is associate professor of Church History and Baptist Heritage at the Campbell University Divinity School. She was educated at Appalachian State University (BS), Southwestern Baptist Theological Seminary (M.Div.), and the University of North Carolina (MA, Ph.D.). Prior to coming to Campbell University in 2003, she was associate professor of Religion at Georgetown College. She has written numerous articles in the field of Church History, and in 1997 she was named to the Pew Young Scholars in American Religion Program.

W. Glenn Jonas, Jr., is the Howard Professor of Religion and chairman of the Department of Religion and Philosophy at Campbell University. He has served in both academic and ministerial capacities for a number of years. He is a graduate of Mars Hill College (BA), Southwestern Baptist Theological Seminary (M.Div.), and Baylor University (Ph.D.). He has contributed articles to a variety of journals and periodicals and is the author of *A Critical Evaluation of Albert Henry Newman, Church Historian* (1992) and a coauthor of *A Journey of Faith: Introduction to Christianity* (Mercer, 2002).

Sandy D. Martin is professor of Religion at the University of Georgia. He was educated at Tougaloo College (BA), Columbia University, and Union Theological Seminary (Ph.D.). He has authored numerous articles and two books, including *Black Baptists and African Missions: The Origins of a Movement, 1880–1915* (Mercer, 1989).

Don A. Sanford is historian emeritus for the Seventh Day Baptist Historical Society in Janesville, Wisconsin. He was educated at Milton College (BA), Alfred University School of Theology (BD), and the University of Wisconsin—Whitewater (MS). He is the author of *A Choosing People: The History of the Seventh Day Baptists.*

Walter B. Shurden is professor of Christianity and executive director of the Center for Baptist Studies at Mercer University in Macon, Georgia. He was educated at Mississippi College (BA) and New Orleans Baptist Theological Seminary (BD, Th.D.). He has published fifteen books and numerous articles in the area of Baptist Studies. Before coming to Mercer University, he taught at the Southern Baptist Theological Seminary, McMaster Divinity College, and Carson-Newman College. A member of the First Baptist Church in Macon, he has also been a member of the Cooperative Baptist Fellowship from its inception in 1990.

Philip E. Thompson is associate professor of Systematic Theology and Christian Heritage at North American Baptist Seminary in Sioux Falls, South Dakota. He was educated at Mars Hill College (BA), Union Theological Seminary in Virginia (MDiv), and Emory University (PhD). He has published scholarly articles in numerous journals such as *Perspectives in Religious Studies*, *American Baptist Quarterly*, *Interpretation*, *Baptist History and Heritage*, *Review and Expositor*, and *Pro Ecclesia*. He is an active member in a number of professional organizations, including the National Association of Baptist Professors of Religion.

Deborah Van Broekhoven is executive director of the American Baptist Historical Society and managing editor of the *American Baptist Quarterly*. She was educated at Barrington College in Rhode Island (BA) and Bowling Green State University (MA, Ph.D.). She taught history and American studies for twenty years, most recently at Ohio Wesleyan University. She has written extensively about women abolitionists, including *The Devotion of These Women: Rhode Island in the Antislavery Network* (2002).

C. Doug Weaver is assistant professor of Religion at Baylor University. Before coming to Baylor in 2003, he served as professor of Christianity and chair of the Division of Religion and Philosophy at Brewton-Parker College. He was educated at Mississippi College (BA) and the Southern Baptist Theological Seminary (M.Div., Ph.D.). He is the author of several books, including *The Healer Prophet: William Marrion Branham* (Mercer); *From Our Christian Heritage* (Smyth & Helwys); *Second to None: A History of the Second Ponce de Leon Baptist Church*; and *Every Town Needs a Downtown Church: A History of First Baptist Church, Gainesville, Florida* (Baptist History and Heritage). He also serves as the current editor of *The Whitsitt Journal*.